"What more can be said about C. S. Lewis that has not already been said? Selby has defied the odds by reconfiguring some of the well-traversed themes in Lewis's writings into a coherent spiritual theology which is at once familiar, yet refreshingly new. Aficionados of Lewis will not be disappointed."

Simon Chan, former Earnest Lau Professor of Systematic Theology, Trinity Theological College, Singapore

"Have you ever wondered why so many Christians confess the goodness of God's creation yet hesitate to enter into its pleasures with unabashed joy? If so, these pages are for you. By drawing on the whole corpus of Lewis's work, Gary Selby deftly presents a much-needed corrective to the often joyless and disembodied spirituality of our age. Rich with practical wisdom and illuminating examples, Selby's joyful vision might just revolutionize how you dwell in the world."

Philip D. Kenneson, author of *Life on the Vine: Cultivating the Fruit of the Spirit in Christian Community*

"Gary Selby's *Pursuing an Earthy Spirituality* is a gift to those who love C. S. Lewis and believe that he offers a way of living the Christian faith that is joyful, embodied, and attached to the beauty and pleasure of creation. Drawing from decades of teaching and interacting with students, Selby beautifully reminds us that Lewis lived a spirituality that was at least as deeply rooted in emotion, imagery, beauty, and the body as it was in his keen intellect."

Gary W. Moon, founding executive director, Martin Institute for Christianity and Culture and Dallas Willard Center, Westmont College, and the founding director of Renovaré Institute, author of *Becoming Dallas Willard*

"Here is a timely book that takes seriously C. S. Lewis's own emphasis on God as a 'Glad Creator,' on sheer goodness and joy as the core and center of that creation, which, even in its fallen state, still brings us remnants of 'the enormous bliss of Eden.' In a full and thorough survey of Lewis's work Selby draws out the consistent strand of particularity, earthiness, and praise for God's good creation, rooted and redeemed in the incarnation of Christ that is at the heart of Lewis's gospel, and of his wide appeal. But more importantly Selby shows how much our contemporary modes of spirituality, so often intellectualized and rootless, need to be grounded again and earthed in the story of the God who came down. This is a much-needed book that will send people back to Lewis with new appreciation but also encourage them to take a long hard look at some of our contemporary spirituality, and seek for a little more substance, a little more joy."

Malcolm Guite, chaplain, Girton College, Cambridge, author of *Mariner: A Theological Voyage with Samuel Taylor Coleridge*

PURSUING AN

EARTHY

SPIRITUALITY

C. S. Lewis AND INCARNATIONAL FAITH

GARY S. SELBY

To Sarah —
Thank you for
everything!
Gary Selby

IVP Academic

An imprint of InterVarsity Press
Downers Grove, Illinois

InterVarsity Press
P.O. Box 1400, Downers Grove, IL 60515-1426
ivpress.com
email@ivpress.com

InterVarsity Press® is the book-publishing division of InterVarsity Christian Fellowship/USA®, a movement of students and faculty active on campus at hundreds of universities, colleges, and schools of nursing in the United States of America, and a member movement of the International Fellowship of Evangelical Students. For information about local and regional activities, visit intervarsity.org.

Scripture quotations, unless otherwise noted, are from the New Revised Standard Version of the Bible, copyright 1989 by the Division of Christian Education of the National Council of the Churches of Christ in the USA. Used by permission. All rights reserved.

Cover design: David Fassett
Interior design: Daniel van Loon
Images: blue-green painted background: © enjoynz / iStock / Getty Images Plus
    San Francisco skyline: © Matteo Colombo / Digital Vision / Getty Images
    apple: © ivan-96 / DigitalVision Vectors / Getty Images
    gold texture: © Katsumi Murouchi / Moment / Getty Images
    grey grunge background: © altedart / iStock / Getty Images Plus
    C. S. Lewis 1947: © C. S. Lewis, 1947 by Arthur Strong / Private Collection / Bridgeman Images.

ISBN 978-0-8308-5236-9 (print)
ISBN 978-0-8308-7277-0 (digital)

Printed in the United States of America ∞

InterVarsity Press is committed to ecological stewardship and to the conservation of natural resources in all our operations. This book was printed using sustainably sourced paper.

Library of Congress Cataloging-in-Publication Data
A catalog record for this book is available from the Library of Congress.

| **P** | 25 | 24 | 23 | 22 | 21 | 20 | 19 | 18 | 17 | 16 | 15 | 14 | 13 | 12 | 11 | 10 | 9 | 8 | 7 | 6 | 5 | 4 | 3 | 2 | 1 |
| **Y** | 38 | 37 | 36 | 35 | 34 | 33 | 32 | 31 | 30 | 29 | 28 | 27 | 26 | 25 | 24 | 23 | 22 | 21 | 20 | 19 |

For my students

Never give up on the longing

❧ CONTENTS ❧

PREFACE

It was the kind of moment every teacher dreams of.

Earlier that day I had introduced my students, all college sophomores, to C. S. Lewis's argument about how our decisions shape our character. Lewis emphasized that every day, a hundred times a day, we are making choices, and taken together those choices determine the kind of people we become and, indeed, our eternal destiny. I gave them lots of examples—the decision whether to share a juicy bit of gossip, say, or to put the phone down and really listen to a friend, or let our gaze rest on another person in a lustful way, or even to begin the day with gratitude or a complaint. The problem, I told them, is that these choices are usually so small, so "beneath the radar" of our consciousness that we don't even realize we are choosing. But we are. And if we could just be aware of them and make decisions that point our lives in a good direction, we would be on our way toward becoming the people we aspire to be.

Now, hours later, here were two students from that same class approaching me on the sidewalk. When they saw me, they both lit up, as if they couldn't wait to share some news. "We were just talking about what you said in class," one said excitedly. "And it's true! We really are making choices all the time." The other nodded vigorously and chimed in, "I just never realized it before."

More than anything else, that is the reaction I hope this book will bring. Of course, I want to shed light on Lewis's thinking about the spiritual life, adding in some small way to the immense body of scholarship on Lewis that has been building almost since he first began to write for a Christian audience. But far greater is my hope that readers will see that what Lewis said makes sense. It's true. And it works. Lewis's understanding of the spiritual life resonates with Scripture and Christian theology, and also with our own deepest longings. It offers the possibility for flourishing in this life and a vibrant hope for the life to come. For those who actually practice the spiritual disciplines he offered, life will never be the same.

I wish to express my gratitude to those who have nurtured this project along the way: to Tammy, my wife, who has shared this journey from day one; to my sons, Joel and Tyler, and their wives, Ashley and Katie, who will soon be introducing my grandchildren to Aslan and the wonders of Narnia; to my friends in the Columbia Church of Christ who welcomed the references to Lewis that seemed to show up almost weekly in my sermons; and especially to Maggie Earles and Steve Koziol, who shared and fueled my enthusiasm for Lewis.

I am also grateful to those who have been instrumental in this project in a more immediate way, especially to David McNutt and the team at InterVarsity Press who got excited about this book with me. Thanks, also, to the two anonymous reviewers for their careful and gracious reading of the manuscript. Their insights and suggestions strengthened the book immensely. I also acknowledge my debt to a brief insight offered by Professor Janet Blumberg in a lecture titled "Plato and Augustine in the Writings of C. S. Lewis" given at a Lewis conference almost twenty years ago (which I stumbled upon in a podcast years later). That insight was the first seed of which this book is the fruition.

Finally, I express my deep gratitude and affection to the students throughout my career whose excitement at discovering Lewis kept me coming back to him again and again—the small group who gathered around *The Great Divorce* in a student apartment at George Washington University, the classes and small groups at Pepperdine University, and now my graduate students at Emmanuel Christian Seminary. But especially I am thankful to Ezra Plank and Mark Barneche, directors of Pepperdine's Lausanne, Switzerland, Study Abroad Program, for inviting me to teach a course on Lewis, not once but twice, and for all the students of the Maison du Lac who embraced that exploration with such eagerness. The vision for this book and most of the original manuscript grew out of our conversations. The joy I saw in you was my inspiration.

ABBREVIATIONS

AM	*Abolition of Man*
FL	*The Four Loves*
GD	*The Great Divorce*
HB	*The Horse and His Boy*
LB	*The Last Battle*
LM	*Letters to Malcolm, Chiefly on Prayer*
LWW	*The Lion, the Witch, and the Wardrobe*
M	*Miracles*
MC	*Mere Christianity*
MN	*The Magician's Nephew*
MP	"Membership"
OSP	*Out of the Silent Planet*
P	*Perelandra*
PC	*Prince Caspian*
PP	*The Problem of Pain*
PR	*The Pilgrim's Regress*
RP	*Reflections on the Psalms*
SJ	*Surprised by Joy*
SL	*The Screwtape Letters*
T	"Transposition" (as it appears in Lewis, *They Asked for a Paper*)
THS	*That Hideous Strength*
TWHF	*Till We Have Faces*
VDT	*The Voyage of the Dawn Treader*
WG	"The Weight of Glory"

INTRODUCTION
"RED BEEF AND STRONG BEER"

Red beef and strong beer." Those were the words C. S. Lewis used to describe life under the rigorous tutelage of his beloved mentor, William T. Kirkpatrick, "The Great Knock." Lewis's father had secured Kirkpatrick as a private tutor for his son in order to prepare him for the entrance examinations to Oxford University. Lewis gave a glimpse of Kirkpatrick's character and teaching style in his endearing account of their first meeting. Kirkpatrick was an imposing figure over six feet tall, "very shabbily dressed (like a gardener, I thought), lean as a rake, and immensely muscular," with a billowing mustache and side-whiskers that made him look like Emperor Franz Joseph. After introducing himself, Lewis nervously tried to make polite conversation by pointing out that Surrey, the region of England where Kirkpatrick lived, seemed "wilder" than he'd expected.[1]

Kirkpatrick's response jarred him. "Stop!" he shouted, with a suddenness that made Lewis jump. "What do you mean by wildness and what grounds had you for not expecting it?" Lewis attempted several answers but found each subjected to further interrogation, until he was finally

---

[1] *SJ*, 133-34.

forced to admit that he'd had no clear rationale for applying the term
wildness to that area whatsoever, a conclusion driven home by Kirkpatrick's assertion that Lewis's remark was completely "meaningless."[2]

Lewis went on to describe his tutor as coming closer than anyone he
ever knew to being a "purely logical entity" for whom "the most casual
remark was taken as a summons to disputation." Although he sometimes
chafed under Kirkpatrick's discipline, Lewis learned to think critically,
and about things that really mattered. Looking back, he would say of his
time there, "Some boys would not have liked it; but to me it was red beef
and strong beer."[3]

Lewis's choice of words to describe the crucible of Kirkpatrick's instruction clearly shows his gift for using language to stir our imagination.
It also underscores his appreciation for the earthy, embodied stuff of life.
Lewis loved food, drink, laughter, and good conversation. He relished an
amble in the English countryside, a joy made all the more delightful by
his anticipation of the cozy fire and pint of ale that awaited him in a pub
at day's end. But I also believe that this phrase gives us a clue to what, for
Lewis, it meant to be spiritual. It points to the possibility that savoring
the sensations of taste and touch, sight and smell and hearing, these
experiences that are often the richest of our earthly lives, represented a
doorway into the presence of God and the first step in the spiritual
journey. This book explores that tantalizing possibility.

SPIRITUAL?

Unfortunately, for many people inside the church and out, becoming
"spiritual" means moving in the opposite direction. Spirituality, they believe, takes us away from the earthy life of "red beef and strong beer." That
was certainly the view I grew up with. As a way of capturing that view of
faith, here is a vivid memory from my life as a young adult, just out of
high school, sitting around the dining room table of a family with whom
I had been deeply connected for several years. The Mossmans were a

---

[2]*SJ*, 134.
[3]*SJ*, 135-35.

fixture in our small community. Dr. Mossman was the town physician, his son was one of my best friends, and I'd dated his daughter, Hannah, in high school. They were lively and engaging and creative, and the times I spent in their farmhouse were always marked by rich conversation and laughter. One memory stands out for me. Dr. Mossman led a small brass ensemble that my brother and I were both part of, which played for various events in our town. One Saturday we had performed for a community function and were back at the Mossmans' house sitting around their dinner table—Dr. Mossman, his son Andy, my brother, and I—talking and laughing together. I especially have an image in my mind of Dr. Mossman with his head thrown back and his mouth wide open, letting loose with a torrent of laughter. As I read back over this account, it all sounds mundane and inconsequential. But it is burned in my memory as a moment of intense pleasure, as witnessed by the fact that I remember it so vividly more than forty years later. In a period of my life riddled with uncertainty and anxiety, that moment around the Mossmans' table gave me a fleeting sense of contentment and well-being, a time when I felt completely at home and filled with joy.

But what strikes me about that experience now is how disconnected it was from the life of faith that I had known for most of my upbringing. I grew up in a deeply religious setting, steeped in Scripture and immersed in the life of the church, all of which I am deeply grateful for. And we did have times of laughter and fun at church (usually after the worship service was over). But what we understood of God and the Christian life seemed to have nothing to do with the kind of pleasure and well-being I felt in that moment around the Mossmans' table. We just didn't have a place for that experience in our theology. It was as if the life of faith and the life of earthy joy were locked in separate rooms, cordoned off in opposite wings of our theological house. For us, as for so many Christians, a chasm existed between what we conceived the "spiritual life" to be and what I glimpsed in that moment of joy and laughter.

Like so many, we believed that the path of discipleship was a path toward emptiness and deprivation, where sacrifice was valued for its own sake and where Christian piety entailed detachment from our bodies and from experiences of physical sensation. When I have explored this popular conception with students, I have typically shown them two photographs side by side and asked the question, "Who's more spiritual?" The first photograph is an iconic image of a Christian saint. He is depicted largely in two-dimensional space, which makes him look especially otherworldly. The corners of his mouth are turned slightly downward in a look of deep thought or detachment or perhaps disapproval. His face is pale, his cheeks are slightly drawn, and his eyes gaze upward to the heavens. Next to that photograph is one of an old guy who looks to be in his seventies, perched on a surfboard and riding a low, gentle wave rolling in at a diagonal to the shore. His face is plastered with a silly grin that beams joy and contentment. For most, it is obvious who is more spiritual. It's the saint. Next, I show them a photograph of a woman sitting by herself on a pew in a large auditorium. It's clearly a church. She is leaning forward in prayer with her head bowed, her forehead resting against the pew in front of her. Next to that photograph is one of a little boy, nine or ten years old, who has just taken a bite out of a juicy red apple. His mouth is full, and a little of the apple still hangs on the edge of his lip. With his whole face, his eyes, even the wrinkle of his nose, he is smiling broadly. That is some apple! Again, who is spiritual? Without a second thought my students answer, "Obviously, it's the woman who is praying."

While I don't want to disparage the holiness of the saints or our need for prayer, I find it significant that when many of us Christians think about what it means to be "spiritual," our minds immediately run in the direction of otherworldliness, of detachment from the physical. We have taken on what we might call a gnostic view of spirituality, according to which becoming spiritual means moving further and further away from the material, from our bodies, and more and more into our heads. When we gather as a community, in that moment when we believe ourselves to be most fully in the presence of God, we sometimes ask God to help us to remove from our minds the things of the world.

A number of contemporary thinkers have traced this tendency to draw back from the stuff of life to Enlightenment philosophy's enduring influence on contemporary Western culture. As one example, Christian philosopher James K. A. Smith explored its roots in the thought of René Descartes, who famously declared *cogito ergo sum*, "I think, therefore I am." Descartes's axiom insinuated that our cognitive rationality functions independently of our bodies and our emotions, suggesting that we could be fully human only to the extent that we bracket out everything but our capacity for abstract reasoning. That paradigm of human existence, which splits mind from body, reaches into every area of our lives, shaping our assumptions about what we can know and leading us to be wary of emotions and distrustful of our bodies. Its influence reaches even to the way we have approached religion, as Smith trenchantly pointed out:

> While the mall, Victoria's Secret, and Jerry Bruckheimer are grabbing hold of our gut by means of our body and its senses—in stories and images, sights and sounds, and commercial versions of "smells and bells"—the church's response is oddly rationalist. It plunks us down in a "worship" service, the culmination of which is a forty-five minute didactic sermon, a sort of holy lecture, trying to *convince* us of the dangers by implanting doctrines and beliefs. . . . The church still tends to see us as Cartesian minds. While secular liturgies are after our hearts, . . . the church thinks it only has to get into our heads.[4]

In a similar vein, psychologists Warren Brown and Brad Strawn's fascinating exploration of contemporary neuroscience and Christian discipleship offered a parallel critique of the understanding many have of the spiritual life:

> In the predominant modern view of spirituality, neither one's physical body, nor other persons, nor church communities, are relevant. Spirituality is both disembodied (that is, manifest in the inner state of the soul,

---

[4]James K. A. Smith, *Desiring the Kingdom: Worship, Worldview, and Cultural Formation* (Grand Rapids: Baker Academic, 2009), 126-27 (emphasis in original).

which we experience as emotions and feelings) and disembedded (an entirely individual state not directly relevant to any other person). Spirituality is an inner reality—one that is only distantly related to ourselves as physical/social beings, or to the nature of our relationships with other people or communities.[5]

When it comes to spirituality, our modern view of the self has sometimes led us to retreat into what philosopher Matthew Crawford called the world "within our heads."[6]

LEWIS'S ALTERNATIVE

Lewis called this tendency to retreat from earthy life "negative spirituality,"[7] and he devoted much of his writing to exposing and refuting it as an utter misunderstanding of God's nature and purpose for humans. Although he addressed it explicitly in many places, his critique of negative spirituality also frequently shows up more indirectly in his works of fiction and fantasy, as the following brief example shows. In the second book of his science fiction trilogy, *Perelandra*, the story's main character, Elwin Ransom, is miraculously transported to Venus at the dawn of that planet's creation. Soon after his arrival, the evil scientist Dr. Weston, who has developed the technology of interplanetary travel, also arrives on the planet, which sets up Lewis's captivating, imaginative account of Venus's version of the temptation story of Genesis 3. As the plot unfolds, it dawns on Ransom that he has been brought there to prevent the planet's first inhabitants from repeating Adam and Eve's sin, a challenge that he is willing to accept until he realizes in a flash that thwarting Weston will mean engaging him in physical, hand-to-hand combat. He is instantly

---

[5]Warren S. Brown and Brad D. Strawn, *The Physical Nature of Christian Life: Neuroscience, Psychology, and the Church* (New York: Cambridge University Press, 2012), 4. See also Owen C. Thomas, "Interiority and Christian Spirituality," *Journal of Religion* 80, no. 1 (2000): 41-60.

[6]Matthew B. Crawford, *The World Beyond Your Head: On Becoming an Individual in an Age of Distraction* (New York: Farrar, Straus and Giroux, 2015), 51. Crawford traces these contemporary trends to the philosophy of Immanuel Kant, who sought to separate the human intellect from the physical world in order to generate moral laws that somehow transcended the messiness of actual human existence.

[7]*M*, 194.

repulsed by that possibility, not only because he finds the prospect of touching Weston's body unnerving and abhorrent but also because, as a religious person, he has always imagined the "spiritual" to be entirely a matter of the will and the mind, not the body, so that the battle against temptation takes place primarily in one's head. The objection is immediately thrown back at him in the knowledge that the "unhappy division between soul and body" commonly assumed by Christians was never God's original design. "Even on earth," he admits, "the sacraments existed as a permanent reminder that the division was neither wholesome nor final. The Incarnation had been the beginning of its disappearance."[8] Thus, in what almost appears as an aside, Lewis reveals what he sees as the error of a spirituality cut off from the physical body.

Not only did Lewis view negative spirituality as a theological error, he also believed that it was the enemy of living joyfully here on earth now and a threat to our hope for the future. To be sure, Lewis unquestioningly embraced the centrality of the cross, and his writings persistently highlight how difficult, indeed how painful, it can sometimes be to embrace true repentance and discipleship. His vision of the joyful Christian life, far from being one of riotous dissipation, was actually marked by an exacting self-awareness and disciplined intentionality. But behind all of this was his insistence that we empty ourselves, not simply in order to be empty but so that God might fill us with the life that is truly life. His view reflected what the New Testament said about Jesus Christ himself, "who for the sake of the *joy* that was set before him endured the cross" (Heb 12:2, emphasis added). When we elevate the negative to a position of the highest value, we rob ourselves of joy and undermine the vibrancy of our message to the world.

Lewis also offered a rich alternative to negative spirituality, what we might call a spirituality of "red beef and strong beer." His alternative was rooted in his understanding of the human self as rational, yet also as emotional and imaginative—deeply moved by beauty—and, finally, as

[8]*P*, 162-63.

embodied. To use his terms from *The Abolition of Man*, we are not just head. We are head, chest, and belly.[9] His understanding of the human person in turn gave rise to an approach to Christian discipleship that involved cognitive functions but also emotions, imagination, and bodily sensations. We see that alternative played out in his own spiritual journey as he was drawn more and more to God through his experiences of beauty and longing, his glimpses of what he called "Joy."[10] Moreover, this earthy view of spirituality runs like a thread through his writings of fiction and fantasy. At the mere hint of the return of the Christ figure, Aslan, to Narnia, the bleak winter snow suddenly melts, primroses bloom, birds begin to sing, and the beauty of a luscious springtime breaks out in the land. When Ransom first finds himself on Venus at the dawn of that planet's creation, he experiences tastes and smells and sights that are overwhelming in the intensity of pleasure they bring. After a mere taste of the juice from a gourd that grew wild on one of the planet's floating islands, he muses that "for one draught of this on earth wars would be fought and nations betrayed."[11] When in *The Great Divorce* the shadowy characters from hell make a visit to the mere outskirts of heaven, what they encounter there is so beautiful and so real that it hurts.

In his nonfiction writing, Lewis similarly invited us to see God as the glad Creator. He pointed to concrete practices that embraced physical pleasure as a principle conduit through which God makes the glory of heaven known on earth. Lewis explained that the act of praise is a crucial dimension of enjoyment—enjoyment's consummation—so that the praise of God is integrally connected to our enjoyment of God. He showed how, by being persistently attentive to our most mundane pleasures and by practicing the discipline of adoration, we might come to receive even the simplest of pleasures as a tiny theophany, in as instantaneous a way as when we hear a particular sound and automatically

---

[9]*AM*, 15-16.

[10]Lewis capitalized the word *Joy* as a way of distinguishing the complex mixture of emotions he was experiencing (pleasure mingled with deep longing, sadness, and nostalgia) from mere feelings of elation.

[11]*P*, 42.

recognize it as the song of a bird, or when we see marks on a page and spontaneously recognize a word. Finally, Lewis gave us a way to receive these pleasures and beauties as glimpses of heaven so that, by constant practice, we cultivate the virtue of hope.

This book traces the theme of earthy spirituality through the writings of C. S. Lewis. It explores his alternative to negative spirituality by focusing on two core dimensions of true Christian spirituality, the elements of consciousness and choice. Lewis believed that becoming spiritual meant growing in self-awareness, expanding one's consciousness of the world and others, and, most importantly, expanding one's consciousness of the presence of God. And he believed that spirituality involved obeying God more and more out of free, uncoerced choice. This book also explores Lewis's conviction that the natural, physical world was the handiwork of a joyful Creator and that it was infused with God's glory so that physical pleasures could be welcomed as "'patches of Godlight' in the woods of our experience."[12] He believed that true spirituality involved exercising consciousness and choice in the realm of the physical so that when we bring the disciplines of consciousness and choice to our physical experience, the physical is "taken up" into, or united with, the spiritual, a view that was rooted in his understanding of the incarnation, resurrection, and ascension of Christ.[13] Finally, this book unfolds the happy implications of his approach to spirituality for our pursuit of Christian discipleship and, especially, for the way that we might sanctify physical pleasures through practices of attention, gratitude and adoration, and self-control.

We begin in chapter one by examining the experience that he called "Joy," the odd mingling of desire, beauty, sadness, and longing that all of us have felt and that, he eventually came to see, was a longing for God.

---

[12]*LM*, 91.
[13]Lewis uses the phrase "taken up" in *The Four Loves* to describe the way that natural loves are taken up into and transformed by divine love (*FL*, 184), as well as in *Reflections on the Psalms*, where it refers to the way non-religious discourse is "taken up" into Scripture (*RP*, 115). For Lewis, the concept is rooted in the incarnation and ascension of Christ (see *M*, 176-78, and *T*, 180).

We explore that experience in our own lives, and we trace the role it played in Lewis's journey to faith. Especially, we note how, in Lewis's early life, as for many Christians today, joy and religion seemed disconnected, almost as if they were in conflict with each other.

In chapter two, we explore the view of God that gave rise to the tension between joy and religion. In his early years, before he became an atheist, Lewis viewed God as distant, harsh, and territorial. As he grew older, he came to see God as the "transcendental Interferer."[14] But as he continued to pursue joy, that repeated experience brought him not simply to a conviction about the reality of God's existence but much more to an understanding of God's nature—to God as the "glad Creator,"[15] the God of joy.

Chapter three focuses on the understanding of spirituality that Lewis believed grew out of the view of God he had known as a young person, what he called "negative spirituality."[16] As he understood it, negative spirituality tends to value sacrifice as an end in itself. It also tends to intellectualize faith and separate it from all that is physical, including sensory pleasure. We conclude by noting why Lewis saw negative spirituality as the enemy of vibrant Christian life and hope.

Chapter four examines Lewis's alternative to negative spirituality, which was centered in the two essential qualities of consciousness and choice. First, Lewis held that we become spiritual as we become more and more aware—aware of ourselves, aware of others and of the world around us, and, most of all, aware of God. Second, we become spiritual as we grow in agency, that is, as we become ever more aware of our capacity to choose and as we obey the will of God increasingly out of free choice.

In chapter five, we show how these core elements of the spiritual life, consciousness and choice, play a central role in the development of character. Lewis challenged us to pay close attention to the cumulative effect

---

[14]*SJ*, 172.
[15]*M*, 194.
[16]*M*, 138.

of what often seem like our most insignificant choices and innermost passing thoughts since these micro-level decisions determine the kind of persons we are becoming. As examples of this principle, we explore the role of consciousness and choice in dealing with emotions, cultivating humility, confronting negative attitudes, and nurturing compassion toward others.

Chapter six applies these two dimensions of the spiritual life to our physical lives, especially to the earthy experience of eating. We explore the way Lewis invites us to bask in God's joyful presence as it comes to us even in the humblest pleasures of our lives, by embracing the disciplines of attention, gratitude and adoration, and self-control.

Chapter seven focuses on the way that seeking community with others plays a crucial role in our personal spiritual growth. Against his natural inclinations, Lewis himself realized that rubbing shoulders with people who are different from us, those whom we might otherwise avoid, has an uncanny power to expand our self-awareness and our consciousness of God. We explore the way that in his writings and his life Lewis modeled curiosity, empathy, and humility as he challenged us to embrace what he came to see as the "fantastic variety of the saints."[17]

Chapter eight explores the impact that Lewis's understanding of "earthy spirituality" can have on the vibrancy of our hope for heaven. Especially, we explore the tantalizing question Lewis encouraged us to ask in our moments of joy, pleasure, and beauty: If these far-off, momentary glimpses of God's presence are so rich and wonderful here, in a world marred by sin and cursed by suffering, what must the life be like that awaits us in heaven?

Finally, we conclude by returning to the theme with which we began, that of joy. We trace that theme through the Bible, exploring how the joy of the Lord runs like a golden thread through all of Scripture, and we show how it provides coherence to all that we understand of living a Christian life.

---

[17]*MP*, 36.

WHY C. S. LEWIS STILL MATTERS

Once, when asked where he wanted the royalties for his books to go after his death, C. S. Lewis predicted, "After I've been dead five years, no one will read anything I've written."[18] As one person quipped, "He would have made a lousy estate planner."[19] In the years since his death Lewis has become the "Elvis Presley of Christian publishing."[20] Within a decade of launching its C. S. Lewis Signature Classics in 2001, HarperOne reported sales approaching ten million.[21] His Narnia series is now in its third film adaptation. When the Huffington Post asked its readers to name one religious book that had most changed their lives, the number one choice was *The Screwtape Letters*.[22] And when *Christianity Today* asked contributors and church leaders to nominate the ten best religious books of the twentieth century, far and away the most popular author was Lewis, and the top choice was *Mere Christianity*. The editors said, "We could have included even more Lewis works, but finally we had to say: 'Enough is enough; give some other authors a chance.'"[23]

What these sources demonstrate about Lewis's enduring influence I have seen directly in the lives of students over the past twenty-five years of university teaching and ministry. More times than I can count I have found myself invited to explore Lewis's writings with students at gatherings that range from late-night fraternity reading groups to campus ministry retreats to spiritual formation training workshops

[18]Lyle W. Dorsett, *Seeking the Secret Place: The Spiritual Formation of C. S. Lewis* (Grand Rapids: Brazos Press, 2004), 20.
[19]John Blake, "Surprised by C. S. Lewis: Why His Popularity Endures," *CNN Belief Blog*, December 10, 2010, http://religion.blogs.cnn.com/2010/12/17/surprised-by-c-s-lewis-why-his -popularity-endures/.
[20]Blake, "Surprised by C. S. Lewis."
[21]Sarah Pulliam Bailey, "C. S. Lewis Still Inspires 50 Years After His Death," Religion, Huffington Post, November 22, 2013, www.huffingtonpost.com/2013/11/22/cs-lewis-50-year-death_n _4325358.html.
[22]"Top 100 Religious Books," Religion, Huffington Post, updated September 14, 2012, www .huffingtonpost.com/2012/09/14/top-100-influential-relig_n_1836687.html?slideshow=true #gallery/246516/0.
[23]"Books of the Century: Leaders and Thinkers Weigh In on Classics That Have Shaped Contem-porary Religious Thought," *Christianity Today*, April 24, 2000, www.christianitytoday.com /ct/2000/april24/5.92.html.

to undergraduate and graduate academic courses. For most, the experience has been life changing. As one student put it, "I will never see the world in the same way again."

For these as for so many others, Lewis provides an intellectually defensible account of Christian faith, in marked contrast to the common view of faith as wishful fantasy (and nonbelief as the only intellectually honest response to the empirical data of the universe). Lewis also gives them theological coherence, by which the biblical narrative and their own personal experiences of joy and longing as well as suffering and pain seem to make sense. They find practical wisdom on topics ranging from prayer and temptation to relationships, emotions, and even good writing. Because he was so well read in historical theology—from Athanasius and Augustine to Anselm and Aquinas, just to name a few from the *A* section—Lewis provides access to a rich theological tradition that most would otherwise never encounter.

But most of all, Lewis gives us a way of living out the faith that is joyful and full of vitality—as God intended it to be. Lewis urges us to pay close attention to the rich, often mundane experiences of pleasure and delight that mark our days and to view these wonderful sensory experiences as glimmers, from an unimaginable distance, of the very glory of God. He bids us wonder at what the nature of God must be to have created this. And he invites us to imagine what it might mean to live eternally in the presence of this God. In offering all of this, he presents a way of living well, a way of living that embodies the Christian message as truly good news. And whatever else is true of our lives, we who claim to follow God, the glad Creator, ought to be known as people who live well.

CHAPTER ONE

AN INCONSOLABLE SECRET

OUR LONGING FOR JOY

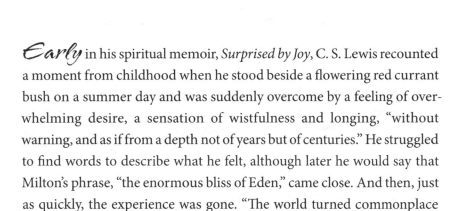

Early in his spiritual memoir, *Surprised by Joy*, C. S. Lewis recounted a moment from childhood when he stood beside a flowering red currant bush on a summer day and was suddenly overcome by a feeling of overwhelming desire, a sensation of wistfulness and longing, "without warning, and as if from a depth not of years but of centuries." He struggled to find words to describe what he felt, although later he would say that Milton's phrase, "the enormous bliss of Eden," came close. And then, just as quickly, the experience was gone. "The world turned commonplace again." The sensation had lasted for just a brief instant and yet, he realized all other pleasures were nothing compared to this.[1]

Most of us have known that experience, that fleeting glimpse of paradise that steals over us unbidden, often when we are not looking. I remember sitting on a bus crowded with commuters one fall morning, quite early. I was looking over my notes for the class I would teach later that day when the bus passed a small lake at the base of a sloping hillside blanketed by oaks and maples ablaze in the full color of autumn. I looked up and instantly felt the sensation of sweet desire, the ache of beauty, the

---

[1]*SJ*, 16.

mixture of longing and sadness all flood over me. Lewis later called it "the scent of a flower we have not found, the echo of a tune we have not heard, news from a country we have never yet visited."[2]

The oddest things can trigger these feelings: a particular view, a memory, certain smells or sounds. For the narrator of Marcel Proust's famous novel, *Remembrance of Things Past*, a mere bite of a madeleine cookie dipped in a hot drink unleashed a stream of nostalgia:

> No sooner had the warm liquid mixed with the crumbs touched my palate than a shudder ran through me and I stopped, intent upon the extraordinary thing that was happening to me. An exquisite pleasure had invaded my senses, something isolated, detached, with no suggestion of its origin. And at once the vicissitudes of life had become indifferent to me, its disasters innocuous, its brevity illusory—this new sensation having had on me the effect which love has of filling me with a precious essence; or rather this essence was not in me, it was me. . . . Whence did it come? What did it mean?[3]

In those moments we are lifted out of our anxiety and self-consciousness. The sensation of timelessness breaks into our experience, a sensation captured in Paul Tillich's pregnant phrase, the "eternal Now."[4] But then, just as suddenly, the moment is gone and we are plunged back into the "reality" of our day-to-day lives.

What are we to make of those experiences? Do they have anything to do with God or with the life of faith? What would it mean for us if they did? In his famous sermon to the citizens of Athens, recorded in Acts 17, the apostle Paul explained that God, who had given humans "life and breath and all things" (Acts 17:25), had deliberately left traces of divine love all around us, in the hope that we would seek God and find life— although, he added, God is not far from each of us. Lewis came to see

---

[2]*WG*, 5.

[3]Marcel Proust, *Swann's Way*, trans. C. K. Scott Moncrieff and Terence Kilmartin (New York: Vintage Books, 1989), 48.

[4]Tillich described how at certain moments eternity "breaks powerfully into our consciousness." Paul Tillich, *The Essential Tillich: An Anthology of the Writings of Paul Tillich*, ed. F. Forrester Church (Chicago: University of Chicago Press, 1999), 127.

these moments of blissful longing as signs of God's presence, traces of God's love that captivated his heart. That sensation, which he called joy, fell upon him before he even had words to describe what it was. In his early years, it became alternatively an obsession and a haunting that sometimes made day-to-day life a challenge. But eventually those strands of joy formed the cord through which God drew Lewis to faith. They also became the foundation for one of his most compelling arguments for the existence of God and the basis for what he had to say about the spiritual life. For Lewis, joy held the secret of living with gladness in the moment and hope for the heavenly life to come, a realization that came out of a personal spiritual journey marked in its early years by a persistent tension between joy on the one hand and religion on the other. And so, although this book is not a biography, we begin with a brief account of his journey, tracing that tension between his religious life and these glimpses of what he called the "inconsolable secret."[5] First, however, let us consider our own glimpses of joy.

THE ENORMOUS BLISS OF EDEN

In a haunting episode from *The Pilgrim's Regress*, which he published in 1933 soon after becoming a Christian, Lewis offered this image of joy. At the beginning of the story, the main character, John, who is languishing under the yoke of oppressive religion, has a glimpse of beauty that stabs his heart with desire. One day when he is out wandering along a road by a stone wall, he notices something odd up ahead—a window in the wall. He approaches the window, and when he looks through it, he sees trees and primroses.

---

[5]*WG*, 3. A number of excellent biographies of Lewis are available, including these: Alister E. McGrath, *C. S. Lewis—A Life: Eccentric Genius, Reluctant Prophet* (Carol Stream, IL: Tyndale House, 2013); Devin Brown, *A Life Observed: A Spiritual Biography of C. S. Lewis* (Grand Rapids: Brazos Press, 2013); George Sayer, *Jack: A Life of C. S. Lewis*, rev. ed. (Wheaton, IL: Crossway, 2005); Humphrey Carpenter, *The Inklings: C. S. Lewis, J. R. R. Tolkien, Charles Williams, and Their Friends* (London: HarperCollins, 1997); and Roger Lancelyn Green and Walter Hooper, *C. S. Lewis: A Biography* (New York: Harcourt, Brace, Jovanovich, 1974). For a brief but very informative overview of Lewis's life, see Art Lindsley's essay, "C. S. Lewis: His Life and Works," *C. S. Lewis Institute*, www.cslewisinstitute.org/node/28.

He remembered suddenly how he had gone into another wood to pull primroses, as a child, very long ago—so long that even in the moment of remembering the memory seemed still out of reach. While he strained to grasp it, there came to him from beyond the wood a sweetness and a pang so piercing that instantly he forgot his father's house, and his mother, and the fear of the Landlord, and the burden of the rules. . . . A moment later, he found that he was sobbing.[6]

Although our own experiences might differ in detail, most of us have known what it feels like to have that ache of longing fall upon us, to yearn deeply for that place, that possession or achievement, that relationship that will finally fulfill us, that will take us out of our loneliness, anxiety, and striving. We have all had experiences that we look forward to or remember or daydream about that make our hearts throb with desire. They are glimpses of Eden.

Mine often involve the memory of times away from the typical routines and demands of my life—a camping trip we once took to the Grand Canyon when my boys were small or the week we would spend each summer with dear college friends in Maine. In one especially vivid memory, my wife and I are in a tiny village in the Sierras, set in a small valley ringed by mountains crowded with tall pines that give way to soaring granite cliffs. It is early in the morning. The sky is a deep blue. The air is cold. I can see my breath. The snow on the ground, hardened during the night's freeze, crunches under my boots. As I walk, I catch the scent of pine mixed with wood smoke.

As that last example shows, the sensation of desire often comes over me in the presence of nature's beauty—the view of mountains covered with frost that I see from my office window when I look up from my desk or the scene I caught from the bus on that early morning commute. Being near the sea has that power over me. I hear the rhythm of the surf as waves break on the shore again and again. An ocean breeze caresses my cheek. The sun is warm on my face. The smell of the sea brings back

---

[6]*PR*, 24.

a flood of memories from childhood vacations at the ocean. But I have also experienced it listening to music or at certain moments when I am watching a movie or reading a good book.

The feeling sometimes comes when I look ahead to some event in the future—a trip I hope to take, the approach of fall, or maybe the first snow of winter. I often experience it when I daydream about the coming of Thanksgiving or Christmas. In my vision, I am surrounded by my family. The house is filled with the sound of conversation and laughter and the smell of food.

Just thinking about these moments creates intense longing in me. It aches and stabs. I want to be there so badly. I know what it is to look forward to those moments—to have the kind of feeling, Lewis said, that comes over us when we first fall in love or we daydream about taking a journey to a distant country.[7] When I know that one of those times is coming, the anticipation of being there is almost overwhelming; indeed, part of the richness of the experience is the anticipation itself. Because I know that when I am there, all will be well. I will be completely content; all of my worries and cares will fade away. I will be lifted out of insecurity and self-consciousness. All my fears about the future or my regrets from the past will melt away. I will be able to enjoy the people I am with completely. Finally, I will be *There*.

I also know what it is like to look back on those experiences in the past. I remember them as being perfect (not like my life at present). My mind re-creates of those times a memory of paradise.

But, if I am honest with myself, I know that when I'm actually in those moments, they are never quite as perfect as I thought they would be. I have been given the gift over the years of vacations in the mountains or by the seashore, as well as wonderful family gatherings. In so many ways they were magical, and they remain the source of many of my richest memories. But I know that, in the moment, they were not perfect. There were still stresses and worries, traces of tension. Running through all was

---

[7]*MC*, 119.

the painful sense that the time was flying, like sand slipping through my fingers. When the long-awaited moment finally comes, it's as if I've been eagerly awaiting Christmas morning and at last have opened my gifts, and then I look around with a sense of loss and disappointment and ask, "Is this all?"

More than any other author I have ever read, Lewis has helped me make sense of that experience. He invited us to consider the possibility that our own longing, this "inconsolable secret,"[8] might be a window on the nature of God, a clue to the purpose for which we were made, and the key to living the good life. His conviction of that possibility grew out of a struggle to come to terms with his encounters with Joy, a struggle that lay at the heart of his own spiritual journey.

Joy Versus Religion: Lewis's Spiritual Journey

As *Surprised by Joy* makes clear, much of Lewis's early spiritual journey was marked by a tug-of-war between the opposing forces of faith and religious observance on the one hand and these recurring glimpses of joy on the other. He described his earliest years, when he was a small child, as an idyllic time often spent in imaginative play with his older brother, Warnie. This was also the time when he had his first glimpses of joy. During these years, he was clearly exposed to religion, but it was a religion in which God was a distant figure and in which faith had nothing to do with joy. We get a hint of the nature of his view of God when his mother, Flora, became sick and eventually died. The year was 1908, and Lewis was just nine years old. He had been taught that God would grant his prayers if only he would pray with enough faith, so he set about trying to muster a sense of conviction within himself (which was what he thought it meant to have faith) in order to secure her healing, almost as if by sorcery. As he saw it, God was a magician who might, if conditions were right, grant his wish and then go away and leave him alone.

---

[8]*WG*, 3.

In the years of adolescence that followed, the battle lines between religion and joy seemed to move back and forth in Lewis's life. At first religion seemed to gain the upper hand while joy retreated into the background. In the fall of 1908, his father, Albert Lewis, engulfed in his own grief over Flora's death, sent his two sons to the Wynyard School, a boarding school that Lewis called "Belsen," after the concentration camp in Nazi Germany.[9] The school was ruled by a despotic, mentally ill headmaster the students called "Oldie." There, Lewis became a believer in the sense that he attended church and tried to actually practice his religion, but it was a fearful faith dominated by what Lewis characterized as a persistent, oppressive "fear for my soul."[10] Almost at the same moment, the glimpses of joy he had known in his earliest years vanished from his life entirely.

The lines shifted, however, when at age thirteen he was sent to a second boarding school, the Cherbourg School, which he called "Chartres," and where, by his own admission, he lost his faith. Although a number of influences hastened this process—among them dabbling in the occult and being exposed to parallels between Christianity and pagan mythology, all overlaid with the deep pessimism toward the universe that he had imbibed early in his life—what he most remembered about his loss of faith was simply how eager he was to be rid of it, so onerous had it been. It was a burden from which he "longed with soul and body to escape."[11] Ironically, this was also the moment of rebirth, when the rich experiences of joy returned to his life.

The two decades that followed represent the season of Lewis's life when he was first an atheist and then an Idealist, holding to a philosophical position that admitted the possibility of some impersonal force or Spirit guiding history.[12] Throughout this time, he arduously resisted the prospect that Christianity might be true. Yet it was also the period

---

[9]For the identification of the schools Lewis attended, see McGrath, *C. S. Lewis—A Life*, 26.
[10]*SJ*, 33.
[11]*SJ*, 62.
[12]On Lewis's embrace of Idealism, see *SJ*, 208-11.

when the quest for joy became his master passion. In 1913, he transferred to a third boarding school, Wyvern College, which he attended for just one year. It was a year marked by the contrast between his "inner" and "outer" lives. The outer life was marked by the overwhelming drudgery of surviving the school culture's ruthlessly competitive social hierarchy, which was centered on sports, and the school's system of involuntary servitude known as "fagging." Lewis's inner life, by contrast, was suffused with glimpses of joy so extravagant and beautiful that they almost hurt. After one year in this purgatory, he found release in the person of William T. Kirkpatrick, who tutored Lewis over the next two years in his home in order to prepare him for Oxford. Lewis came away from his time with Kirkpatrick more deeply confirmed in his atheism but also with a sharpened intellect and a lifelong passion for logical argument—a facility that would play a crucial role in his coming to faith, by compelling him to make sense of the recurring experiences of joy. He would speak of Kirkpatrick with reverence and gratitude for the rest of his life.

Lewis successfully completed his scholarship examinations in the winter of 1916 and was admitted to Oxford the following summer, but before he could begin in earnest, he enlisted in the army and, in November 1917, found himself in the frontline trenches of northern France where he witnessed the carnage of the First World War and where he was wounded in April of the following year.[13] Returning to Oxford in January 1919 at the end of the war, he spent the next four years studying Greek and Latin literature, philosophy and ancient history, and English literature, before being appointed as a tutor in philosophy at University College in 1924 and, the following year, a fellow and tutor in English literature at Magdalen College, where he served until his appointment to the chair of Medieval and Renaissance Literature at Cambridge University in 1954.

As Lewis recounted it, it was during this time, when he was a student and then a fellow at Oxford, that his quest to find joy reached its most fevered pitch. He became something of an expert in Norse mythology

---

[13]*SJ*, 158.

in the belief that it would lead him to joy, but once he had built the temple, he awakened only to discover that "the God had flown."[14] His earlier boarding school experience had already convinced him that ambition offered no answer, and over time he considered but finally eliminated both sex and the occult as possibilities. During this period he also found the defenses he had erected against God beginning to crumble. He came to realize that his favorite writers, if not all actual believers, were "dangerously tinged with something like religion, even at times, with Christianity."[15] He found himself surrounded by close friends whom he truly respected and enjoyed, who were either Christians or at least sympathetic to Christianity, among them Owen Barfield, J. R. R. Tolkien, Hugo Dyson, and others. And in a development we will consider in greater detail in the next chapter, he was forced to the logical conclusion that there had to be a source to which these experiences of joy were pointing, if not in the natural world then in a world beyond this one. From there, it was but a short distance to that point when, on a summer evening in 1929, with great reluctance, he surrendered to God.[16] As we shall see, coming to terms with the experience of joy not only led him to admit that there was "another country" ruled by the God he had all his life avoided; it also hinted at the fundamental character of that God—the God of joy. In this way, what for most of Lewis's early life had been completely separate, these experiences of longing and his faith in God, finally came together, a process driven by the haunting of our "inconsolable secret."[17]

THE INCONSOLABLE SECRET IN LEWIS'S WRITINGS

In a number of his early writings, we find traces of Lewis's haunting glimpses of joy. One compelling expression of that longing occurs in the first book he ever produced, an edition of poetry titled *Spirits in Bondage:*

---

[14]*SJ*, 165.

[15]*SJ*, 214.

[16]*SJ*, 228. McGrath, with others, has argued that the correct date was actually 1930. See his *C. S. Lewis—A Life*, 146.

[17]*WG*, 4.

A Cycle of Lyrics.[18] Lewis published the book in 1919, just after returning
from World War I—and before he had returned to Christianity, or even
theism. Published under the pseudonym Clive Hamilton (his first name
and his mother's maiden name), the slim volume contained poems he
had been writing as early as his teen years, along with others that he
wrote during the war. In some we hear anger at a God who, at this point,
Lewis doesn't even believe exists.[19] In others we get a hint, rare in Lewis's
writings, of the suffering he witnessed during World War I. But especially
we sense the stabs of longing. Yet at this stage in his journey, there was
no God to which they pointed. The best Lewis could hope for was to
savor those rare moments in the midst of the hopelessness of mundane
human existence. One particularly poignant expression was the poem
"Dungeon Grates," which depicts joy as a tiny stream of light coming
through the bars of a prison.[20]

Lewis began the poem by trying to convey what he saw as the human
condition, that of being caught in an endless chain of cause and effect,
within a meaningless, materialistic universe. We are trapped in a grim
and hopeless world, inescapably entangled in the gears of "unrelenting
fate," and we would die from the utter dreariness of it all were it not for
the rare, unsought glimpses of beauty that steal over us, those moments when we sense a "fragrant breath" that comes wafting to us from
the distant country for which we ache "with overstrong desire."[21] We
cannot control those moments; no amount of effort on our part will
produce them—they are beyond our will. Instead, they come upon us

---

[18]C. S. Lewis, *Spirits in Bondage: A Cycle of Lyrics*, ed. Walter Hooper (New York: Harcourt Brace
Jovanovich, 1984).

[19]Lewis said of this period, "I was at this time living . . . in a whirl of contradictions. I maintained
that God did not exist. I was also very angry with God for not existing. I was equally angry with
Him for creating a world" (*SJ*, 115).

[20]C. S. Lewis, "Dungeon Grates," in *The Collected Poems of C. S. Lewis: A Critical Edition*, ed. Don
W. King (Kent, OH: Kent State University Press, 2015), 88-89. In an essay published some
twenty-five years later, Lewis described another moment when a small beam of light shone in a
dark place, not a dungeon but a toolshed. Only then he spoke not simply of looking at the beam
but of looking *along* the beam and, by it, seeing the world. C. S. Lewis, "Meditation in a Toolshed," in *God in the Dock: Essays on Theology and Ethics*, ed. Walter Hooper (Grand Rapids:
Eerdmans, 1970), 212-15.

[21]"Dungeon Grates," 88.

when we are not expecting them. And yet, in those glimpses of transcendence, we are "one with the eternal stream of loveliness," that ocean of beauty in which we long to "sport and swim."[22] Much later, Lewis returned to this notion of our hunger for oneness with the beauty we see around us in his "Weight of Glory" sermon, where he described our response to the beauty of nature as a longing not simply to gaze from the outside but "to be united with the beauty we see, to pass into it, to receive it into ourselves, to bathe in it, to become part of it."[23] As a Christian, he came to see that experience as a foretaste of what awaits us:

> At present we are on the outside of the world, the wrong side of the door. We discern the freshness and purity of morning, but they do not make us fresh and pure. We cannot mingle with the splendors we see. But all the leaves of the New Testament are rustling with the rumor that it will not always be so. Some day, God willing, we shall get in.[24]

But again, at the point in his journey when he published *Spirits in Bondage*, Lewis possessed no answer for this persistent longing.

In some poems from the same collection, Lewis railed in anger at the meaningless universe, as in the poem titled "In Prison," where he cried out

> For the pain of man . . .
> Against the hopeless life that ran
> Forever in a circling path.[25]

---

[22]"Dungeon Grates," 89.

[23]*WG*, 8.

[24]*WG*, 8.

[25]C. S. Lewis, "In Prison," in King, *Collected Poems of C. S. Lewis*, 84. Although Lewis was attracted to what he called this "Promethean defiance" early in his life, he came to see as a logical contradiction the very idea that a meaningless universe could, through a process of random, "natural" selection, produce creatures who are aware of that meaninglessness and who expect that it should be otherwise. As he put it in *Mere Christianity*, "A man feels wet when he falls into water, because man is not a water animal: a fish would not feel wet. . . . If the whole universe has no meaning, we should never have found out that it has no meaning" (*MC*, 45-46). He called this "a futility which seems to vitiate Lord Russell's stirring essay" (*SJ*, 205)—a reference to Bertrand Russell's famous essay, "A Free Man's Worship." This observation served as one of the foundations for his arguments for the existence of God in *Mere Christianity* (45-46), *Miracles* (17-36), and *The Problem of Pain* (1-15).

In others, he wished he had never known the siren call of desire, as when he romanticized the life of the "stout, suburban people" who "water flowers and roll the lawn" then "sit and sew and talk and smoke" while he sits alone in the cold, wet night vexed by "homeless longing."[26] How much better to be these "solid folk" who, "after their work and doze and smoke, are not fretted by desire."[27] But having been touched by that longing, the most positive response he could muster as he ended "Dungeon Grates" was to express a resigned determination to hold onto the memory of that glimpse of light. Perhaps we will find in that glimpse the strength to bear the dreary hopelessness of the universe, the strife that mars our social relationships, and the burdens and disappointments and pain of our lives:

> One moment was enough . . .
> We have seen the Glory—we have seen.[28]

Like the theme to which a musical composition returns again and again, we hear throughout the poems in this collection the despair of finding himself trapped in a meaningless existence, yet haunted by the glimpse of something more.

However, the book in which Lewis described the experience most explicitly was *Surprised by Joy*. In the opening pages, he recounted one of his earliest memories from around the age of seven, when his brother, Warnie, showed him a little "toy garden" he had created on the inside lid of an old cookie tin, "covered with moss and garnished with twigs and flowers. . . . That was the first beauty I ever knew." He went on to say, "As long as I live my imagination of Paradise will retain something of my brother's toy garden." During this same time from early childhood, he recalled, he and his brother would gaze at a series of knolls that were visible from the nursery window, which they called "the Green Hills." His

---

[26]C. S. Lewis, "In Praise of Solid People," in King, *Collected Poems of C. S. Lewis*, 98-99.

[27]We will meet the "solid folk" again in Lewis's fantasy, *The Great Divorce*, where they represent the glorious condition of humans who have embraced the utter reality of heaven. But here, without the perspective of Christian faith, Lewis could only romanticize that state as one of blissful ignorance of the inconsolable ache.

[28]"Dungeon Grates," 89.

description of them captures the ache that would become a theme of his life—though not that far away, they seemed "quite unattainable. They taught me longing—*Sehnsucht*."[29]

Later in the book, he described other such recurring moments from young childhood (including the one when he was standing next to the flowering red currant bush), one of which came to him when he read Beatrix Potter's *Squirrel Nutkin*, a book that haunted Lewis with what he could only call "the Idea of Autumn."[30] Again, the book evoked such longing, and he found himself returning to it in order to arouse that sense of desire. A third glimpse he found in poetry, particularly in a passage from Longfellow's *Saga of King Olaf*, where he read these words:

I heard a voice that cried,
Balder the beautiful
Is dead, is dead—

Although he knew nothing of Balder, somehow the poetry lifted him up "into huge regions of northern sky." As with his other experiences of joy, the longing that came over him was "almost sickening" in its intensity and then, almost as quickly, it was gone.[31] In every case, he was left with the yearning to feel it again.

By contrast, he saw his passage into adolescence as a journey into the desert or into winter. He was shipped off to that first "concentration camp" of a boarding school (Wynyard) and the indiscriminate cruelty of Oldie, the headmaster, and then soon after enrolled at the school he called "Chartres" (the Cherbourg School), where he abandoned his faith

---

[29]*SJ*, 7. Paul Brazier offers a helpful explanation of this German concept, which, he observed, is not easily translatable because "it is more than simply a word—it is 'a yearning,' 'a longing.' . . . A yearning for, a longing for, implies an object, an object of desire, but there is so often with *Sehnsucht* no object, it is the sensation itself. Therefore, *Sehnsucht* is often seen to have mystical overtones relating to something unattainable. It is . . . characterized by a fervent and passionate desire or longing, a yearning or craving, a hunger or even an addiction. In many ways this feeling, the concept of this desire, is destructive, negative, even seen by some as self-defeating because of the regret and, simultaneously, the deeply corrosive sense of unattainability and loss." Paul Brazier, *C. S. Lewis—Revelation, Conversion, and Apologetics* (Eugene, OR: Pickwick, 2012), 29.
[30]*SJ*, 16.
[31]*SJ*, 17.

and where he learned to smoke and to take on the dress, speech, and demeanor of pompous dandy.[32] Early in his time at Chartres he came to know ambition and had many experiences of pleasure, but "the authentic 'Joy' . . . had vanished from my life: so completely that not even the memory or the desire of it remained."[33]

But then one day everything changed. Joy returned. It is a mark of the kind of religion Lewis had been taught that this rediscovery of joy only happened after he had ceased believing in God. He described that moment in language that will be familiar to anyone who has read of Aslan's return to Narnia in *The Lion, the Witch, and the Wardrobe*; he said that it was as if the "long winter" had suddenly given way to "a landscape of grass and primroses and orchards in bloom, deafened with bird songs and astir with running water."[34] The winter ended so abruptly when he happened on a literary magazine that someone had left lying on a classroom table one afternoon. As he entered the room, he saw a headline that read "Siegfried and the Twilight of the Gods" and, below it, an image drawn by the famous illustrator Arthur Rackham. That magazine cover instantly took him back to those powerful experiences from childhood that he had all but forgotten. Overcome with what felt "almost like a heartbreak," he found that he had returned "at last from exile and desert lands to my own country."[35] Then, just as quickly, the moment was gone and he found himself in the same drab, unswept classroom. But from that moment on, he was determined to recapture that sensation.

Through all of these experiences, Lewis traced the common thread of joy, which he defined as "an unsatisfied desire which is itself more desirable than any other satisfaction."[36] Joy, he insisted, was different from happiness or pleasure (the latter of which we, at least, have some power to produce for ourselves). Joy might just as easily be described as a kind of bittersweet sadness, and yet no one who had truly known that feeling would trade it

---

[32]*SJ*, 68.
[33]*SJ*, 72.
[34]*SJ*, 72.
[35]*SJ*, 73.
[36]*SJ*, 17-18.

for any other gratification the world could offer. It was this uncanny melding of transcendent bliss, intense longing, and bittersweet sadness that I felt that fall morning on the bus riding past the lake and the trees in fall color, a sensation all of us have known in our own glimpses of Eden.

As Lewis made clear, these momentary visions of bliss mingled with longing and sweet sadness were the richest experiences of his life. Although he came to realize that the longing's fulfillment was unattainable, that it was always over the next hill or around the next bend, he also found that simply to feel the longing itself, unfulfilled though it was, was more to be sought than any other satisfaction that might be attained in his life. As chapter two will show, when Lewis moved further through his education and into his early career as a scholar, the juxtaposition of desire's intensity with its ultimate frustration in this life became a vexing existential problem for him. Complicating the matter, of course, was the logical conviction he came to that the universe could not be dismissed as meaningless or random, indeed, that attempting "to keep our minds, even for ten seconds at a stretch, twisted into the shape that this philosophy demands" was simply impossible.[37] Coming to terms with that problem would be a key to his conversion—and would provide him with one of his most compelling arguments for the reality of heaven. Although he offered that argument in several places, one of the most explicit is in his "Weight of Glory" sermon, where he spoke movingly of the "inconsolable secret . . . which hurts so much that you take your revenge on it by calling it names like Nostalgia and Romanticism and Adolescence," that secret which is our "desire for our own far-off country."[38] In our search for desire's fulfillment we likewise come to realize that the longing does not reside in the things that aroused it—the music, the book, the sexual encounter, the accomplishment, the vacation, wherever the place or image was that we thought would bring joy. Rather, we find that

---

[37]C. S. Lewis, "The Empty Universe," in *Present Concerns: Essays by C. S. Lewis*, ed. Walter Hooper (San Diego: Harcourt Brace Jovanovich, 1986), 83-84. Lewis cites the ironical alternative to seriously contemplating nihilism, which was recommended by David Hume—retreating into a game of backgammon.

[38]*WG*, 4.

it only came *through* them. . . . These things, the beauty, the memory of
our own past—are good images of what we desire; but if they are mistaken for the thing itself they turn into dumb idols, breaking the hearts
of their worshippers.[39]

Thus, he concluded, "We remain conscious of a desire which no natural
happiness will satisfy." Yet he looked around and realized that every other
desire we have finds its fulfillment in *this* country, save this one, which
is the longing that haunts us above all others. Might this tell us that we
were ultimately made for *another* country? While a man's hunger does
not prove that he will get bread, surely it "does prove that he comes of a
race which repairs its body by eating and inhabits a world where eatable
substances exist."[40] For Lewis, then, this excruciating desire, uniquely
potent and yet unattainable in this life, would eventually become the key
to his understanding of God's vision for human existence. But not yet.

SIGNPOSTS

On the final page of *Surprised by Joy* Lewis asked, "But what, in conclusion,
of Joy?" He answered by saying that after he became a Christian, the
subject "lost nearly all interest for me."[41] It wasn't that he no longer felt
the pull of that deep longing. But now he realized that its value really lay
in the way it pointed to something beyond itself. In one sense, this was
true. He came to believe that the longing was never intended for fulfillment in this life, but only in God. Once he realized its true purpose,
finding it in this life no longer held the urgency that it once did.

But this is not the entire story. Although these glimpses of Eden no
longer had power over him in the way they had before he came to faith,
they nevertheless remained a foundational element of his spiritual life,
pointing him to the presence and goodness of the God he had come to
know. As he would put it in "The Weight of Glory," they are the "faint,
far-off results of those energies which God's creative rapture implanted

---

[39] *WG*, 4-5, emphasis in original.
[40] *WG*, 6.
[41] *SJ*, 238.

in matter when He made the worlds."[42] In Lewis's view of the spiritual life, they were sacraments, signs of grace and gifts from God, the glad Creator.

Lewis would also come to see in these experiences the foundation of our hope, a perspective also captured on the final page of *Surprised by Joy*. He described what it was like to find a signpost when we are lost in the woods. We all excitedly gather around it. But once we've found our way and are passing signposts regularly, we no longer stop and gaze at them as we did at first. Of course, they encourage us, and we are grateful to the One who put them there. "But we shall not stop and stare, or not much; not on this road. Though their pillars are of silver and their letters of gold, 'We would be at Jerusalem.'"[43] As signposts, they were never ends in themselves but instead pointed beyond themselves to God. Lewis would frequently warn against the dangers of focusing on pleasures apart from the presence of God. In *The Great Divorce*, hell turns out to be the place where you can have anything you want, just by wishing it to be— the kind of place that most of us imagine (and that most advertising offers) as pure paradise. Yet the people there are quarrelsome, lonely, and miserable. Even the new, larger house that one gains by wishing it into existence cannot keep out the rain. And yet, Lewis also came to believe that as Christians, we ought to savor these experiences as glimpses of the coming glory vouchsafed to us who now live in this "valley of tears."[44] Thus, for Lewis, what began in that nursery before he had the language to put it into words became the basis for his understanding of God, as well as a theme running throughout much of his writing.

In almost thirty years of talking about that longing with audiences young and old and at dramatically different stages of faith, I have yet to find one that hasn't felt it, in spite of Lewis's advice in the opening pages of *Surprised by Joy* to anyone who had not experienced that ache, that they should put the book down and move on. Rather, what I always see come over people's faces is a knowing, if also a faraway, wistful look.

---

[42]*WG*, 14.
[43]*SJ*, 238.
[44]*LM*, 92.

We've all felt it. And I always ask these questions: What do these glimpses of joy mean? What might they be pointing us to? To folks who are not yet followers of Jesus, I acknowledge that they might not mean anything. But wouldn't that be the ultimate tragedy, if the richest, most exquisite moments of our lives, when we are overcome with transcendent longing, didn't point to anything, but instead were just a cruel joke played on us by our brains. On the other hand, what if they *do* mean something? What if they actually *are* signposts pointing us to the purpose for which we were made? Wouldn't that be a possibility more wonderful than we can imagine? Wouldn't it at least be worth serious consideration? For Christians, of course, the question goes deeper. What do these experiences tell us about the nature of God and the life that God intends for us? What would it mean for us if our faith and our deepest longing were brought, finally, together?

That is the question that runs through all of Lewis's Christian writings. He believed that we are each imprinted with a desire that, for all our attempts to fulfill it in other ways, is really the longing for one thing: heaven. In *The Problem of Pain*, he said that, although he had sometimes wondered if we desired heaven at all, more often he was convinced that we have never desired anything else. The longing for heaven is "the secret signature of each soul, . . . the thing we desired before we met our wives [or husbands] or made our friends or chose our work, and which we shall still desire on our deathbeds, when the mind no longer knows wife [or husband] or friend or work." All our lives this "unattainable ecstasy" has hovered just beyond our consciousness. In our happiest moments we have only known "hints of it—tantalizing glimpses, promises never quite fulfilled, echoes that died away just as they caught your ear." And yet, he said wistfully, if you should ever find it, "if there ever came an echo that did not die away but swelled into the sound itself—you would know it. Beyond all possibility of doubt you would say 'Here at last is the thing I was made for.'"[45]

---

[45]*PP*, 133-34.

CHAPTER TWO

NOT SAFE—BUT GOOD

GOD AS THE GLAD CREATOR

Safe?' said Mr. Beaver. 'Don't you hear what Mrs. Beaver tells you? Who said anything about safe? 'Course he isn't safe. But he's good. He's the King, I tell you.'"[1] Earlier, as the four Pevensie children, Peter, Susan, Lucy, and Edmund, led by the good Mr. Beaver, had trudged through the snows of Narnia—where it was winter but never Christmas—their guide had gathered them close and told them, in a whisper, "They say that Aslan is on the move." Lewis wrote, "A very curious thing happened. None of the children knew who Aslan was . . . ; but the moment the Beaver had spoken these words everyone felt quite different." For the three oldest children, it was like a "dream so beautiful that you remember it all your life and are always wishing you could get into that dream again."[2] But now, as they sat around the Beavers' dinner table after a tasty meal of fresh pan-fried trout, and Mr. Beaver revealed that Aslan, the King of Narnia, was a Lion, they were not so sure.

---

[1]*LWW*, 75-76.

[2]*LWW*, 64. For their younger brother, Edmund, who on an earlier venture into Narnia had agreed to betray his sisters and brother to the White Witch in exchange for Turkish Delight and a position of royal power, Aslan's name brought "a sensation of mysterious horror."

As the story unfolded, Peter, Susan, and Lucy made their way to a place called the Stone Table, where they were to meet the King. Edmund had already stolen away from the Beavers' house while the others were deep in conversation and gone to the Witch's castle, where he found not the delicious candy and hot chocolate he had hoped for but stale bread crusts and insipid water and, instead of royal power, imprisonment. On their way to meet Aslan, the other three children began to see everywhere around them signs of Aslan's presence. Narnia was coming alive with springtime.

But ironically it was Edmund, by then also on his way to the Stone Table, a grim prisoner in the White Witch's sledge, who was most touched by Narnia's rebirth. As Lewis depicted it, Edmund's journey of repentance actually began with his dawning awareness of the first hints of spring. It was an awakening that roused all his physical senses as if from sleep. He first heard a "strange, sweet, rustling, chattering noise" that he realized was running water, and he saw "streams chattering, murmuring, bubbling, splashing and even (in the distance) roaring. And his heart gave a great leap (though he hardly knew why) when he realized that the frost was over."[3] The cold landscape came to life:

> Wherever you looked, instead of white shapes you saw the dark green of firs or the black prickly branches of bare oaks and beeches and elms. Then the mist turned from white to gold and presently cleared away altogether. Shafts of delicious sunlight struck down onto the forest floor and overhead you could see a blue sky between the tree-tops.[4]

Soon Edmund saw crocuses springing up around the foot of an old tree, "gold and purple and white," and then he heard an even more enchanting sound, a bird chirping from the branch of a tree, answered by the "chuckle of another bird a little further off," so that, as if by signal, "there was chattering and chirruping in every direction, . . . and within

---

[3]*LWW*, 114.
[4]*LWW*, 116.

five minutes the whole wood was ringing with birds' music."[5] Aslan—and springtime—had come to Narnia.

Taken together, these threads from Lewis's beloved children's fantasy show how Lewis came to understand the character of God, represented in the Chronicles of Narnia by Aslan, a figure of Christ. God is relentless in goodness and fierce in love, and ultimately God overturns Narnia's perpetual winter through Aslan's willing self-sacrifice on the Stone Table, Narnia's parallel to the cross. Yet behind all of that is God's identity as the glad Creator whose very appearance awakens a jubilant spring.

But it was not always this way. For much of his early life, Lewis saw God as harsh and exacting, as an impediment in his quest for the good life. The tug-of-war he experienced between joy and religion owed much to that view of God. Sadly, he was not alone in that view. For many people inside the church and out, God seems disconnected from their own richest experiences of pleasure and longing. Even for those who remain in the faith, their conception of God gives rise to a kind of Christian life that seems dull and unfulfilling and fails to nurture their flourishing as persons.[6] And yet Lewis eventually came to a radically different view of God, one in which his experiences of joy were integrally connected to his understanding of God's character. He came to see God's joyful presence as the fulfillment of his deepest longings, especially the longings evoked by the beauty of the world around him.[7] In this chapter, we trace

---

[5]*LWW*, 117.

[6]See David Kinnaman and Gabe Lyons, *Unchristian: What a New Generation Really Thinks About Christianity . . . and Why It Matters* (Grand Rapids: Baker Books, 2007), who summarized young adults' view of Christians and Christianity in this way: "Christians are boring, unintelligent, old-fashioned, and out of touch with reality." Few believe that "an active faith helps people live a better, more fulfilling life. Church . . . has no spiritual verve. . . . The faith is boring" (119, 120, 121).

[7]In much of what Lewis wrote about seeing God's glory in the beauty of nature, he reflects the influence of Augustine, who wrote of how, even in a universe marred by sin, we experience "divine generosity" in "the manifold diversity of beauty in sky and earth and sea; the abundance of light, and its miraculous loveliness, in sun and moon and stars; the dark shades of woods, the color and fragrance of flowers; the multitudinous varieties of birds; . . . the mighty spectacle of the sea itself, putting on its changing colors like different garments, now green, with all the many varied shades, now purple, now blue." These goods "flow as it were from the fountain of God's goodness even into a nature corrupted by sin and condemned to punishment." Augustine, *City of God*, trans. Henry Bettenson (Harmondsworth, UK: Penguin Books, 1972), 22.24.

that wonderful transformation in Lewis's understanding of God, and we explore the perspective he gave us for making sense of our own encounters with that exquisite, inconsolable desire.

THE DISTANT LANDLORD

We find a hint of the God Lewis knew in his early years from his poignant account of his mother's death from cancer when he was just ten years old, which we alluded to in chapter one. When her case was pronounced hopeless, he sought to produce within himself the confidence that she would be healed, in keeping with what he had been taught about how the prayer offered with sufficient faith would make the sick well. Then, when she died, he set himself to praying in the belief that she would be miraculously raised. What is most unexpected about Lewis's account, however, is how little the failure seemed to affect him. At this point, he said, he felt neither love nor even fear toward God. Rather, God was more like a magician who, after granting Lewis's fervent wish, would just disappear.[8] Even at an early age, Lewis knew God as distant and aloof.

That same aloofness, this time mingled with harsh strictness, characterized another early portrait of God, this one from Lewis's allegory, *The Pilgrim's Regress*. This portrait seems to fit what we know of his early religious life, which was pervaded by profound fearfulness and by futile, desperate attempts to fulfill his required nightly prayers by producing an internal sense (Lewis called them "realizations"[9]) that he had prayed with enough faith that he could finally allow himself to fall, exhausted, into bed. Several episodes in the early life of the allegory's main character, John, capture the negative, oppressive character of religion in the land of Puritania where John lived. One day John ventured into the woods and began to pick primroses. His mother came running from the garden in a panic, snatched him up, smacked his hands, and sternly warned him never to enter the wood again. Several years later, he took his little sling out into the garden intending to "have a shot at a bird" when cook came

---

[8]*SJ*, 20-21.
[9]*SJ*, 62.

running, smacked him soundly, and warned him never to kill any birds from the garden, for if he did, he would incur the wrath of the Steward, the man charged by the Landlord to enforce the rules of the country.[10] A few years after that, John was taken to meet the Steward himself, who instructed him in the ways of the Landlord. The Steward told him that the Landlord owned all the country and that it was "*very, very* kind of him to allow us to live on it at all—very, very kind" (emphasis in original). The Steward, clearly a caricature of the sanctimonious clergyman, kept repeating "very kind" in such a "queer sing-song voice" that John began to be afraid. Then the Steward took a big card, written all over in small print, down from a peg on the wall and handed it to John, telling him that it contained the list of "all the things the Landlord says you must not do."[11] Lewis described the card in this way:

> Half the rules seem to forbid things he had never heard of, and the other half forbade things he was doing every day and could not imagine not doing; and the number of the rules was so enormous that he felt he could never remember them all.[12]

When the Steward asked, "I hope that you have not already broken any of the rules?" John's heart began to pound.

> Because, you know, if you did break any of them and the Landlord got to know of it, do you know what he'd do to you? . . . He'd take you and shut you up forever and ever in a black hole full of snakes and scorpions as large as lobsters—forever and ever. And besides that, he is such a kind, good man, so very, very kind, that I'm sure you would never *want* to displease him.[13]

Again, God was distant, harsh, territorial, and unconcerned for the good of people. God had given humans an impossible list of rules and threatened them with eternal punishment for violating them—a stark reality that could not be masked by all of the Steward's hollow claims of

---

[10]*PR*, 20.
[11]*PR*, 21.
[12]*PR*, 21-22.
[13]*PR*, 22, emphasis in original.

God's kindness. Much later, in *Mere Christianity*, Lewis echoed this view
when he described how most people approached Christian morality:
"People often think of Christian morality as a kind of bargain in which
God says, 'If you keep a lot of rules I'll reward you, and if you don't I'll
do the other thing.'"[14] No wonder the Steward, after asking John if he had
ever broken one of the rules, removed his mask and said—in his one
moment of authentic disclosure—"Better tell a lie, old chap, better tell a
lie. Easiest for all concerned."[15]

Somewhat later in Lewis's early adulthood, as he began to sense the
reality of God assaulting the fortress of his atheism, a related perception
of God came to dominate his thinking, one present in that early childhood
hope that God would heal his mother and then leave Lewis alone. This
was God as divine interferer. It owed much to what Lewis claimed was a
"lopsidedness of temperament," his intense desire not to be interfered
with. When it came to food, he could forgive blandness much more
quickly than what he suspected was excessive seasoning. So also in his
life, he was ready to endure monotony with far greater patience than any
sort of inconvenience or interruption, and what he insisted on above all
else was not to be interfered with.[16]

This desire not to be interfered with had been nourished by his relationship with his father, a sentimental, effusive, and somewhat mercurial man
with whom Lewis and his brother had a difficult relationship. In one particularly humorous episode, he described how his father would occasionally, and quite spontaneously, take the afternoon off of work and come
home to discover his sons reading contentedly in the garden. He would
join them, dressed, of course, in one of his overcoats, and would then
invite them to squeeze onto a bench exposed to the full glare of the sun
so that pretty soon, he would begin to wilt in the heat. Exclaiming that it

---

[14]*MC*, 86.
[15]*PR*, 22.
[16]*SJ*, 116-17. Lewis captured this natural disposition in what he described as his ideal day—a day
that involved no interference with those activities that brought him pleasure (*SJ*, 141-43). We can
appreciate the burden Lewis took on in devoting several hours per day responding personally,
often by hand, to the vast amount of mail from followers who wrote to him after he began to
publish books about Christianity.

was too hot, he would then order the party indoors, an order with which his sons would disappointedly but dutifully comply.[17]

What Lewis came by naturally and in his relationship with his father, he brought to his conception of God—a strong desire not to be interfered with. As a teenager embracing the cold rationalism of his tutor, William T. Kirkpatrick, and the materialist philosophy to which he thought it inevitably led, Lewis found himself looking out on a world that was hopeless and forbidding but at least was "free from the Christian God." Lewis expressed outrage that he had been brought into existence without his consent, and he located his "horror of the Christian universe" in the fact that "it had no door marked *Exit*."[18] Later, when recounting his journey toward conversion, he framed the story as one in which his Adversary was slowly but inexorably closing in on him. He used the metaphor of a chess match to describe the major turning points in his religious life, recounted in chapters from *Surprised by Joy* titled "Check" and "Checkmate." To anyone who might speak glibly of a person's search for God, he retorted that this would be like the "mouse's search for the cat."[19] He hated authority, valuing above all else his absolute autonomy, and at the center of the Christian faith, he believed, was a God who demanded absolute obedience. In his final attempts to defend himself from God, he spoke of God's "steady, unrelenting approach," and when he finally surrendered to theism, it was submission to "Him whom I so earnestly desired not to meet."[20]

The conception that emerges from these varied passages in Lewis's works, then, is of a God who was distant, removed from the concerns of people. To the degree that God was present, God was jealous and

---

[17]*SJ*, 124-25. This account is part of one of the most detailed portraits of his father that Lewis ever gives (*SJ*, 120-26). It is delightful in its humor, yet also poignant in the affection Lewis showed toward his father and also in the regret he felt over his inability to respond to his father's intense loneliness and desire for his sons' friendship. But it might also be taken as an example for how parents might honor their children by learning to *listen* to them, a theme Lewis emphasized in his treatment of *storge*, or "affection," in *The Four Loves* (42-44).

[18]*SJ*, 171.

[19]*SJ*, 227.

[20]*SJ*, 228.

self-protective, enforcing rules—mainly prohibitions—with threats of eternal punishment. For Lewis, the God he seemed to know in his early years was the negation of all that he found beautiful and good. This understanding of God helps to explain the central dynamic of Lewis's early spiritual journey, which, we noted, consisted in a tug-of-war between joy and religion, set at odds against each other and vying for the place of prominence in his heart. It was almost as if these two important features of his life, his religion and his longing for these recurring experiences of transcendence, pulled in opposite directions so that as one increased the other diminished. During the time he was a pupil at his first boarding school (Wynyard) as a child, he began to learn about Christian teachings but in a way that made him constantly fear for his soul. At the same moment that he was embracing this fearful Christianity, he was also seeing "a great decline in my imaginative life," by which he meant a loss of those experiences of joy.[21] Later, by contrast, when the experiences of joy began to return in early adolescence, they did so at the same time that he was losing his faith. Because Lewis saw God as the harsh, self-protective enemy of human happiness, he naturally could not imagine that joy and religion had anything to do with each other.

In fact, in *Surprised by Joy*, Lewis emphasized that his adolescence actually represented two separate stories, one of joy and one of "reality." As he put it, "I am telling a story of two lives. They have nothing to do with each other: oil and vinegar, a river running beside a canal, Jekyll and Hyde. Fix your eye on either and it claims to be the truth."[22] On the one side had been his brief experience with Christianity as an oppressive and fearful religion and later, when his faith waned, the stark reality and empty futility of daily existence leading eventually to death. This was his day-to-day life, and, as his education developed, it became especially the life of his intellect. And yet there was that other life of glimmered moments of ecstasy "when you were too happy to speak," when you felt like

---

[21]*SJ*, 33-34.
[22]*SJ*, 119.

the beauty "might break you with mere richness."[23] Those glimpses of joy were often closely intertwined with sensory pleasures:

> What keen, tingling sunlight there was! The mere smells were enough to make a man tipsy—cut grass, dew-dabbled mosses, sweet pea, autumn wood, wood burning, peat, salt water. The sense ached. I was sick with desire; that sickness was better than health.[24]

He would later come to realize that those encounters with joy offered him something that, ironically, had been completely absent from his religion. They were actually moments of adoration, a "kind of quite disinterested self-abandonment to an object which securely claimed this by simply being the object it was."[25] Of course, this is what God ultimately should have evoked in him. Yet the God he had come to believe in was so disconnected from his experiences of beauty that, while God might have evoked fear or dread, this God did not call forth a response of worship. He actually felt more awe toward the Norse gods he knew weren't real than he did toward the God in whom he claimed to believe. Eventually, Lewis surmised that during this period of his life, he had, in mercy, been "sent . . . back to the false gods there to acquire some capacity for worship against the day when the true God should recall me to Himself."[26] But until that day came, these sweet ecstasies bore no connection to what he saw as the real world, much less to the reality of God. Rather, they were "but momentary flashes, seconds of gold scattered in months of dross, each instantly swallowed up in the old, familiar, sordid, hopeless weariness."[27]

FROM DIVINE INTERFERER TO GLAD CREATOR

What changed all of this for Lewis? Among the many influences on his life that moved him toward faith, two factors seem to predominate.

---

[23] *SJ*, 118.
[24] *SJ*, 118-19.
[25] *SJ*, 76, emphasis added.
[26] *SJ*, 77.
[27] *SJ*, 119.

One was simply his dawning awareness of God's relentless goodness, an awareness that grew out of his pre-conversion sense that God was closing in on him. Although he made clear that he was conscious of his own freedom to choose, what dominated the period of his life before his conversion was a sense that God was pursuing him, that God was constantly pressing him to surrender.

In his fantasy *The Great Divorce*, Lewis described a series of characters who travel on a bus from hell to heaven and who are each invited to stay—but in order to stay, each must relinquish some attitude or belief or behavior, some souvenir of hell, that they have been convinced they cannot live without. Each visitor from hell is met by an angelic guide, someone they had known on earth who was now in the glorious new body of heaven, and whose task it is to help them stay. In each case, the heavenly guides (Lewis calls them the "solid people") do all in their power—pleading, cajoling, arguing, challenging, grasping at even the flimsiest of straws—in order to get the visitors from hell simply to stay and partake of heaven's bliss. This was Lewis's way of capturing what he came to believe—that God's desire to save us and to bring us joy were unremitting, and that the gates of hell were locked on the hell side. This is what Lewis came to see of God from his own journey, as he reflected on the way God had welcomed him despite his stubborn efforts to resist God's entreaties at every turn. He marveled at the "Divine humility" that would "open the high gates [even] to a prodigal who is brought in kicking, struggling, resentful, and darting his eyes in every direction for a chance of escape."[28] Central to the transformation of his understanding of God was coming to know in his own life the fierce love of the God who would go to any length, short of overruling a soul's final, stubborn refusal, in order to save.

But the other element that changed his view of God was his pressing need to come to terms with the recurring experience of joy, to overcome what Malcolm Guite described as the "profound divorce between what

---

[28]*SJ*, 228-29.

his reason told him, what he felt he could know and affirm philosophically, on the one hand, and the deepest intuitions or apprehensions of
his imagination on the other."[29] As we noted in the last chapter, among
the most formative influences on his intellectual development was
William T. Kirkpatrick, "The Great Knock," under whose tutelage Lewis
learned to think clearly and critically. As an adult, Lewis loved logic, he
relished a good argument, and was so well known as a debater that in
1941, when a group of students established the Oxford Socratic Club, a
society for debating issues about faith and reason, they naturally chose
him as their first president.[30] Most importantly, perhaps owing to his
time with Kirkpatrick, Lewis was fiercely committed to intellectual
honesty. In a poem he wrote several years before his embrace of theism
he depicted reason, represented by the goddess Athene, as "a virgin,
arm'd, commercing with celestial light," and he solemnly warned that the
person who sins against her defiles his own deepest nature: "no cleansing
makes his garment white."[31] At the same time, Lewis could not dismiss
the stirrings of his imagination, represented by Athene's counterpart
Demeter, "warm, dark, obscure, and infinite," bringing delight and
beauty, but also pain. The poem concluded with his plea for a way to
bring reason's "intellectual sight" together with imagination's "dim
exploring touch."[32]

What brought him to that convergence between reason and imagination was a process that looks much like the kind of argument that

---

[29]Malcolm Guite, "Telling the Truth Through Imaginative Fiction: C. S. Lewis on the Reconciliation of Athene and Demeter," in *C. S. Lewis at Poets' Corner,* ed. Michael Ward and Peter S.
Williams (Cambridge: Lutterworth, 2016), 16.

[30]For an account of the establishment of the Socratic Club, see Alister E. McGrath, *C. S. Lewis—
A Life: Eccentric Genius, Reluctant Prophet* (Carol Stream, IL: Tyndale House, 2013), 250-52; and
Walter Hooper, "Oxford's Bonnie Fighter," in *Remembering C. S. Lewis: Recollections of Those Who
Knew Him,* ed. James T. Como (San Francisco: Ignatius Press, 2005), 241-308. See also the de-
lightful account by the club's founder, Stella Adwinkle, "Memories of the Socratic Club," in
C. S. Lewis and His Circle: Essays and Memoirs from the Oxford C. S. Lewis Society, ed. Roger
White, Judith E. Wolfe, and Brendan N. Wolfe (Oxford: Oxford University Press, 2015), 192-94.

[31]C. S. Lewis, "Set on the Soul's Acropolis the Reason Stands," in *The Collected Poems of C. S. Lewis:
A Critical Edition*, ed. Don W. King (Kent, OH: Kent State University Press, 2015), 238. See also
Guite's insightful analysis of this poem, "Telling the Truth," 16-19.

[32]Lewis, "Set on the Soul's Acropolis," 238.

appears several times in his writings, the process of elimination.[33] We encounter this argumentative form, of course, in his articulation of the "trilemma" (the idea that Jesus was a liar, a lunatic, or the Lord),[34] but it also shows up in his arguments for theism in *Mere Christianity* (where he eliminates first materialism, then pantheism, and finally dualism),[35] as well as in *The Lion, the Witch, and the Wardrobe*, when Professor Kirk challenges the Pevensie children to logically analyze the claims of their sister Lucy that she has found a magic kingdom through the door of an old wardrobe,[36] and, finally, in his novel *Till We Have Faces*, when the character Orual considers the claim of her half-sister, Psyche, that she is married to a god and living in a splendid castle, none of which Orual has yet seen.[37]

Lewis's own spiritual journey followed the same process, writ large. To be sure, Lewis was not "forced" into faith by logical argument, and it would be a gross misreading of his writings to reduce that process to merely an intellectual operation.[38] As Lewis made clear, imagination, aesthetic beauty, and myth all play a crucial role in awakening us to the reality of God. These are the "good dreams" God had sent to the human race to prepare us for God's presence,[39] giving us, in Guite's words, the "imaginative anticipation of truths to which reason has not yet attained." Indeed, Lewis's entire body of Christian writing—certainly his novels and fantasies but also those stirring poetic passages in his nonfiction work—these were all predicated on the assumption that "stories and poetry . . . kindle the imagination for

---

[33]*Convergence* is Smilde's term for the reconciliation between reason and imagination. See Arend Smilde, "Horrid Red Herrings: A New Look at the 'Lewisian Argument from Desire'—and Beyond," *Journal of Inklings Studies* 4, no. 1 (2014): 33-92.

[34]*MC*, 54-56.

[35]*MC*, 31-51.

[36]*LWW*, 43-45.

[37]*TWHF*, 117-18.

[38]Smilde argues convincingly that the so-called "argument from desire" often attributed to Lewis actually represents a misreading of his work. Rather, Lewis spoke in terms of a "dialectic of Desire" lived out through one's experience, a dialectic that involves pursuing and then abandoning every false object of desire at the moment that its falsity becomes apparent. Smilde, "Horrid Red Herrings," 35-42.

[39]*MC*, 54.

Christ." And so, as Guite concluded, "appeals to imagination are not simply a decorative idea, a sweetening of the doctrinal pill in Lewis's apologetic writing, but are woven essentially into the fabric of what he says."[40] This was certainly Lewis's own experience, one in which, he said, "my imagination was, in a certain sense, baptized; the rest of me, not unnaturally, took longer."[41]

Rather, his conversion was the result of his intellect and his imagination working together, over the course of many years.[42] In his early years, he associated the feeling of joy with "Northernness," his term for the constellation of imagery, music, mythology, and even elements of nature that, in his mind, all revolved around Norse legend. As we noted above, after the drought of his early adolescence, the sensation of joy had come "riding back to me on huge waves of Wagnerian music and Norse and Celtic mythology."[43] Lewis subsequently plunged himself into reading the sagas, collecting recordings of Wagner's operas, and learning Norse history, to the point that, by his own count, he could have passed a rigorous exam on the topic. But he found that the more he knew, the less he enjoyed. At other points, he dabbled in spiritualism and the occult, but was protected from this "spiritual debauch," not only by his fear of "awakened childhood horrors" but simply by "the known nature of Joy." The "ravenous desire to break the bounds, to tear the curtain, to be in the secret," all of which occultism offered him, "revealed itself, more and more clearly the longer I indulged it, to be quite different from the longing that is Joy."[44] And so he eliminated the occult as the source of joy. Like many people, Lewis also sought its fulfillment in sex, and one of his more humorous remarks on his quest relates to the insight that while sex brought pleasure, it did not bring joy. It was not a question of morality but, rather, of relevance:

[40]Guite, "Telling the Truth," 19, 25, 19-20.
[41]SJ, 181.
[42]In the preface to the third edition of *The Pilgrim's Regress*, Lewis was careful to point out that he discovered each of the options he had pursued as the source of joy to be false, "not by intelligence but by experience" (*PR*, 8).
[43]SJ, 165.
[44]SJ, 176-77.

You might as well offer a mutton chop to a man who is dying of thirst as offer sexual pleasure to the desire I am speaking of. I did not recoil from the erotic conclusion with chaste horror exclaiming, "Not that!" My feelings could rather have been expressed in the words, "Quite. I see. But haven't we wandered from the real point?"[45]

"Joy," he concluded, "is not a substitute for sex; sex is very often a substitute for Joy."[46]

Lewis thus found that every answer to the search came up short, and of course he thought he had already eliminated God as a possibility.[47] For a time, he concluded that there must not be any objective reality to which the longing was attached and decided instead that "what I wanted was a 'thrill,' a state of my own mind." But this, he came to see, was a deadly error: "Only when your whole attention and desire are fixed on *something else*—whether a distant mountain, or the past, or the gods of Asgard—does the 'thrill' arise. It is a by-product" (emphasis added).[48] What finally drove him to this realization—and, to use his chess metaphor, forced him into checkmate—was discovering the theory of "Enjoyment" and "Contemplation" in philosopher Samuel Alexander's book *Space, Time, and Deity*, a technical concept that would inform much of Lewis's thinking and writing for the rest of his life.[49] Alexander's theory sought to distinguish the object on which one is focusing from the actual act of focusing on it, that is, from consciousness of that object as an event in the mind. As Lewis explained it, when one sees a table, one contemplates the table, and "enjoys" the act of seeing the table.[50] But then, if one turns to thinking about what it means

---

[45]*SJ*, 170.

[46]*SJ*, 170.

[47]Around the same time, Lewis encountered a number of authors whom he deeply respected who, in one way or another, believed in some kind of reality beyond the "frontier" of this world, among them Yeats, Maeterlinck, and especially George MacDonald, as he expressed his views in *Phantastes, A Faerie Romance* (first published in London: Fifield, 1905; see *SJ*, 174-75, 179-81). Still later, writers like George Herbert and G. K. Chesterton challenged him to consider the possibility that the object of his desire might actually be God (*SJ*, 214).

[48]*SJ*, 168.

[49]Samuel Alexander, *Space, Time, and Deity: The Gifford Lectures at Glasgow, 1916-1918* (Gloucester, Mass.: Peter Smith, 1979).

[50]*SJ*, 217.

to "see" the table, one is no longer contemplating the table itself but is now contemplating the act of "seeing." Lewis also believed that the experience of "enjoyment" included the attendant emotions, sensations, and so on that come from the "contemplation" of whatever one is seeing or hearing or thinking *about*. So in one of his own examples, we contemplate the object of our hope—some happy event we anticipate in the future—and we enjoy the feelings of hopefulness that come with that anticipation.[51] Or to use another of his examples, when we grieve, we contemplate the reality of the beloved's death and enjoy the feelings of grief and loss.[52]

The pivotal insight from Alexander's conception of contemplation and enjoyment, which Lewis instantly realized to be true, was that one could not contemplate an object at the same time that one contemplates the act of thinking about it or the feelings produced by that object. The moment we turn our attention from the object of our contemplation to the feelings themselves, the feelings go away. As he explained, you can't focus on your feelings of fear and the thing you are afraid of at the same time. Turn your attention from the object of your dread to the feelings themselves and the feelings cease. That distinction made sense to Lewis instantly but then, almost as quickly, he began to realize the consequences of that acceptance— consequences he called "catastrophic."[53] Looking back over his whole life, he suddenly understood why the sensation of joy would instantly disappear the moment he realized that he was experiencing it—he had attempted to contemplate the feelings themselves, which it was impossible to do without driving them away. But even more importantly, he was forced to admit that there must be some object, some thing or some Person, the contemplation of which produced the longing he so desired. In other words, this was the logical conclusion of the entire matter: the very existence of joy "presupposes that you desire not *it* but something other and outer."[54] He had already realized that all glimpses of joy in this

---

[51]*SJ*, 218.
[52]*SJ*, 217.
[53]*SJ*, 218.
[54]*SJ*, 168, emphasis added.

life had proved unfulfilling. But now, he was forced to admit that the desire is always oriented toward something outside of itself. Solely as an event in his mind, joy had no real value. Its only value lay in whatever it was pointing to as its fulfillment. As he put it, each imagined fulfillment had said, finally, "I am only a reminder. Look! Look! What do I remind you of?"[55] And, through this process of elimination, he had come to realize that no fulfillment for this desire existed in this country. He was driven to one inexorable conclusion: we must have been made for another country.

What is crucial for Lewis's understanding of the nature of God, however, was not just that there was another country but also what kind of country it was and, more importantly, what kind of Deity ruled there. As he thought more deeply about Alexander's conception of contemplation and enjoyment, Lewis found himself forced to admit not only the reality of an object to which his desires were pointing, which in the short term seemed the most startling implication. What became far more important over the course of Lewis's life was his realization that the desire "*owes all its character to its object.*"[56] This was the insight that finally connected his experiences of joy to his conception of God. If these flashes of longing, his deepest, most exquisite glimpses of bliss, of delight and beauty, were pointers to God, what must the nature and character of this God be? What must heaven, the country of this God, be like? What would it mean to partake of that glory? In one of his final books, *Letters to Malcolm, Chiefly on Prayer*, Lewis would answer that question by articulating what he called the "secret doctrine that *pleasures* are shafts of the glory as it strikes our sensibility."[57] In those moments, "we are being touched by a finger of that right hand at which there are pleasures forevermore." And he would ask this haunting question: "What must be the quality of that Being whose far-off and momentary coruscations are like this?"[58] Thus, this rule of logic became the thing that finally helped

---

[55]*SJ*, 220.
[56]*SJ*, 220, emphasis added.
[57]*LM*, 89, emphasis in original.
[58]*LM*, 90.

to bring his faith and his experiences of longing and beauty together, ending once and for all the war between them. He now saw those moments of ecstatic bliss as signposts pointing to God. And of course the signposts stood most often within the realm of physical sensation. The place where, for humans, the touch of that divine finger was most present was in the physical world, apprehended through sensory experience— the realm, Lewis pointed out, that God created and uniquely blessed in the incarnation. As he exclaimed, it is this God "who sends rain into the furrows till the valleys stand so thick with corn that they laugh and sing. The trees of the wood rejoice before Him and his voice causes the wild deer to bring forth their young. He is the God of wheat and wine." This understanding of God would frame Lewis's entire conception of the Christian life. Our call, he insisted, was not "to shrink back from all that can be called Nature into negative spirituality," for that would be "as if we ran away from horses instead of learning to ride."[59] To be spiritual, we must learn to ride.

The God of Corn and Oil and Wine

Lewis never lost his sense of awe at God's power and holiness, never lost his awareness that Aslan was not safe, but good.[60] But his own journey to faith showed him that even God's severity was aimed wholly at our salvation. Toward the end of the second book of his science fiction trilogy, *Perelandra*, the character Elwin Ransom glimpses the true nature of the figures of Venus and Mars, who represent archangel guardians of those planets, and he realizes that a "single, changeless expression—so clear that it hurt and dazzled him—was stamped on each."[61] He concluded that what he was seeing was charity, or divine love. Yet, it was "terrifyingly different" from human charity, "ten million miles" from the natural affection that is usually bound up with our own loves. Rather, "pure, spiritual, intellectual love shot from their faces like barbed lightning. It was

---

[59]*M*, 138.
[60]*LWW*, 76.
[61]*P*, 199.

so unlike the love we experience that its expression could easily be mistaken for ferocity."[62] God, in Lewis's mind, was clearly no indulgent, doting grandfather. To the contrary, God was fierce in seeking our salvation. Of course, as Lewis would say in *The Four Loves*, God's unremitting love would ultimately lead to the cross:

> He creates the universe, already foreseeing—or should we say "seeing"? There are no tenses in God—the buzzing cloud of flies about the cross, the flayed back pressed against the uneven stake, the nails driven through the . . . [medial] nerves, the repeated incipient suffocation as the body droops, the repeated torture of back and arms as it is time after time, for breath's sake, hitched up. If I may dare the biological image, God is a "host" who deliberately creates His own parasites; causes us to be that we may exploit and "take advantage of" Him. Herein is love. This is the diagram of Love Himself, the inventor of all loves.[63]

As Lewis saw in his own life, "The hardness of God is kinder than the softness of men, and His compulsion is our liberation."[64]

But Lewis also came to realize that this liberation was liberation into the joy of the God of "corn and oil and wine,"[65] whose glory comes to us even in our momentary experiences of mundane pleasure. And as he would say in "The Weight of Glory," those "reborn in Christ" shall drink "at the fountain-head that stream of which even these lower reaches prove so intoxicating."[66] Such would be our final, glad experience of the glory of God.

Among the many passages in his writings that convey our glimpses of that glory, one of the most charming is the happy encounter that Peter, Susan, and Lucy have on their way to the Stone Table, in the episode with which this chapter began. The children, along with Mr. and Mrs. Beaver, had taken shelter in a cave where they could rest for a while before continuing their journey. They awakened to the sound of bells and

---

[62]*P*, 199-200.
[63]*FL*, 127.
[64]*SJ*, 229.
[65]*M*, 194.
[66]*WG*, 14.

assumed that the White Witch had caught up to them. Mr. Beaver scrambled out of the cave to look, but the person he found was not the Witch at all. He motioned the others to come, so they clambered up a small rise that overlooked the path and there, atop a sledge with reindeer,

> sat a person whom everyone knew the moment they set eyes on him. He was a huge man in a bright red robe (bright as holly-berries) with a hood that had fur inside it and a great white beard that fell like a foamy waterfall over his chest. . . . He was so big, and so glad, and so real, that they all became quite still, . . . but also solemn.[67]

The person they saw, of course, was Father Christmas himself, whose presence signaled the return to Narnia of feasting and celebration and good cheer.[68] At his greeting, Lucy "felt running through her that deep shiver of gladness which you only get if you are being solemn and still."[69] For Lewis, as for the children, the arrival of Aslan brought joy, this King whose very name was like "a dream so beautiful that you remember it all your life and are always wishing you could get into that dream again."[70]

In Exodus 34:6, in the mysterious story where God's presence passes before Moses, it says that "the LORD proclaimed" the divine name to Moses. It was God's way of saying, "This is who I am. This is my nature, my very essence." And what was the name of God?

> The LORD, the LORD,
> a God merciful and gracious,
> slow to anger,
> and abounding in steadfast love and faithfulness. (Ex 34:6)

---

[67]*LWW*, 102-3.

[68]As Michael Ward observed, Father Christmas represents the mythical character of Jupiter, or Jove, an archetypal figure whose presence "animates the imaginative vision of *The Lion, the Witch, and the Wardrobe*." See Ward, *Planet Narnia: The Seven Heavens in the Imagination of C. S. Lewis* (Oxford: Oxford University Press, 2008), 42. Lewis himself described Jove as "Kingly; but we must think of a King at peace, enthroned, taking his leisure, serene. The Jovial character is cheerful, festive, yet temperate, tranquil, magnanimous. When this planet dominates we may expect halcyon days and prosperity. . . . He is the best planet, and is called The Greater Fortune, *Fortuna Major*." C. S. Lewis, *The Discarded Image: An Introduction to Medieval and Renaissance Literature* (Cambridge: Cambridge University Press, 2012), 106.

[69]*LWW*, 103.

[70]*LWW*, 64.

This was the God Lewis came to know—and the God that he invited us to know. In his imaginative writings, he sought to paint pictures and evoke images that would plant a vision of this God deep in our own imaginations, through such characters as Aslan, Father Christmas, and Maleldil. But Lewis also gave us a way of cultivating this vision of God in our daily lives, by attending to our longings, our experiences of beauty, and our sensations of pleasure, and then looking beyond them to the God who has given them to us. In so doing, he believed, we would come to know this God who abounds in steadfast love.

CHAPTER THREE

THIS BLEAK FANTASY

NEGATIVE SPIRITUALITY
AND THE CHRISTIAN LIFE

In the first volume of Lewis's science fiction trilogy, *Out of the Silent Planet*, the character Elwin Ransom is knocked out and dragged into a spaceship by the story's two evil villains: Edward Weston, referred to several times already, a famous physicist who intends to colonize the planet Mars, or Malacandra, in order to preserve the human race, and Dick Devine, a greedy opportunist who simply wants to get as much as he can of the planet's plentiful gold ("sun's blood") and bring it back with him to Earth. Very early in the story, Ransom awakens and realizes with a jolt of despair that he is being taken against his will into outer space. But after he gets over his initial panic, he actually begins to find the experience delightful. As their vessel journeyed "through depth after depth of tranquility, far above the reach of night, he felt his body and mind daily rubbed and scoured and filled with new vitality." Although Weston attributed his good feeling to solar rays that did not normally reach the Earth's surface, Ransom became aware of "another and more spiritual cause for his progressive lightening and exultation of heart. A nightmare, long engendered in the modern mind by the mythology that

follows in the wake of science, was falling off him." Like most of the
people of his age, Ransom had all his life envisioned outer space as a
place of "black, cold, vacuity" and "utter deadness."[1]

When we explore what Lewis wrote about spirituality, what is remarkable about this brief episode from *Out of the Silent Planet* is how
closely his language captures the kind of imagination he believed most
people had of the "spiritual life"—that it was a life similarly cold and
empty, marked more by deadness than vitality. As if to accentuate the
connection between Ransom's view of space and the common view of
spirituality, Lewis described Ransom's awakening as a "spiritual" one.
Flooded by these exquisitely pleasurable sensations, Ransom realized
that to call this "empyrean ocean of radiance" by the label "space" was a
"blasphemous libel": "he felt life pouring into him from it every
moment. . . . He had thought it barren: he now saw that it was the womb
of the worlds." Space, he decided, was the wrong word. "Older thinkers
had been wiser when they named it simply the heavens—the heavens
which declared the glory."[2] With this, Lewis sought to re-enchant the
universe, to recapture that sense of all creation being alive with the
presence of God, which had been lost in the modern view of the world.
As if to be sure that we did not mistake his point, Lewis ended this rhap-
sodic dream in Ransom's mind by evoking the words of the psalmist,
"The heavens declare the glory of God" (Ps 19:1 KJV).

In our last chapter, we explored Lewis's early view of God as the divine
interferer whose nature and purposes seemed to have nothing to do with
his glimpses of joy. In this chapter, we examine the understanding of the
spiritual life that Lewis believed grew out of that view of God, an understanding he called "negative spirituality."[3] Lewis used this label to describe an interconnected constellation of ideas about religion that
includes at least three elements. At its core, negative spirituality elevates
sacrifice to a position of ultimate or intrinsic value, where self-deprivation

---

[1] *OSP*, 32.
[2] *OSP*, 32.
[3] *M*, 194.

for its own sake becomes a mark of Christian virtue. Closely related is a second dimension, the impulse to intellectualize faith. Negative spirituality separates the mind (or spirit) from the body and from all that is physical, locating spirituality in the mind. The body, if not inherently evil, is irrelevant or even a hindrance to the spiritual life. Growing out of these two is the third and most obvious characteristic, the rejection of sensory pleasure. Steeped in this view of the world, spiritual growth comes to be viewed as an ever-increasing movement away from all that is material and embodied. Lewis believed that this view was unbiblical and unhealthy, robbing us of joy in the present and snuffing out our hope for the life to come.

NEGATIVE SPIRITUALITY

Lewis opened his sermon, "The Weight of Glory," by pointing out that if you asked "twenty good men" what the highest virtue was, most would reply, "Unselfishness." But if the same question had been asked of "any of the great Christians of old," the answer would have been love. Then he made this observation: "You see what has happened? A negative term has been substituted for a positive, and this is of more than philological importance." This substitution makes the highest ideal not securing good things for others but going without them ourselves, "as if our abstinence and not their happiness were the important point."[4]

Although the New Testament has much to say about self-denial, he insisted, it never presents sacrifice as an end in itself. Rather, we are commanded to deny ourselves in order to follow Christ, and when we trace following Christ to its ultimate end, what we find is almost always an appeal to our desires. Although multiple examples might be offered for this principle, consider how Jesus charged the rich young man who wanted to follow him to "go, sell your possessions, and give the money to the poor, and you will have treasure in heaven" (Mt 19:21), or his promise that anyone who had given up home or family or suffered

---

[4]*WG*, 1.

persecution to follow him would receive "a hundredfold now in this age" and "in the age to come eternal life" (Mk 10:29-30), or his assurance that in denying ourselves, taking up our crosses and following him, losing our lives for his sake, we would find true life (Mt 16:24-25). In each case, the call to self-denial is followed by a promise of reward, and the entire formula assumes that this desire is itself a good thing. As philosopher James K. A. Smith put it, we are teleological creatures, oriented to the world by desire: "To be human is to be animated and oriented by some vision of the good life, some picture of what we think counts as 'flourishing.' And we *want* it. We crave it. We desire it."[5] And that is how God made us. By highlighting this simple principle, Lewis challenged the fundamental notion of spirituality as the negation of desire, attributing it not to Christianity but to the influence of Immanuel Kant and Stoic philosophy. He called our attention to the "unblushing promises" of "staggering" reward offered in Scripture, leading him to this stunning conclusion:

> It would seem that Our Lord finds our desires, not too strong, but too weak. We are half-hearted creatures, fooling about with drink and sex and ambition when infinite joy is offered us, like an ignorant child who wants to go on making mud pies in a slum because he cannot imagine what is meant by the offer of a holiday at the sea. We are far too easily pleased.[6]

This is our problem: we settle for cheap imitations of the joy for which we were made. The answer is not to quell desire, to empty ourselves of joy. Rather, it is to set our aim higher, to expect more. And as we shall see, aiming higher in no way means renouncing the pleasures that come with physical sensation. To the contrary, infinite joy is integrally bound up in our lives as embodied creatures.

Lewis traced the impulse toward negative spirituality to at least two sources. The most fundamental, he believed, was the split between nature and spirit brought on by the fall. In the Christian view, he argued, "the spirit was once not a garrison, maintaining its post with difficulty in

---

[5]James K. A. Smith, *You Are What You Love: The Spiritual Power of Habit* (Grand Rapids: Brazos Press, 2016), 11, emphasis in original.
[6]*WG*, 1-2.

a hostile Nature." Rather, it was "fully 'at home' with its organism, like a king in his own country or a rider on his own horse—or better still, as the human part of a Centaur was 'at home' with the equine part."[7] As evidence that the hostility between body and spirit was not God's original design, Lewis pointed to two unlikely sources—the jokes we make about our bodies and our revulsion at death. One source of much earthy humor is what, objectively, we know to be normal bodily functions, especially those that have to do with digestion and the elimination of waste. Why is it that, when we're sitting in a quiet gathering of people, we feel embarrassed when our stomach emits a loud rumbling sound? What could be more natural? For Lewis, our discomfort was a sign of "an animal which finds its own animality either objectionable or funny. Unless there had been a quarrel between the spirit and the organism, I do not see how this could be." And our horror at death, with its "associated ideas of pallor, decay, coffins, shrouds, and worms," makes no sense unless we know, at some deep level, that this was not our true condition. Our fear of ghosts and our revulsion at corpses reflects our reaction to a division between two things that never should have been divided—our spirits and our bodies. If we were only physical organisms, neither would be intelligible, but when we acknowledge that we were originally created as "a unity and that the present division is unnatural," then our uneasiness makes sense.[8] Lewis understood that the division between body and spirit could lead us into two opposite errors. One is materialism, the belief that we are only a physical organism, which elevates only the physical side of this divide. But the other and equally dangerous error is negative spirituality, the view that ignores the physical and seeks to cut ourselves off from our bodies and from the natural world. In this way, he believed, negative spirituality perpetuates the division between physical and spiritual brought on by sin, rather than welcoming their glad reunion, signaled in the incarnation and ascension of Christ.

[7]*M*, 152.
[8]*M*, 154.

Lewis's reference to Kant in "The Weight of Glory" indicates that, like the authors cited in the introduction of this book, he also traced our impulse toward negative spirituality to the ascendency of Enlightenment philosophy in modern Western culture. In particular, Lewis attributed the separation of spirituality from its natural connection with the physical world to the rise of empiricism and the scientific method. Although Lewis was not an enemy of science itself, he expressed deep concern about modernity's prevailing assumption that true knowledge only came through scientific observation. In the opening to his massive volume, *English Literature in the Sixteenth Century*, Lewis set the context for his landmark study by noting the impact of science's ascendency upon our understanding of what it meant to be human:

> On the practical side it was this that delivered Nature into our hands. And on our thoughts and emotions . . . it was destined to have profound effects. By reducing Nature to her mathematical elements it substituted a mechanical for a genial or animistic conception of the universe. The world was emptied, first of her indwelling spirits, then of her occult sympathies and antipathies, finally of her colors, smells, and tastes. . . . The result was dualism rather than materialism. The mind, on whose ideal construction the whole method depended, stood over against its object in ever sharper dissimilarity. Man with his new powers became rich like Midas but all that he touched had gone dead and cold. This process, slowly working, ensured during the next century the loss of the old mythical imagination.[9]

Lewis believed that the dominance of the scientific method as our fundamental way of knowing led us to view ourselves primarily as minds (as James K. A. Smith put it, "thinking machines"[10]) and placed us above and at odds with the created order. It led, moreover, to a "disenchantment" of the physical world, robbing nature of the constant, throbbing presence

---

[9]C. S. Lewis, *English Literature in the Sixteenth Century, Excluding Drama* (Oxford: Clarendon Press, 1954), 3-4. For a contemporary philosophical response to this enduring dichotomy between mind and body in Western culture, see Hubert Dreyfus and Charles Taylor, *Retrieving Realism* (Cambridge, MA: Harvard University Press, 2015).

[10]James K. A. Smith, *Desiring the Kingdom: Worship, Worldview, and Cultural Formation* (Grand Rapids: Baker Academic, 2009), 43.

of God. No longer were the "heavens . . . telling the glory of God" or the "firmament proclaim[ing]" God's "handiwork" (Ps 19:1). Now nature was a thing, an object of study by the human mind and something to be controlled by human agency. From this point on, he believed, the human mind stood in opposition to all that was physical and embodied, with singularly unfortunate implications for Christians' understanding of what it meant to be spiritual.

THE UNIVERSE . . . A RATHER REGRETTABLE INSTITUTION

From all indications, Lewis knew intimately the effect of negative spirituality in his own life. As we noted in previous chapters, his early experiences of religion were fearful and oppressive, with the result that he actually welcomed the loss of faith as a relief. But, by his own account, a significant influence was the "deeply ingrained pessimism" that had taken over his mind as a result of external influences to which joyless faith had made him vulnerable. His mother's death, when he was so young, was certainly one such influence. Another was his father's constant chorus of lament over being always one step from poverty—even though in reality his family lived a comfortable, middle-class life. Lewis came to believe that his life would be an unending grind of drudgery and toil, a belief captured in something he once said to a friend at school: "Term, holidays, term, holidays, till we leave school, and then work, work, work till we die." The principal source of this pessimism, however, even more than the death of his mother, was actually something that grew out of the reality of his embodied condition—"the clumsiness of my hands." It seems Lewis suffered from a physical defect in his thumbs that made even the simplest tasks requiring fine motor coordination virtually impossible to perform, a continual source of frustration to him. "Whatever you wanted to remain straight, would bend; whatever you tried to bend would fly back to the straight; all knots which you wished to be firm would come untied; all knots you wanted to untie would remain firm." This constant frustration produced in him from a very early age the expectation that nothing would work out the way he wanted it to.

Remarkably, however, Lewis was also experiencing at the very same time those rich, embodied moments of bliss that might have pointed him in the opposite direction, moments hinting at the world as a place of wonder, and his body, his endowment with "retinas and palates" as he would later put it, as a conduit of heavenly glory. But again, his "very simple theology" offered no place for that. Instead, the predominating influences shaping his view of the world all seemed to be negative, even down to being prohibited by a master at his boarding school from giving money to a beggar at the school gate. Although not unhappy, he said, he came to the firm conviction that the world was "a rather regrettable institution." His own comfort, his glimpses of longing, these he came to see with suspicion; even a child, after all, will acknowledge that all around him there is desert, even though he sits, for the moment, "in an oasis." Again, the utter divide between joy and his understanding of God gave him no defense against this pessimism. His faith simply did not offer the possibility that he would later embrace with all his being, that the misfortunes which bred such hopelessness were shadows, and that joy was pointing to the one thing that was real and solid. For him, it was the opposite; despite such flashes of overwhelming gladness and beauty, he concluded with the ancient poet Lucretius:

> Had God designed the world, it would not be
> A world so frail and faulty as we see.[11]

Such was the view of life that Lewis's experiences of faith left him.

This Bleak Fantasy

Given the tyranny of negative spirituality in his own early life, it is not surprising that much of what Lewis wrote after becoming a Christian was dedicated to challenging this view of faith and offering an alternative. He focused on the way that this view, with its conception of spirituality as a state of mind, divorced the life of faith from physical, embodied existence. He called it "a life without space, without history, without environment,

---

[11]*SJ*, 63-65.

with no sensuous elements in it."[12] In this view "we feel, if we do not say, that the vision of God will come not to fulfill but to destroy our nature; this bleak fantasy often underlies our very use of such words as 'holy' or 'pure' or 'spiritual.'"[13] He warned that this conception of spirituality forces a divorce between what we imagine spirituality to be—"a life in Christ, a vision of God, a ceaseless adoration"—and the physicality that at every moment presses on our awareness: "When we seem nearest to the vision of God in this life, the body seems almost an irrelevance."[14] To be spiritual, in this view, is not to "taste and see that the LORD is good" (Ps 34:8). It is, rather, somehow to distance ourselves from the very capacity for sensory engagement with physical creation that lay at the heart of the psalmist's compelling invitation. It is to stop tasting altogether.

Negative spirituality also became a theme in Lewis's fictional writings. One poignant example occurs in a scene from his novel *Till We Have Faces*, when the story's narrator, Orual, journeyed to the Grey Mountain in order to retrieve the remains of her sister, Psyche, who had been left tied to a tree as a sacrifice to the god of the mountain. Orual represents the character in whom natural, familial love and protectiveness have been corrupted into a jealous and ultimately cruel form of possession so that she wields her martyrdom, her sadness at not being adequately appreciated, as a tool for controlling her sister. But, like Lewis, she also saw the gods as divine interferers intent on depriving humans of all pleasure and happiness. At one point, after several hours of riding in cold shadows, she and her companion, Bardia, came suddenly into full, warm sunlight. She looked out on "a vast tumble of valley and hill, woods and cliffs, and more little lakes than I could count." All around her "the whole colored world was heaped up and up to the sky." She heard a lark singing, and yet was also touched by the "huge and ancient stillness."[15] Orual found

---

[12]*M*, 176.
[13]*T*, 177. Two versions of Lewis's "Transposition" sermon are in print. I am using the expanded version published in his collection *They Asked for a Paper: Papers and Addresses* (London: Geoffrey Bles, 1962), 166-82. An earlier version is included in his collection *The Weight of Glory and Other Addresses* (1949; repr., Grand Rapids: Eerdmans, 1965).
[14]*M*, 189.
[15]*TWHF*, 95.

herself in the midst of such beauty that would make even the most closed, sullen heart glad. But not Orual:

> My struggle was this. You may well believe that I had set out sad enough; I came on a sad errand. Now, flung at me like frolic or insolence, there came as if it were a voice—no words—but if you made it into words, it would be, "Why should your heart not dance?" It's a measure of my folly that my heart almost answered, "Why not?" I had to tell myself over like a lesson the infinite reasons it had not to dance. My heart to dance? Mine whose love was taken from me?[16]

Almost did the beauty of nature around her cause her to dance, which might have opened her heart to a sense of proportion and even to genuine love. The scene is especially ironic for the way that Orual failed to connect the splendor of her surroundings with the presence of the divine all around her—she was on the mountain of the god and it was exquisitely beautiful, but, like Lewis, she refused to acknowledge that these two things might be connected. Instead, determined to nurture her own misery—and because "mere seemliness, if nothing else, called for it"[17]— she pushed joy away as she went about her sad errand. Her elevation of misery as the mark of seemliness, her rejection of the beauty invading her senses, captures what Lewis saw as the essence of negative spirituality.

In some cases, Lewis even placed the call for negative spirituality on the lips of characters who represented evil itself. At one point in *The Lion, the Witch, and the Wardrobe*, the White Witch and her human prisoner came across what Lewis described as a "merry party":[18]

> a squirrel and his wife with their children and two satyrs and a dwarf and an old dog-fox, all on stools round a table. Edmund couldn't quite see what they were eating, but it smelled lovely and there seemed to be decorations of holly and he wasn't at all sure that he didn't see something like a plum pudding.[19]

---

[16]*TWHF*, 95-96.
[17]*TWHF*, 96.
[18]*LWW*, 112.
[19]*LWW*, 111.

At the very moment her sledge ground to a halt, the fox had risen and was about to offer a toast. "What have we here? Stop!" the White Witch cried. "What is the meaning of all this gluttony, this waste, this self indulgence? Where did you get all these things?"[20]

Finally, the fox stammered out an answer: "F-F-F-Father Christmas." The White Witch bit her lip so hard that a drop of blood appeared on her white cheek as she raised her wand. "Instantly, where the merry party had been there were only statues of creatures (one with its stone fork fixed forever half-way to its stone mouth) seated round a stone table on which there were stone plates and a stone plum pudding."[21] Whereas merry feasting, courtesy of Father Christmas, heralded Aslan's return to Narnia, the White Witch brought stingy asceticism, a rejection of all pleasure and gladness.

In *Perelandra*, we also see hints of negative spirituality in the character of Dr. Weston (who represents the serpent from the story of the fall in Gen 3), as he subtly planted in the mind of the "Green Lady" (a figure of Eve) a preoccupation with "the nobility of self-sacrifice and self-dedication" as a way of drawing her away from Maleldil (i.e., God)—a preoccupation that led her more and more to ignore the plain fact that she had been given "a happiness so great that hardly any change could be for the better."[22] But perhaps Lewis's most trenchant attack on negative spirituality occurs in his classic fantasy *The Screwtape Letters*, when he satirically depicted the advice of Screwtape, a senior devil, to his nephew Wormwood, who had been assigned to prevent a particular human (referred to as the "patient") from embracing Christianity. At one point in the story, Screwtape railed against human experiences of mirth. He spoke of the dangerous similarities between laughter and "that detestable art which the humans call Music," noting that something like the latter occurs in Heaven "—a meaningless acceleration in the rhythm of celestial experience quite opaque to us."[23] He advised his apprentice tempter,

---

[20]*LWW*, 111-12.
[21]*LWW*, 112-13.
[22]*P,* 132-33.
[23]*SL*, 57-58.

Wormwood, against allowing his patient even so much as an experience
of fun, since fun

> is closely related to Joy—a sort of emotional froth arising from the play
> instinct. It is very little use to us. It can sometimes be used, of course, to
> divert humans from something else which the Enemy would like them to
> be feeling or doing: but in itself it has wholly undesirable tendencies; it
> promotes charity, courage, contentment, and many other evils.[24]

But he saved his angriest tirade for the kind of laughter that is pure joy,
such as one might see "among friends and lovers reunited on the eve of
a holiday." Laughter of this kind, he warned, "does us no good and should
always be discouraged." Not only might it lead to spiritual outcomes
inimical to the goal of drawing the patient away from faith, he sputtered,
"the phenomenon is of itself disgusting and a direct insult to the realism,
dignity, and austerity of Hell."[25]

A LANGUISHING HOPE

As these passages show, Lewis was keenly interested in challenging the view
that spirituality had as its ultimate goal the emptying of desire or the negation of the self. He aimed particularly at a conception that divorced mind
from body and that placed the spiritual in the realm of mind. Perhaps because Lewis had known negative spirituality intimately within his own life,
he was able to address with great clarity why it could be so damaging to
spiritual health. He noted that the failure to see body and mind as an integrally united whole led to all kinds of confusion and anxiety, and he observed that we have a perverse tendency to focus on whichever of the two
most happens to thwart our own spiritual growth at the moment. At times
we relegate sinfulness entirely to the realm of the body while ignoring the
evil taking root in our character. In *Mere Christianity*, for example, Lewis
distinguished between "sins of the flesh" and "spiritual sins," by which he
meant habits of attitude and disposition, and he insisted that

---

[24]*SL*, 58.
[25]*SL*, 57-58.

the sins of the flesh are bad, but they are the least bad of all sins. All the worst pleasures are purely spiritual: the pleasure of putting other people in the wrong, of bossing and patronizing and spoiling sport, and back-biting, the pleasures of power, of hatred. For there are two things inside me, competing with the human self which I must try to become. They are the Animal self, and the Diabolical self. The Diabolical self is the worse of the two. That is why a cold, self-righteous prig who goes regularly to church may be far nearer to hell than a prostitute. But, of course, it is better to be neither.[26]

The sins of the spirit, of course, run so deep and can be so much more insidious and opaque to us, and because the mind-body dualism of negative spirituality denigrates the body, we can easily assume that the physical is the realm of the really bad sins.

At other times, however, this confusion takes us in the opposite direction, leading us to ignore our daily, earthy existence when we ought to be paying it more attention. Thus, in counseling Wormwood on how to tempt the patient away from God, Screwtape urged Wormwood to keep the patient's mind

on the inner life. He thinks his conversion is something inside him and his attention is therefore chiefly turned at present to the states of his own mind—or rather to that very expurgated version of them which is all you should allow him to see. Encourage this. Keep his mind off the most elementary duties by directing it to the most advanced and spiritual ones.[27]

In particular, he urged Wormwood to exploit the patient's difficult relationship with his mother by building up in the house between them "a good settled habit of mutual annoyance; daily pinpricks." Although Wormwood could not keep the patient from praying for his mother, he could render those prayers innocuous by making sure "that they are always very 'spiritual,' that he is always concerned about the state of her soul and never with her rheumatism."[28] Keep his aspirations to virtue, in

---

[26]*MC*, 94-95.
[27]*SL*, 20.
[28]*SL*, 20-21.

other words, confined to abstract concepts or romantic fantasies, and do not let him think about how those virtues might actually enter the realm of his mundane, physical life (how he eats, drinks, or treats his mother). As long as the impulse toward virtue remains lodged in his intellect as an abstraction and does not enter the particularities of his actual day-to-day life, that impulse, Screwtape said, "will not keep a man from our Father's house," and it "may make him more amusing when he gets there."[29] In this case, then, the split between mind and body leads the patient to conceive of virtue as an abstract ideal that resides in the mind and that has nothing to do with his body, with his earthy, mundane life. Given how much our attitudes and dispositions are shaped by what we do with our bodies, the result is that he would be prevented from ever becoming truly Christian through and through.

Among the pernicious effects of negative spirituality that Lewis highlighted, three are especially important for the understanding of the spiritual life emphasized in this book. First, the tendency to see the spiritual as separate from our embodied existence often brings us needless distress over the condition of our spiritual health. We diagnose as spiritual malaise what may be merely a symptom of our physical state—the need for food or sleep, for example. Lewis likely experienced the same confusion in his early life as a Christian, during the period when he was trying to achieve what he called his "realizations" in prayer to which we have alluded several times.[30] He had been taught that in order for his prayers to be effective and acceptable to God, he needed to think about what he was saying, which, for Lewis's tender conscience, became a form of self-condemnation. The moment he would finish his prayers, he would begin to question whether he had truly been thinking about what he had been saying. His stricken conscience would conclude that he had not, and would compel him to set about saying his prayers again, this time trying harder to muster by sheer willpower a "certain vividness of the imagination and the affections."[31] His

---

[29]*SL*, 38.
[30]*SJ*, 62.
[31]*SJ*, 61.

description of the memory of this period was especially touching: "How it all comes back! The cold oilcloth, the quarters chiming, the night slipping past, the sickening, hopeless weariness. This was the burden from which I longed with soul and body to escape."[32]

Lewis later spoke with great passion about the danger of measuring the success of our worship by the psychological state that it produces within us. Just because we experience a particular state of mind or emotion, this in no way guarantees that the content of our worship bears any resemblance to true Christianity. What is more, such an approach comes very close to idolatry in its expectation that, by means of our own performance, we can somehow control the presence or the actions of God, to "extort 'by maistry' what God does not give," as Lewis said, quoting "old Walter Hilton's warning."[33] But as the final line of the above passage suggests, what made this approach to prayer so pernicious was simply that, in his attempts to produce his "realizations," Lewis was swimming against the overwhelming tide of his own body, as "night after night, dizzy with desire for sleep and often in a kind of despair," he sought to control the psychological outcome of his prayers. It is no wonder that he said of his loss of faith, "Oh, the relief of it!"[34]

In *Letters to Malcolm*, Lewis similarly counseled Malcolm about the impact of our bodies on the quality of our prayers. When he spoke of being "at the top of one's form" in prayer, he was careful to say that he was speaking of the whole person: "The condition of the body comes in; for I suppose a man may be in a state of grace and yet very sleepy."[35] Later he addressed Malcolm's concern that he had been feeling "flattened rather than joyful" by telling Malcolm that what he was experiencing was not spiritual malaise but simply exhaustion: "The body (bless it) will not continue indefinitely supplying us with the physical media of emotion."[36] The danger for Malcolm was attributing to a spiritual problem his need for physical rest.

---

[32]*SJ*, 62.
[33]*SJ*, 62.
[34]*SJ*, 60, 62.
[35]*MC*, 16.
[36]*LM*, 46.

The Screwtape Letters likewise highlights this effect of spirituality when Screwtape responds to Wormwood's naive hope "that the patient's religious phase is dying away." Apparently, the Christian to whom Wormwood had been assigned had experienced a cooling off in his spiritual fervor. Screwtape responded by pointing out that humans are "amphibians—half spirit, half animal" (to which Screwtape, ever the champion of negative spirituality, added parenthetically that God's "determination to produce such a revolting hybrid" was one of the things that led Satan to "withdraw his support" in the first place). Although humans possess a spirit that belongs to the eternal world, "as animals they inhabit time. This means that while their spirit can be directed to an eternal object, their bodies, passions, and imaginations are in continual change." The closest they come to constancy is "undulation— the repeated return to a level from which they repeatedly fall back." This ongoing cycle of troughs and peaks is tied to their physical existence and includes "periods of emotional and bodily richness and liveliness" that "alternate with periods of numbness and poverty." The patient's "dryness and dullness," which Wormwood thought was his own workmanship, was "merely a natural phenomenon which will do us no good unless you make good use of it."[37] Screwtape went on to explain techniques for exploiting this natural condition of embodiment, for example, by appeals to sensuality (especially sexual temptation) or, even better, by calling the patient's attention to the dryness and creating within him a sense of anxiety over the seeming loss of his faith. The task, Screwtape wrote, is rather simple: "Direct his attention to the appropriate passages in scripture, and then . . . set him to work on the desperate design of recovering his old feelings by sheer will-power, and the game is ours."[38] Behind all of this is the mistaken separation of flesh from spirit, which leads us to try to produce what we think are "spiritual" states of thinking and feeling in our minds, all the time remaining unaware how profoundly they are affected by what is happening in our bodies.

---

[37]*SL*, 44-45.
[38]*SL*, 50.

A second, closely related effect of the divorce of physical from spiritual happens when we attempt to generate feelings of spiritual fervor in response to abstract, disembodied theological concepts like grace or holiness or the supremacy of Christ, and we question the state of our spiritual health when the dial does not seem to move. Here again we see Lewis as a young boy trying to achieve his "realizations," attempting to generate sufficient emotional intensity in the act of praying that he could be sure that he had prayed with enough "faith" for his prayers to be acceptable to God.[39]

A brief episode narrated in *Letters to Malcolm* likewise captured Lewis's concern about this misunderstanding. Lewis began by explaining his preconception about what it meant to worship or adore God: "I had thought that one had to start by summoning up what we believe about the goodness and greatness of God, by thinking about creation and redemption and 'all the blessings of this life.'"[40] Note what Lewis described here—the attempt to fix his attention on an abstract theological idea in hopes that it would generate the kind of impulse to worship that he had felt in his encounters with "Northernness." Malcolm countered this mistaken view by turning to a small, murmuring brook of cool, clean water, splashing his hot face, and then asking Lewis, "Why not start with this?" Lewis used this brief encounter to insist that physical sensation rather than ideas or concepts is more often the springboard for encountering the glory of God. As he went on to say, "You were not—or so it seemed to me—telling me that 'Nature,' or 'the beauties of Nature,' manifest the glory. No such abstraction as 'Nature' comes into it."[41] Again, note the distinction between the idea of nature as an abstract construct and the actual sights, smells, sounds, and feel of this moment. Lewis thus upended the pernicious way of thinking that actually places us in a no-win situation of trying to manufacture emotions that are integrally tied to bodily experience but in response to conceptions and ideas that

---

[39]*SJ*, 62.
[40]*LM*, 88.
[41]*LM*, 89.

exist only in our minds. The concept of Nature (with a capital *N*) is a mental, immaterial idea that removes us from actual sensory experience, from "that cushiony moss, that coldness and sound and dancing light." And although Lewis valued theological concepts and devoted a great deal of labor to explaining them, what he wanted us to see was that the sensations we take in through our bodies represent a crucial gateway to true adoration.

In *The Screwtape Letters* we find a perverse exploitation of this same tendency to see the spiritual as some kind of idealized abstraction, in almost the mirror image of Lewis's discussion of adoration noted above. Although the patient had just become a Christian—a potentially catastrophic development—it was as yet merely a minor setback. Among those factors working in Wormwood's favor was the patient's mistaken conception of what it meant to be spiritual, in this case, a naive expectation of what true Christians should look like. As Screwtape explained, "At his present stage, you see, he has an idea of 'Christians' in his mind which he supposes to be spiritual but which, in fact, is largely pictorial. His mind is full of togas and sandals and armor and bare legs." With this expectation in his mind, the patient comes to church and sees a "half-finished, sham Gothic erection on the new building estate," and inside,

> the local grocer with rather an oily expression on his face bustling up to offer him one shiny little book containing a liturgy which neither of them understands, and one shabby little book containing corrupt texts of a number of religious lyrics, mostly bad, and in very small print.[42]

As he sits down in his pew, he looks around and sees the very kind of people he has always tried to avoid. Especially, Screwtape counseled, "Make his mind flit to and fro between an expression like 'the body of Christ' and the actual faces in the next pew." In this case, then, his view of spirituality was expected to drive him away from the embodied reality of the church. The patient could not see the possibility that in the pew next to him sat "a great warrior on the Enemy's side." All he could see was "those neighbors [who]

---

[42]*SL*, 15-16.

sing out of tune, or have boots that squeak, or double chins, or odd clothes," which leads him to conclude "that their religion must therefore be somehow ridiculous."[43] His false conception of spirituality would thus cause him not to see the beauty of a life of deep faith etched in those earthy faces all around him. In this second outgrowth of negative spirituality, then, we end up living in our heads, focusing on abstract ideas and concepts and unsuccessfully attempting to muster religious zeal in response to them, all the while ignoring the rich signs of God's presence that come to us moment by moment in pleasurable, physical sensation, and through the people with whom we daily rub shoulders.

The final outcome of this turn to negative, disembodied spirituality is that we lose the fervency of our hope. Ultimately, Lewis's response to this danger was to emphasize heaven's "earthiness," its quality of solidness and excruciating beauty, and also to highlight the close correspondence between our greatest joys here and what awaits us in heaven, so that even our greatest pleasures are mere shadows of the glory that we anticipate. But he also addressed that vibrant hope's opposite, the notion of heaven as some kind of disembodied "spiritual state," which grew out of negative spirituality. In "The Weight of Glory," he gave voice to a common reaction to the language of glory associated with Scripture's accounts of heaven, noting that, at first glance, glory seemed to mean either fame or luminosity:

> As for the first, since to be famous means to be better known than other people, the desire for fame appears to me as a competitive passion and therefore of hell rather than heaven. As for the second, who wishes to become a kind of living electric light bulb?[44]

In *Mere Christianity* we encounter what came close to sheer irritation from Lewis when he responded to those "facetious people who try to make the Christian hope of 'Heaven' ridiculous by saying they do not want 'to spend eternity playing harps.'" Lewis dismissed this response by

---

[43]*SL*, 15-16.
[44]*WG*, 8.

saying, "The answer to such people is that if they cannot understand books written for grown-ups, they should not talk about them."[45] At one point in *The Great Divorce* the narrator responds to something MacDonald has just said with this question: "Then those people are right who say that Heaven and Hell are only states of mind?"[46] MacDonald's response is instructive:

> "Hush," said he sternly. "Do not blaspheme. Hell is a state of mind—ye never said a truer word. . . . But Heaven is not a state of mind. Heaven is reality itself. All that is fully real is Heavenly. For all that can be shaken will be shaken and only the unshakable remains."[47]

In each case, Lewis challenged the implication of negative spirituality for our understanding of heaven, not only because he believed that it was wrong but because it also rendered living with hope impossible. As he put it in *Miracles*, "Where our fathers, peering into the future, saw gleams of gold, we see only the mist, white, featureless, cold and never moving."[48] Believing heaven to be "merely a state of mind," our hold on hope, named along with faith and love in 1 Corinthians 13 as one of the three final theological virtues, grows weak and dim.

TOUCHED BY GOD'S FINGER

In my early years as a teacher, I would go through something like a crisis of faith at the end of every school year. In the weeks leading up to finals, I would be hanging on by a thin thread waiting for it all to end and daydreaming about the glory of having an expanse of time ahead of me with no schedule, no demands. That would be paradise. But when it finally came, I would feel at sea, listless, without direction, with no motivation for reading, praying, doing anything productive. Of course, I'd also feel guilty for feeling that way, and I'd wonder if I'd lost my drive and my faith—and whether it would ever come back.

---

[45]*MC*, 120-21.
[46]*GD*, 65.
[47]*GD*, 65.
[48]*M*, 193.

Lewis's critique of negative spirituality contains helpful wisdom for how we face that kind of experience, especially in what he said about how negative spirituality leads us to separate the body from the spiritual and to misdiagnose as a spiritual problem what is more often something going on in our bodies or emotions. What I came to realize in those times was that I was just emotionally and physically exhausted from the crush of a demanding school year. Added to that was my growing awareness of how much the rhythms of the university provide structure to the flow of my life, and what it meant when those were no longer around me. Nothing had happened to my faith. My physical and emotional batteries were just a bit low. I knew that I was susceptible to some temptations unique to those low physical and emotional energy points, but beyond that God and I were fine. All would be well.

Lewis's critique of negative spirituality as the rejection of desire has also helped me see my own desires and impulses in a new way. Often we give in to them unreflectively, or if we do notice them, we try to squelch them, and may feel guilt and shame that they have even come over us. Lewis challenges us to take a dramatically different approach. He invites us to pay attention to them and to probe the deeper meanings they might hold for us. I can remember being in a high-end clothing store and coming across a rack of button-down shirts made from a sturdy but soft cotton broadcloth. I immediately wanted one of those shirts. No matter that it looked almost identical to three shirts I already owned. I wanted *this* shirt, I craved this shirt, almost as if buying this shirt would be the answer to the deepest longings of my heart. In the past I would just go ahead and buy it. In other similar situations, if the craving was for something I'd consider unhealthy or sinful, I'd try to push it away and feel ashamed of the impulse itself. What Lewis invited us to do in those moments is to interrogate that desire, as if we were taking it out and putting it on the table in front of us and examining it carefully. Following that wisdom means asking a question: This impulse that's come over me—what is the deeper desire within me that it touches? Will this new shirt (or whatever it is that I crave) really give it to me, or is it just offering me a cheap imitation of that for which I am truly restless, which, as Augustine reminded us, is the presence of God?[49] I might still buy the shirt, but at least I'm learning to see all the impulses and cravings that come over me as signs of that deeper longing for my true heart's desire. In my best days, I pray for the faith to trust that what I'm longing for is God. This is what Jesus emphasized when, in the Sermon on the Mount, he urged us to do our "acts of righteousness"—praying, fasting, and giving—in secret, and not in order to win the praise of others. It's not so much that doing religious things for others' approval breaks some divine rule. Rather, it's because in doing so, in seeking the praise of others, we have settled for a cheap imitation of the "reward" we truly long for, to be noticed and blessed by our "Father in heaven" (Mt 6:1-18).

But most of all, by reconnecting the physical and spiritual and especially by emphasizing that what we do with our bodies is integrally connected to our spiritual lives, Lewis invited us to anticipate the reconciliation of the physical and the spiritual—the healing of "our disease" as he put it. Although the complete healing is beyond our imaginations, "some glimpses and faint hints we have: in the Sacraments, in the use made of sensuous imagery by the great poets, in the best instances of sexual love, in our experiences of the earth's beauty."[50] Lewis re-enchanted the physical world with the glory of God, and he offered us the possibility of embracing physical joys as pointers to God. Lewis highlighted this possibility in a crucial moment in *The Screwtape Letters* when the patient recovers his own sense of God's presence. It happens in a moment when he is immersed in the physical creation. As the book had progressed, Wormwood had been increasingly successful in luring the new Christian further and further away from God. But then, in one truly catastrophic moment, he let the patient "slip through his fingers." And what, according to Screwtape, led to this disaster?

> You first of all allowed the patient to read a book he really enjoyed, because he enjoyed it and not in order to make clever remarks about it to his new friends. In the second place, you allowed him to walk down to the old mill

---

[49] Augustine, *Confessions*, trans. Henry Chadwick (Oxford: Oxford University Press, 1991), 1.1.
[50] *M*, 190.

and have tea there—a walk through country he really likes, and taken alone. In other words you allowed him two real positive Pleasures. Were you so ignorant as not to see the danger of this?[51]

Far from being irrelevant or a hindrance, this experience of mundane, sensuous pleasure became the patient's path back to God. In the same way, Lewis will challenge us to be faithfully attentive to our own moments when we are immersed in the sensation of physical pleasure and to intentionally receive that pleasure as a gift from God. For, when we are faithfully attentive in those moments, we come to realize that "we are being touched by a finger of that right hand at which there are pleasures for evermore."[52]

---

[51]*SL*, 66-67.
[52]*LM*, 90.

CHAPTER FOUR

A NEW KIND OF CONSCIOUSNESS

THE ALTERNATIVE
TO NEGATIVE SPIRITUALITY

At the heart of all morality, Lewis believed, lies our capacity to choose. He highlighted this principle with great poignancy in his last and, as he viewed it, his most mature novel, *Till We Have Faces*. At one point in the story, Orual traveled to the Grey Mountain in search of Psyche's remains after she had been left there as a sacrifice to the god of the mountain. She discovered that Psyche was alive and now claimed to be married to the god Cupid and living in an elegant, sumptuous palace. By all appearances, Psyche was vigorous and radiant and, if it were possible, even more beautiful than she had been before. Orual saw in Psyche's eyes "unspeakable joy."[1] But Orual refused to accept her sister's word or even the evidence of her own sight because of what that acceptance would mean for her. She told herself, "If this is true, I've been wrong all my life," and she admitted to herself the foreboding sense that Psyche was "slipping out of my hands."[2] Orual became aware in her own mind, almost as if she were outside of herself observing her own processes of thought,

---

[1]*TWHF*, 123.
[2]*TWHF*, 115, 118.

that at the very moment when she deliberately turned away from the overwhelming evidence before her, "something began to grow colder and harder inside me."[3] As their conversation continued and it became clear that Psyche had transferred her devotion from Orual to her husband, Orual found herself aware that she faced a stark moment of decision: "I saw in a flash that I must choose one opinion or the other; and in the same flash knew which I had chosen."[4] That evening, after she and Psyche had separated for the night, she was unable to sleep, and so she walked back to the river that separated them. Lifting up her eyes and looking once more into the mist across the water, she saw

> that which brought my heart into my throat. There stood the palace, grey—as all things were grey in that hour and place—but solid and motionless, wall within wall, pillar and arch and architrave, acres of it, a labyrinthine beauty. As she [Psyche] had said, it was like no house ever seen in our land or age.[5]

But still Orual refused to acknowledge the reality of what Psyche had claimed, or even to allow Psyche to enjoy the happiness that, by all appearances, she had been given. In this way, Lewis highlighted the progression of choices that led Orual deeper and deeper into a kind of insanity of possession, reflected first in a moment when Orual flew into a crazed frenzy and tried to forcibly coerce her sister to come back with her and later when she heartlessly manipulated Psyche into doing what the god had expressly forbidden, to look on his face—the act that destroyed Psyche's happiness and forced her into the sad life of a wandering exile.

But in book two, Orual's defenses began to crumble. She met a man who years earlier had been caught in a dalliance with Redival, the sister closest to her in age, whom Orual had scorned as little more than a whore. He revealed to her a side of Redival she had never considered—how much Redival had loved Orual when it had been just the two of

[3] *TWHF*, 122.
[4] *TWHF*, 126.
[5] *TWHF*, 132.

them; how cast aside she had felt when Orual's beloved tutor, the Fox, had come; and later when Psyche had been born. For the first time, Orual became aware of how, by her own actions, she had impelled the very behaviors she so loathed in Redival. Soon afterward, her trusted counselor, Bardia, died, and she visited his wife, Ansit, who accused Orual of exploiting him until every drop of his life had been spent. At first, Orual was angry and defensive and, for a moment, even considered using her power as queen to order Ansit's execution. But, in an instant, she knew that what Ansit said was true, that she had devoured Bardia. She even recalled times when she would invent reasons to keep him in the palace late at night simply to assuage her own loneliness. But for all this, she insisted that she had truly loved Psyche—until finally, in a vision, she was brought to the gods so she could make her charge against them, that they had robbed her of Psyche's love. However, when she stood naked and exposed before the gods, her veil stripped away, what came out of her mouth was not the story she had concocted to perpetuate her self-deception but the ugly truth of her own self-centeredness and possessiveness:

> Oh, you'll say you took her away into bliss and joy such as I could never have given her, and I ought to have been glad of it for her sake. Why? What should I care for some horrible, new happiness which I hadn't given her and which separated her from me?[6]

Orual acknowledged that she would rather her sister had been torn to pieces than taken away from her, and her torrent of anger and bitterness all led up to this cry: "She was mine. *Mine.* Do you not know what the word means? Mine!" And in that moment, all was silent and she knew with certainty "that this, at last, was my real voice." She had finally allowed the truth to enter her consciousness. But, miraculously, this became her moment of grace and redemption. Lewis powerfully captured the central place of self-awareness as the turning point in Orual's life in the climactic scene from which the novel drew its title, when she

---

[6]*TWHF*, 292.

asked why, until the truth "can be dug out of us," should the gods "hear the babble that we think we mean? How can they meet us face to face till we have faces?"[7] And in that dramatic scene Lewis unveiled what he saw as the crux of the spiritual life, what he sought to offer as the alternative to negative spirituality.

In the previous chapter, we explored the widely held view that sees spirituality as moving further and further away from all that is material and embodied. Lewis called this "negative spirituality," and he believed that it was unhealthy because it cuts us off from the physical reality that constantly presses on our senses. We diagnose as spiritual malaise what might simply be hunger or the need for sleep. We engage in the often futile exercise of attempting to generate feelings of spiritual fervor in response to theological concepts that, robbed of their embodied elements, have become lifeless abstractions. Believing heaven to be "merely a state of mind," our hold on the virtue of hope languishes. In this chapter, we consider Lewis's alternative, an alternative that ran throughout Orual's gripping story as well as many other of his writings. At the heart of that understanding of spirituality lay two vital components, consciousness and choice.

CONSCIOUSNESS AND CHOICE

Although Lewis believed that our physical bodies were prime sites for the practice of spirituality, it is vital to note that ultimately he believed spirituality had nothing inherently to do with the presence or absence of materiality. Instead, it centered on the role in the life of the Christian of two essential qualities, consciousness and choice.[8] In his philosophical treatment of human suffering, *The Problem of Pain*, Lewis speculated on the nature of human existence before sin entered into the world. He

---

[7]*TWHF*, 294.

[8]In appendix A of his book *Miracles: A Brief Study*, in a brief essay titled "On the Words 'Spirit' and 'Spiritual,'" Lewis made an explicit distinction between the common view of *spiritual* as "the opposite of 'bodily' or 'material'" versus *spiritual* as the "rational element" of human personhood—that is, the part of humans involving awareness and choice. This latter, "supernatural" sense, he said, was "the most useful way of employing the word" (*M*, 205).

conjectured that although human-like creatures might have existed for
ages, there came a moment when

> God caused to descend upon this organism, both on its psychology and
> physiology, a new kind of consciousness which could say "I" and "me,"
> which could look upon itself as an object, which knew God, which could
> make judgments of truth, beauty, and goodness, and which was so far
> above time that it could perceive time flowing past.[9]

As his description clearly shows, consciousness and choice were at the
center of pre-fall human existence. Lewis speculated that paradise might
have been marked by the unmarred and, in some sense, unlimited
exercise of these two qualities. Through them, humans "ruled and illuminated" their "whole organism"[10]—perhaps to the point of even being
aware of and controlling their own digestion and circulation:

> This power the first man had in eminence. His organic processes obeyed
> the law of his own will, not the law of nature. His organs sent up appetites
> to the judgment seat of will not because they had to but because he chose.
> Sleep meant to him not the stupor which we undergo, but willed and
> conscious repose—he remained awake to enjoy the pleasure and duty
> of sleep.[11]

Perhaps, Lewis wondered, "processes of decay and repair in his tissues"
were even under the control of consciousness and choice. When humans
turned away from God in what we call the fall, he believed that what they
lost was this full consciousness. Their wills became corrupted, and they
lost that sense of being at home in their bodies. Consequently, Lewis saw
the process of turning back to God and embracing the life of God—the
process of spiritual growth—as being centered in the recovery of those
two central elements of personhood.

First, becoming spiritual means growing in self-awareness—seeing
oneself for who one truly is—and expanding one's consciousness of
others, the world around us, and most importantly, the presence of God.

---

[9]*PP*, 77.
[10]*PP*, 78.
[11]*PP*, 78.

This is what Orual turned away from as she moved deeper into an irrational, almost insane possessiveness toward her sister, and when she finally embraced honest self-awareness, it became her doorway to salvation. Lewis also illustrated this expanding consciousness in an episode in *Perelandra* when Ransom discovered what he named the "bubble trees" on one of Venus's floating islands. He saw what at first looked to be large, spherical bulbs of glass hanging from tree branches through which the refracted sunlight sent out a stream of rainbow colors. He reached up to touch one, and it instantly burst, showering him with a spray of deliciously fragrant ice-cold water. Lewis described Ransom's ecstatic baptism in these words:

> His nostrils filled with a sharp, shrill, exquisite scent that somehow brought to his mind the verse in Pope, "die of a rose in aromatic pain." Such was the refreshment that he seemed to himself to have been, till now, but half awake. When he opened his eyes—which had closed involuntarily at the shock of moisture—all the colors about him seemed richer and the dimness of that world seemed clarified. A re-enchantment fell upon him.[12]

In that moment, it was as if he had been aroused from a stupor. In the same way, Lewis believed that spirituality involved an awakening of consciousness in the mind and heart of the Christian.

On the other hand, the tempter Screwtape pointed to the opposite impulse when he characterized most temptation as confusion and misdirection, a "darkening . . . [of the patient's] intellect."[13] Whenever the patient was under the spell of fear or lust or anger, Screwtape told Wormwood to keep his attention focused on the *object* of his anger, and do not let come into his awareness, "I am having feelings of anger," "I am afraid," and the like.[14] Later in the story, when the patient was welcomed into a new "set" of urbane, sophisticated people whose approval he valued, Wormwood was to make him talk about things and engage in

---

[12]*P*, 47.
[13]*SL*, 106.
[14]*SL*, 35-36.

activities that he did not really enjoy so that he ended up being confused about what actually gave him pleasure in the first place.[15] In all of this, Screwtape cautioned, one must carefully manage the "dim uneasiness" that might come over the patient as he slipped more deeply into sin: "If it gets too strong it may wake him up and spoil the whole game."[16]

Integrally related to the first quality of spirituality, consciousness, is the second element that Lewis placed at the heart of the spiritual life, that of choice, or agency. For Lewis, the ability to choose freely was the hallmark of *agape*, divine love: "In God there is no hunger that needs to be filled, only plenteousness that desires to give. The doctrine that God was under no necessity to create is not a piece of dry scholastic specu-lation. It is essential."[17] In a similar vein, holiness consists not simply in doing the right thing but in doing the right thing freely and intentionally, more and more out of completely uncoerced choice. When, in *Pere-landra*, Ransom attempted to counter the persistent attacks by Dr. Weston on the resolve of the "Green Lady" to disobey Maleldil, his task was made excruciating by the fact that what the tempter said to get her to declare independence from Maleldil's will was so close to the truth, as he ac-knowledged to himself: "It must be part of the Divine plan that this happy creature should mature, should become more and more a creature of free choice, should become, in a sense, more distinct from God and from her husband in order thereby to be at one with them in a richer fashion."[18] In other words, the growing separateness between herself and God would become what enabled her to choose God's will. Ransom experienced this same dimension of spirituality himself when, after his delicious shower by the bubble tree, he instantly thought "how easy it would be to get up and plunge oneself through the whole lot of them and to feel, all at once, that magical refreshment multiplied tenfold."[19] As with Orual, Ransom was somehow able to stand outside of himself and

---

[15]*SL*, 63.
[16]*SL*, 62.
[17]*FL*, 175.
[18]*P*, 133.
[19]*P*, 48.

observe himself facing a choice. In his case, he realized that seeking to repeat that bliss would somehow be a sacrilege, and so he decided to turn away from enjoying it a second time.

Although this theme appears repeatedly in Lewis's writings, perhaps the most extensive exposition of the role of choice in the spiritual life comes in *The Great Divorce* on the lips of George MacDonald, one of the "solid people" from heaven and the guide assigned to the narrator, who is actually Lewis himself.[20] MacDonald at first explained how it was that the "ghosts" from hell had been allowed to visit heaven, stating that whether the place from which they had come was truly hell would depend on their decision about whether to stay or not. He said that for those who remained in hell, it would seem that they had always been in hell, whereas for those who chose heaven, the brief sojourn in hell would simply be a kind of purgatory. This prompted Lewis to ask more questions, but rather than entertaining theological speculation, MacDonald instead brought their focus back to the central place of choice itself in the final state of each person's soul. Lewis asked how anyone could ever choose hell, to which MacDonald replied, citing Milton, "The choice of every lost soul can be expressed in the words, 'Better to reign in Hell than serve in Heaven.'" For each soul in hell, he continued, "there is always something they insist on keeping even at the price of misery," in the same way that a spoiled child chooses to miss out on playing and enjoying his dinner rather than admit he was wrong and apologize.[21] Thus, the kind of person that we become and the ultimate state of our souls, MacDonald insisted, would be the result of the choices we make:

> There are only two kinds of people in the end: those who say to God, "Thy will be done," and those to whom God says, "*Thy* will be done." All that are in Hell, choose it. Without that self-choice there could be no Hell. No soul that seriously and constantly desires joy will ever miss it. Those who seek find. To those who knock it is opened.[22]

---

[20]*GD*, 60-69.
[21]*GD*, 66.
[22]*GD*, 69, emphasis in original.

As this statement suggests, Lewis's entire theology demanded a central place for human choice, that freedom which, MacDonald says, is "the gift whereby ye most resemble your Maker and are yourselves parts of eternal reality."[23]

Certainly, Lewis believed that God's presence and grace lay behind all of this—that God was at work in drawing people toward faith and life, and that even God's respect for human freedom was itself a sign of grace. Indeed, he said, "our tiny, miraculous power of free will only operates on bodies which His continual energy keeps in existence."[24] Lewis hinted at the relationship of grace and human freedom in *The Problem of Pain* when he talked about the difference between the relationship of a human to his or her pet and that shared between a lover and the beloved.[25] If I have a pet dog, regardless of what "silly anthropomorphic exaggerations" I may attribute to that animal, the reality is that I am its owner. Our relationship exists for my well-being, and to that end I freely interfere with my dog's natural state in order to "make it more loveable [e.g., to me] than it was in mere nature."[26] How different that is from the relationship between the lover and the beloved, which, we recognize

---

[23]*GD*, 129. In the final pages of *The Great Divorce* (130-31), Lewis offered an image that he hoped would address the apparent contradiction between human choice and the foreknowledge of God, who sees the universe from a vantage point outside of time. The narrator is given a vision of a chessboard on which he sees chessmen go "to and fro doing this and that" (*GD*, 130). The chessmen represent humans as they see themselves—and especially as they make choices about their lives. But surrounding the chessboard is a "great assembly of gigantic forms all motionless, all in deepest silence." He realizes that these giant figures are the "immortal souls" of the men and women on the chessboard who are moving about within time, represented by the chessboard itself. The movements of each chessman seem merely to be a mimicry or pantomime of the eternal nature of the giant figures watching the board. The narrator is immediately plunged into despair, for it appears that the movements of the men and women were predetermined by the nature of the giant figures, in which case all that we experience of free will is a mirage. And if this was the case, then the role of choice in the eternal state of one's soul is a sham. MacDonald, however, raises the possibility that the opposite might also be the case—that what he saw of the immortal souls was actually an anticipation of the choices being made on the chessboard. In this way, Lewis hoped to show that despite the appearance of God's eternal knowledge and our free will being in contradiction (precisely *because* we exist in time), they are nevertheless both true. Beyond this, however, MacDonald counseled "Do not ask of a vision in a dream more than a vision in a dream can give" (*GD*, 131).

[24]*PP*, 30-31.

[25]*PP*, 31-34.

[26]*PP*, 31.

instinctively, demands the autonomy to enter the relationship freely. As Screwtape put it, whereas Satan wants "cattle who can finally become food," God has "the curious fantasy of making all these disgusting little vermin into what He calls His 'free' lovers and servants," beloved children who are "united with him but still distinct."[27] For this reason, Screwtape explained, God's "scheme" forbids his overriding the human will. To do so would be useless: "He cannot ravish. He can only woo."[28]

We see this tension between freedom and grace in Lewis's own journey toward faith. Before his conversion, Lewis clearly perceived that he was being "wooed" toward God, drawn almost inexorably toward faith. But he also recognized that the choice to open himself up fully to that process would be his and his alone. In one particularly dramatic instance, he wrote, the reality that he faced a choice, that he *was* choosing, came to him in a moment of almost miraculous clarity. He was on a bus heading up Headington Hill in Oxford when he became aware of a fact about himself—that he was resisting something, almost as if he were desperately trying to keep a door shut. He felt himself being given, in that instant, a free choice about whether he would allow the door to open. He knew that the decision would be life changing, and yet, oddly enough, he felt no emotion surrounding the decision. As he put it, "I was moved by no desires or fears. In a sense I was not moved by anything. I chose to open, to unbuckle, to loosen the rein." He would describe it as the closest thing to a "perfectly free" action he would ever take.[29]

Not surprisingly, much of Lewis's own self-awareness came after his conversion. Looking back, he could acknowledge that his atheism had not reflected a purely intellectual honesty. He was, as he said himself, "desperately anxious to get rid of my religion,"[30] and he admitted that what he found in Kirkpatrick, his nonbelieving tutor, was really support for a stance that he had already chosen.[31] As materialism became less

---

[27]*SL*, 46, 17, 47.
[28]*SL*, 46.
[29]*SJ*, 224.
[30]*SJ*, 61.
[31]*SJ*, 140.

and less a satisfactory answer to the question of human existence, he had still clung desperately to it because it had contained no God, no "transcendent Interferer."[32] Still later, when he found himself forced to acknowledge some Being outside of the material universe, he had settled for a time on what he called "Absolute Mind," because it was "safely and immovable 'there.' It would never come 'here,' never (to be blunt) make a nuisance of Itself."[33] He was even able to look back and chide himself at how ridiculously he had rationalized away his discovery that the writers he truly loved—MacDonald, Chesterton, Johnson, Spenser, Milton—all had been marked by the same curious oddity, their allegiance to Christ.[34]

If *The Screwtape Letters* is any indication, Lewis also recognized the central role of awareness and choice in the day-to-day life of the Christian. He especially captured how susceptible we are to closing ourselves off from honest self-awareness. In the letter where Screwtape counseled Wormwood on how to exploit the patient's difficult relationship with his mother, noted in the previous chapter, his strategy centered on that "most useful human characteristic, the horror and neglect of the obvious."[35] (*SL*, 20-23). Done well, Wormwood would "bring him to a condition in which he could practice self-examination for an hour without discovering any of those facts about himself, which are perfectly clear to anyone who has ever lived in the same house with him or worked in the same office."[36] Especially, Screwtape advised Wormwood to bring to the patient's awareness those particular tones and facial expressions of his mother's that he found "almost unendurably irritating"—that "particular lift of his mother's eyebrows which he learned to dislike in the nursery"—and plant in his mind the suggestion that she knew how annoying it was and did it deliberately. Do not let him consider the "immense improbability" of this assumption and, certainly, don't let him suspect that "he has tones

---

[32]*SJ*, 172.
[33]*SJ*, 210.
[34]*SJ*, 213.
[35]*SL*, 20.
[36]*SL*, 20-21.

and looks that similarly annoy."[37] The end result of this "game" would be to build up within both the patient and his mother a kind of impossible, and unreasonable, double standard to which they were both blind:

> Your patient must demand that all his own utterances are to be taken at their face value and judged simply on the actual words, while at the same time judging all his mother's utterances with the fullest and most over-sensitive interpretation of the tone and the context and the suspected intention. She must be encouraged to do the same to him. Hence from every quarrel they can both go away convinced, or very nearly convinced, that they are quite innocent. You know the kind of thing: "I simply ask her what time dinner will be and she flies into a temper." Once this habit is well established you have the delightful situation of a human saying things with the express purpose of offending and yet having a grievance when offense is taken.[38]

Note how that one word, *simply*, hides the patient's true desire to wound his mother from his own consciousness. Again, central to Screwtape's advice is preventing honest self-awareness in the patient, the kind of honesty about himself that might lead him to repent and start making the choices that bring him closer to God.

CHOOSING DAMNATION

One of the ways Lewis emphasized the importance of consciousness and choice in our spiritual development was to portray what happens when characters repeatedly choose to close themselves off from honest self-awareness and from God. We see this process in the character Orual when she plunged into a crazed panic brought on by her fear of losing possession of Psyche. We also see several similar examples in the Narnia books. Very early in *The Magician's Nephew*, for example, Uncle Andrew, who had rationalized his own bad behavior so habitually that he now lived under the delusion that he was above the principles of basic morality—such imperatives as telling the truth and keeping

---

[37]*SL*, 22.
[38]*SL*, 22-23.

one's word—underwent a flash of self-awareness and a momentary opportunity for repentance when his nephew Digory told him, "You're simply a wicked, cruel magician like the ones in the stories. Well, I've never read a story in which people of that sort weren't paid out in the end, and I bet you will be. And serve you right."[39] Lewis stated,

> Of all the things Digory had said this was the first that really went home. Uncle Andrew started and there came over his face a look of such horror that, beast though he was, you could almost feel sorry for him. But a second later he smoothed it all away and said with a forced laugh, "Well, well, I suppose that is a natural thing for a child to think."[40]

For one instant, a door opened for self-awareness and the possibility of change, for the possibility of becoming more than merely a "beast." But then, just as quickly, Uncle Andrew slammed the door shut.

Lewis especially emphasized that the result of constantly resisting that opportunity to see oneself honestly and make different choices was ultimately the loss of self, the loss of one's consciousness and ability to choose—the very qualities that make us spiritual beings in the first place. Toward the end of *The Last Battle*, for example, Ginger the cat, one of Narnia's talking animals who had used his powers of speech and reasoning for diabolical purposes, ended up losing both in a dramatic episode that left him frantic and wailing, his eyes like green saucers and his fur and tail so bristled that he appeared twice his normal size. One of the other talking animals standing nearby made this observation, poignant for its use of an impersonal pronoun to describe what the cat had become: "*It* can't talk. *It* has forgotten how to talk! *It* has gone back to being a dumb beast. Look at *its* face."[41] In his depiction of Ginger the cat, Lewis provided an imaginative glimpse of the fall, where choosing to turn one's will away from the good results in the loss of the central elements of personhood, consciousness and choice.

---

[39] *MN*, 27.
[40] *MN*, 28.
[41] *LB* 137, emphasis added.

But the most frightening example of this process is what happens to the figure of Dr. Weston in *Perelandra*. Weston claimed to have embraced a form of spirituality, a participation in some impersonal force or spirit, which he asserted was actually the same as Ransom's "religion." At first, he was the same old Weston, speaking in his pompous lecturing voice. But then he began to speak in another voice, that of a gangster's whisper, which sent shivers of fear and disgust over Ransom as Ransom felt a growing sense of the presence of evil before him.[42] At one point in their conversation, Weston erupted in "cackling laughter, almost an infantile or senile laughter," causing Ransom to recoil in horror.[43] Still later, Ransom found what he thought might be a thread of contact between them, a bridge across which, even now, he might bring Weston back, and that was the fact that both of their views required a total giving up of oneself. Excitedly he held that possibility out to Weston, when he was suddenly interrupted:

> "Idiot," said Weston. His face was almost a howl and he had risen to his feet. "Idiot" he repeated. "Can you understand nothing? Will you always try to press everything back into the miserable framework of your old jargon about self and self-sacrifice?" . . . Then horrible things began happening. A spasm like that preceding a deadly vomit twisted Weston's face out of recognition. As it passed, for one second, something like the old Weston reappeared—the old Weston, staring with eyes of horror and howling, "Ransom! Ransom! For Christ's sake don't let them—" and instantly his whole body spun round as if he had been hit by a revolver-bullet and he fell to the earth, and was there rolling at Ransom's feet, slavering and chattering and tearing up the moss by the handfuls.[44]

Later, as Weston's body was fully taken over by demonic forces, he became Ransom's tormenter. He repeated Ransom's name over and over again, torturing Ransom with the sheer monotony of his abuse, slowly trying to chip away at Ransom's sanity. At other times, he engaged in

---

[42]*P*, 92.
[43]*P*, 94.
[44]*P*, 96.

obscene gestures and contortions, and even mocked the words of Jesus on the cross. By this point, the narrator no longer described this creature as "Weston" but as "Weston's body," and eventually as the "Unman." All that had made him a human person had literally wasted away. In one especially poignant passage, Lewis described what could only be called the damnation of a human soul:

> The forces which had begun, perhaps years ago, to eat away at his humanity had now completed their work. The intoxicated will which had been slowly poisoning the intelligence and the affections had now at last poisoned itself and the whole psychic organism had fallen to pieces. Only a ghost was left—an everlasting unrest, a crumbling, a ruin, an odor of decay. "And this," thought Ransom, "might be my destination; or hers."[45]

Where spirituality was ever-increasing consciousness and agency, damnation was imbecility. Ironically, as Weston surrendered himself, he was at the same time, little by little, relinquishing both his consciousness and his power to choose, abandoning the very qualities that made him human.

"NARNIA, AWAKE!"

Lewis's fictional writings also provide positive, imaginative glimpses of these spiritual qualities in the lives of his characters. In *The Magician's Nephew*, Lewis tells of how Narnia came to have talking animals in the first place. Just after Narnia's creation, Aslan gathered a collection of animals around him and gave them the gift of speech and self-awareness. Evoking the Gospel of John's account of when Jesus breathed the Holy Spirit on the apostles, Aslan breathed "a long warm breath" on them and said, "Narnia, Narnia, Narnia, awake. Love. Think. Speak. Be walking trees. Be talking beasts. Be divine waters." They answered him, "Hail, Aslan. We hear and obey. We are awake. We love. We think. We speak. We know."[46] With his breath he thus elevated the beasts of Narnia to the level of spiritual beings. Their endowment involved not just speech but

---

[45]*P*, 130.
[46]*MN*, 138-39.

the capacity to be awake—they now possessed self-awareness and choice, the two qualities essential to being able to love.

Later in *The Horse and His Boy*, we find one of those talking beasts, the Narnian horse Bree, invited to embrace the kind of honest self-awareness that would open the door to true spirituality. Bree had a good heart, but he was haughty, deeming himself superior in courage and virtue to other horses and even to some people. But then, there came a moment of severe testing when he and the other talking horse, Hwin, along with Shasta the urchin boy and Aravis, a noble family's daughter fleeing a forced marriage, were running for their lives trying to escape a ferocious lion (who turns out to be Aslan). Overcome by fear, Bree kept running, but Shasta leapt from his back and turned to face down the lion. Later, when Bree and Hwin were being cared for at the house of the Hermit, with time to reflect on their journey, Bree felt paralyzed by shame and disgrace and lay with his face toward the wall in despair: "I who called myself a warhorse and boasted of a hundred fights, to be beaten by a little human boy. . . . I've lost everything."[47] He did not so much admire Shasta's courage as he felt the humiliation of his own failure. As they were talking the Hermit quietly approached and said,

> My good Horse, you've lost nothing but your self-conceit. No, no, cousin. Don't put back your ears and shake your mane at me. If you are really so humbled as you sounded a minute ago, you must learn to listen to sense [e.g., to honest self-examination]. You're not quite the great Horse you had come to think, from living among poor dumb horses. Of course you were braver and cleverer than *them*. You could hardly help being that. It doesn't follow that you'll be anyone very special in Narnia. But as long as you know you're nobody special, you'll be a very decent sort of Horse, on the whole.[48]

Bree was given, in that moment, the chance to see himself and his world with stark clarity, and, painful as the expansion of consciousness was, he embraced it and followed the path of repentance. Later, when he met Aslan, he admitted in a shaken voice, "I'm afraid I must rather be a fool,"

---

[47]*HB*, 161.
[48]*HB*, 161-62, emphasis in original.

to which Aslan replied, "Happy the Horse who knows that while he is still young. Or the Human either."[49]

We see the same two elements at work in the process by which the Green Lady in *Perelandra* became "older," that is, wiser and more spiritual, a process in which she became aware of her own capacity for choosing or rejecting the will of Maleldil. Her aha moment came during a conversation with Ransom when he reminded her of when they first had met. He had initially spied her on one of the floating islands from across the water that separated them and had observed her face fall in the moment she first looked on him, a clear sign that she had been expecting someone else, the King. Remembering that moment, she had a sudden insight about what it meant to choose the will of Maleldil, which she explained using an analogy of looking for something to eat:

> One goes into the forest to pick food and already the thought of one fruit rather than another has grown up in one's mind. Then, it may be, one finds a different fruit and not the fruit one thought of. One joy was expected and another is given. But this I had never noticed before—that in the very moment of the finding there is in the mind a kind of thrusting back, or setting aside. The picture of the fruit you had *not* found is still, for a moment, before you. And if you wished—if it were possible to wish—you could keep it there. You could send your soul after the good you had expected, instead of turning it to the good you had got. You could refuse the real good; you could make the real fruit taste insipid by thinking of the other.[50]

Lewis here offered stunning insight into the nature of disappointment—that it always grows out of frustrated expectation. But running through the Lady's speech was also the realization that at every moment, in every circumstance, we face the choice of whether to notice and welcome what is before us or to keep our minds fixed on what we had hoped for but not received—in which case the gift we have been

---

[49]*HB*, 215-16.
[50]*P*, 68-69, emphasis in original.

offered becomes a disappointment. Most of the time, however, we simply do not operate at the level of awareness where we realize that we are actually choosing to hold onto those expectations. Instead, like Orual, we blame our disappointment on circumstances or other people, or perhaps on God. But in a moment of recognition, the woman realized that in every set of circumstances she was being given the power to choose and, in that ever-growing consciousness, that she could *will* the good that God had sent her. Lest we think this freedom of choice is only a privilege of good circumstances, recall what Victor Frankl famously wrote about observing the identical process among prisoners in the concentration camps of Nazi Germany—a process in which he found the secret of "spiritual freedom":

> We who lived in concentration camps can remember the men who walked through the huts comforting others, giving away their last piece of bread. They may have been few in number, but they offer sufficient proof that everything can be taken from a man but one thing: the last of the human freedoms—to choose one's attitude in any given set of circumstances, to choose one's own way.[51]

In the same way, the Green Lady discovered that, whether she admitted it or not, she *was* choosing, and whatever emotions she felt would be an outcome of that choice, whether she experienced gratitude and gladness or dissatisfaction and regret. She had come to understand the essence of faith: "It is I, I myself, who turn from the good expected to the given good. Out of my own heart I do it." All along, she assumed that she had been "carried on the will of Him I love," but now she realized that she was walking in that will of her own accord. She had assumed that the good things God sent her simply drew her in "as the waves lift the islands," almost against her will. But now, she said, "I see that it is I who plunge into them with my own legs and arms, as when we go swimming."[52] Thus, to be spiritual is, first, to recognize that one is choosing and, in that recognition, to embrace freely the will of God. As Screwtape also realized, it is in freely and

[51]Victor E. Frankl, *Man's Search for Meaning* (New York: Pocket Books, 1984), 86.
[52]*P*, 69.

consciously giving ourselves to God that we find our true identity: "When they are wholly His they will be more themselves than ever."[53]

STANDING UP ON OUR OWN LEGS

As we noted in the previous chapter, in his discussion of what he called the "law of undulation," Screwtape stressed to Wormwood that as an "amphibian—half spirit, half animal," humans are susceptible to the peaks and troughs that inevitably come with physical life, "periods of emotional and bodily richness" that "alternate with periods of numbness and poverty."[54] We emphasized how integrally our perceptions of "spiritual health" are bound up with the state of our bodies so that it is a mistake to automatically attribute the moments when we feel dullness or a lack of fervor to spiritual malaise. But Screwtape went on to talk about why, exactly, God allows these troughs to occur in the life of the Christian and how God uses them in order to nurture the patient's spiritual growth. At the beginning of one's life as a Christian, God is "prepared to do a little overriding," sending "communications of His presence which, though faint, seem great to them, with emotional sweetness, and easy conquest over temptation."[55] But sooner or later,

> He withdraws, if not in fact, at least from their conscious experience, all those supports and incentives. He leaves the creature to stand up on its own legs—to carry out from the will alone duties which have lost all relish. It is during such trough periods, much more than during the peak periods, that it is growing into the sort of creature He wants it to be. Hence the prayers offered in the state of dryness are those which please Him best.[56]

The reason for this is simple: whereas Satan wants food he can absorb into himself, God wants sons and daughters, lovers whose "wills freely conform to His."[57] For this to happen, Lewis realized, we must have awareness and choice, and we grow more and more into an authentic relationship with

---

[53]*SL*, 68.
[54]*SL*, 44-45.
[55]*SL*, 46.
[56]*SL*, 47.
[57]*SL*, 46.

God, more and more spiritual—and more and more human—when we obey God from a condition in which we are increasingly aware that we are choosing and so obey more and more from our own free will. It is in the knowledge of this reality that Screwtape issued his most dire warning:

> Do not be deceived, Wormwood. Our cause is never more in danger, than when a human, no longer desiring, but intending, to do our Enemy's will, looks round upon a universe from which every trace of Him seems to have vanished, and asks why he has been forsaken, and still obeys.[58]

This was Lewis's alternative to the negative spirituality that viewed spirituality as a state of mind, centered in abstract theological ideas and cut off from our embodied nature. In its place was an understanding of spiritual formation centered in an expanding self-awareness and a consciousness of others, of the world, and of God, and a greater and greater level of agency, in which we choose the will of God in a way that is truly free. As chapter five will show, this view of spirituality lies at the heart of true discipleship. More importantly, as we will emphasize in the chapters that follow, this view of spirituality embraces and sanctifies the physical and opens us up to the life-changing possibility of living in community with what Lewis came to call the "fantastic variety of the saints."[59]

As embodied creatures, we are daily given infinite gifts of beauty and pleasure, which come to us through our physical senses. When we receive them with gratitude and discipline, we welcome the very presence of God in a way that reflects Paul's claim that our bodies can actually become a "temple of the Holy Spirit" (1 Cor 6:19). And nothing brings us face to face with our own personalities and habits, or offers richer possibility for growing in character, than living graciously with those who are different from us, with whom we become "joined together" to form a "dwelling place for God" (Eph 2:21-22).

---

[58]*SL*, 47.
[59]*MP*, 36.

CHAPTER FIVE

VERY FAR INSIDE

SPIRITUALITY AND
THE LIFE OF VIRTUE

In one of the few existing recordings of his radio addresses, Lewis, in his sonorous baritone voice, summed up Christian discipleship as

> simply a process of having your natural self changed into a Christ self, and . . . this process goes on very far inside. One's most private wishes, one's point of view, are the things that have to be changed. That's why unbelievers complain that Christianity's a very selfish religion. "Isn't it very selfish, even morbid," they say, "to be always bothering about the inside of your own soul, instead of thinking about humanity?"[1]

With satirical wit, Lewis showed the absurdity of that accusation, drawing on imagery that would have been universally familiar to an audience that had only recently witnessed the ravages of war:

> Now, what would an NCO say to a soldier who had a dirty rifle, and when told to clean it, replied, "But Sergeant, isn't it very selfish, even morbid, to

---

[1]C. S. Lewis, "The New Men," *Beyond Personality*, broadcast March 21, 1944. This excerpt and the following quotations were transcribed by the author. These recordings are available on a number of websites, including www.openculture.com/2014/06/the-only-known-recordings-of -c-s-lewis-1944-1948.html.

be bothering about the inside of your own rifle, instead of thinking about the United Nations?"[2]

"Well," Lewis concluded, "We needn't bother about what the NCO would actually say."[3] His explanation echoed the call in Scripture that we undergo nothing less than a complete transformation, putting away whatever belongs to our "former way of life" (Eph 4:22) and making "every effort" to cultivate the virtues of goodness, knowledge, self-control, perseverance, godliness, and love (2 Pet 1:5-7). What is demanded is to have our character changed, to become people who possess these traits as core, stable qualities of our very personality.

At the same time, Lewis understood that this process of transformation happens in the small, almost imperceptible daily choices that turn our lives in one direction or the other. As he put it in *Mere Christianity*,

> Every time you make a choice you are turning the central part of you, the part of you that chooses, into something a little different from what it was before. And taking your life as a whole, with all your innumerable choices, all your life long you are slowly turning this central thing either into a heavenly creature or into a hellish creature.[4]

Virtue is gained or lost, in other words, at the level of our innermost passing thoughts and in the course of making what seem like our most insignificant choices—choices that usually happen so much beneath the radar of our conscious mind that we may not even be aware that we are making them.

In chapter four, we explored what Lewis offered as the alternative to negative spirituality, to the conception of spirituality as an ever-increasing separation from our bodies and a retreat into realms of mind or abstract idea. For Lewis, these had little to do with the spiritual life. Instead, spirituality had to do with ever-expanding consciousness and ever-increasing agency. We become spiritual as we grow more and more aware of ourselves, others, and God and when our obedience to God reflects more

---

[2]Lewis, "New Men."
[3]Lewis, "New Men."
[4]*MC*, 86.

and more our free choice. As this chapter will argue, consciousness and choice also lie at the heart of Christian discipleship. Lewis recognized, of course, that God is constantly present in this process, seeking always to bring truth to our awareness, as Screwtape warned Wormwood in his advice about thwarting the patient's prayers:

> The Enemy will not meantime be idle. Wherever there is prayer, there is danger of His own immediate action. He is cynically indifferent to the dignity of His position, and ours, as pure spirits, and to human animals on their knees He pours out self-knowledge in a quite shameless fashion.[5]

But Lewis also knew that we acquire virtue only as we welcome that self-knowledge, as we become more and more aware of these "micro-level" choices—the split-second decisions to be grouchy or grateful, to practice empathy or defensiveness—and as we exercise our will and make choices under the guidance of the Holy Spirit that take us in the direction of Christ.

VIRTUE AT THE MICRO-LEVEL

In our last chapter, we noted a number of examples from Lewis's writings that emphasized the role of consciousness and choice in characters' progression toward or away from God. In each case, Lewis took great care to highlight the presence of these two dimensions of spirituality, often giving us an inside view of the character's thinking process or, in the case of Orual in *Till We Have Faces*, putting on the lips of the story's narrator the clear sense not only that the character is choosing but that she knows she is choosing. But in two additional episodes from Lewis's fiction, we find him placing particular stress on how much the quality of our character and spiritual lives results from our small, seemingly insignificant choices. In both cases, they recount unfortunate decisions that take characters away from God and toward damnation.

The first happens at the beginning of *The Lion, the Witch, and the Wardrobe* and concerns the "fall" of the character Edmund. When we

---

[5]*SL*, 26.

first meet Edmund, he is clearly immature, peevish, and self-absorbed, but he is not evil. Before he found his own way into the wardrobe and stumbled onto Narnia, his sister Lucy had already been there, met Tumnus the faun, and come back breathless with excitement about what she had discovered. When she told her story, her brothers and sister did not believe her, but Edmund was especially unkind to her. "He sneered and jeered at her and kept on asking her if she'd found any other new countries in other cupboards all over the house."[6]

But now, standing among the snow-covered trees of Narnia, Edmund knew that the country was real and that Lucy had been telling the truth all along. It was a moment of self-awareness:

> He now remembered that he had been looking for Lucy: and also how unpleasant he had been to her about her "imaginary country" which now turned out not to have been imaginary at all. He thought she must be somewhere quite close and so he shouted, "Lucy! Lucy! I'm here too—Edmund."[7]

When he did not get an answer, he instantly cast her actions in the worst possible light: "She's angry about all the things I've been saying lately."[8]

In what happened next, Lewis highlighted the qualities awareness and choice: "Though he did not like to admit that he had been wrong, he also did not much like being alone in this strange, cold, quiet place; so he shouted again, 'I say, Lu! I'm sorry I didn't believe you. I see now you were right all along. Do come out. Make it Pax.'"[9] Almost at the same moment, he heard the sledge of the White Witch and went out to meet her. She gave him hot chocolate and Turkish Delight and made him agree to bring his brother and sisters back to her palace (in exchange for her promise to make him ruler over his siblings). Immediately after she rode away, Lucy returned from visiting Mr. Tumnus again and was overjoyed to see her brother. "Isn't it wonderful?" she exclaimed. But Edmund, after

[6]*LWW*, 23.
[7]*LWW*, 26.
[8]*LWW*, 26.
[9]*LWW*, 26.

stuffing himself with Turkish Delight and disparaging his siblings before the White Witch, had become even more snappish: "All right," said Edmund, "I see you were right and it is a magic wardrobe after all. I'll say I'm sorry if you like. But where on earth have you been all this time? I've been looking for you everywhere." She told him that she had taken tea with Mr. Tumnus, who had told her all about the evil White Witch. Again, Edmund made a split-second decision not to reveal that he had just been sitting beside that very person. He asked with feigned innocence, "The White Witch? Who's she?"[10] Edmund had now gone from giving himself over to peevishness to perpetrating deception. If he had not yet lied overtly, he was very close.

The two of them then went back to find the others, and Lucy was eager to share the magic of Narnia with their other brother and sister, Peter and Susan. "What fun it will be," she said to Edmund.[11]

> But Edmund secretly thought that it would not be as good fun for him as for her. He would have to admit that Lucy had been right, before all the others, and he felt sure the others would all be on the side of the Fauns and the animals; but he was already more than half on the side of the Witch.[12]

Lucy brought Edmund to the others and exclaimed, "Edmund has seen it too." Lewis wrote, "And now we come to one of the nastiest things in this story. Up to that moment Edmund had been feeling sick, and sulky, and annoyed with Lucy for being right, but he hadn't made up his mind what to do." Peter turned to Edmund and asked him if it was true, and at that pivotal turning point, Lewis said, Edmund "decided all at once to do the meanest and most spiteful thing he could think of. He decided to let Lucy down."[13]

> "Tell us, Ed," said Susan.
> And Edmund gave a very superior look as if he were far older than Lucy (there was really only a year's difference) and then a little snigger and said,

---

[10]*LWW*, 37.
[11]*LWW*, 39.
[12]*LWW*, 39.
[13]*LWW*, 40-41.

"Oh, yes, Lucy and I have been playing—pretending that all her story about a country in the wardrobe is true. Just for fun, of course. There's nothing there really."

Poor Lucy gave Edmund one look and rushed out of the room.[14]

Viewed in terms of the rest of the book, this pivotal exchange lasts no more than a few seconds. But Lewis chose to slow down time and narrate Edmund's innermost thoughts in painstaking detail as a way of giving us a precise window on Edmund's moral failure. He also depicted this turning point as the climactic moment in a series of choices that moved Edmund further and further away from virtue. We see the power of consciousness—Edmund was able to perceive his situation clearly, how he had been wrong and how embarrassing it was going be to admit that fact. He was also aware that he had been forestalling a final decision, playing both sides of the fence. And then he chose. Lewis wanted to make clear that Edmund knew what he was doing, that he was, in a sense, actually observing himself in the process of deciding.

In his account of Edmund's fall, Lewis also highlighted how, in such a short time, the minute choices of disposition that Edmund had been embracing had had a cumulative effect, something he explained in detail in *Mere Christianity*. There he noted that a good many things in our lives might not be worth bothering about if we were only going to live for seventy years. For example, say, my jealousy or my bad temper is gradually getting worse. Because the transformation happens so slowly, almost imperceptibly, it might not be that noticeable even over the course of a human lifetime. "But," he wrote, "it might be absolute hell in a million years: in fact, if Christianity is true, Hell is precisely the correct technical term for what it would be."[15] Here was Lewis's invitation to ask where the small, almost unconscious choices we make a hundred times a day are taking our lives. What does the trajectory look like if we stretch out over eternity the moods and dispositions that we daily give ourselves over to now? As Edmund's story played out, he went on to betray his

---

[14]*LWW*, 41.
[15]*MC*, 73.

brother and sisters to the White Witch, an act of treachery that eventually cost Aslan his life. But Lewis wanted us to see that this foulest of sins was merely the cumulative effect of the kind of person Edmund had been turning into all along.

What Lewis emphasized by means of skillful storytelling technique in the case of Edmund, he highlighted explicitly in *The Great Divorce*, in a conversation with his heavenly guide, George MacDonald, after they met an old woman who had indulged self-pity and complaining over imagined slights for so long that she was in danger of losing her very soul. When Lewis expressed concern over the woman's fate—that she was just an old woman who had gotten into the habit of grumbling—his teacher answered, "That is what she once was. That is maybe what she still is. If so, she certainly will be cured. But the whole question is whether she *is* now a grumbler." "I should have thought there was no doubt about that," Lewis replied, surprised. "Aye, but ye misunderstood me," MacDonald answered. "The question is whether she is a grumbler, or only a grumble." "But how can there be a grumble without a grumbler?" asked the narrator.[16]

What MacDonald said in response beautifully captures the central place of consciousness and choice in the development of our character. He explained that all of us have had states of disposition that began "with a grumbling mood, and yourself distinct from it." In other words, at this juncture we can still observe ourselves grumbling, and we might even criticize our own behavior. At this moment, we still retain the gift of consciousness as we watch ourselves engaging in behaviors that undermine virtue. But, he warned, a dark hour may come when we might actually "will that mood, embrace it." And here we have not only consciousness but also choice, the willful giving of oneself over to the dark mood. At this point, it is still a tiny thing, a decision that would seem in the grand scheme of things infinitesimally trivial. As MacDonald continued, the time still exists when "ye can repent and

---

[16]*GD*, 70-71, emphasis in original.

come out of it again." But what comes of the repeated choice to give oneself over to this negative mood? "There may come a day when you can do that [e.g., repent] no longer." Here Lewis captured the dire outcome of these tiny decisions: "Then there will be no *you* left to criticize the mood, nor even to enjoy it."[17] At that point, we will have become so habituated to the sin that we no longer choose it. It has simply become who we are.

In these two examples, Lewis gave a negative view of how consciousness and choice turn our inner selves, "the part of you that chooses," in the direction of heaven or hell. But his writings also pointed to the positive ways that the process can work as well. One of these was in *Letters to Malcolm, Chiefly on Prayer*, where he addressed the apparent absurdity inherent in Paul's instruction to "let your requests be made known" (Phil 4:6) to the God we believe to be all-knowing. Why should we reveal our desires to God since God already knows them before we even ask? Lewis's answer turned on the nature of what it meant to be known by God. All of us, whether we like it or not, are "known" to God as objects, in the same way that God knows "earthworms, cabbages, and nebulae."[18] But note how, in the practice of prayer, we actually employ the faculties of consciousness and choice:

> When we (a) become aware of the fact—the present fact, not the generalization—and (b) assent with all our will to be so known, then we treat ourselves, in relation to God, not as things but as persons. We have unveiled. Not that any veil could have baffled this sight. The change is in us. The passive changes to the active. Instead of merely being known, we show, we tell, we offer ourselves to view.[19]

By exercising consciousness and choice in this way, Lewis wrote, "We assume the rank of persons before Him. And He, descending, becomes a Person to us." When we practice the core dimensions of spirituality, we take on full personhood before God and enter ever more deeply into

---

[17]*GD*, 72, emphasis in original.
[18]*LM*, 20.
[19]*LM*, 21.

personal relationship with our Creator. As Lewis concluded, God "speaks as 'I' when we truly call Him 'thou.' (How good Buber is!)."[20]

As these examples show, Lewis believed that the road to heaven or hell is ultimately paved by the choices we make, even in the moments when we are not even aware that we are choosing. He also believed that God is constantly at work, prodding us toward greater awareness, bringing possibilities to our consciousness, seeking to guide us in our choosing.[21] Our challenge is to welcome the growing consciousness that God seeks to bring, and to choose wisely.

PRACTICING VIRTUE

Lewis was concerned to show how even the micro-level choices we make indelibly shape our character and the trajectory of our lives. But beyond providing momentary insight into human psychology, what he said about consciousness and choice holds immense practical value for us in our efforts to become better people.

---

[20]*LM*, 21.

[21]Although this book focuses on the human dimensions of consciousness and choice, it is important to note that Lewis gave numerous hints about his belief in the presence and guidance of God in our spiritual formation. He offered several poignant illustrations in the Narnia books, where Aslan seeks to bring awareness and guidance to various characters' choices. One occurs in *Prince Caspian* when Lucy encounters Aslan after she had been disobedient to a vision he had given her of himself, in response to which she was to lead her company in following him (*PC*, 148-50). A second occurs at the end of *The Last Battle* when Aslan tries in vain to awaken a group of dwarves to the reality that they are not in a dark, smelly stable, as they obstinately believe, but at the very border of Aslan's beautiful country (*LB*, 180-86). In both cases, Lewis represents God's prompting as the growl of Aslan. Additionally, in *The Screwtape Letters* Lewis depicts God as being constantly present, always seeking some opening to awaken humans to the divine presence. As one example, Screwtape tells of a patient he had once had whose mind started to go in the direction of God: "The Enemy, of course, was at his elbow in a moment." Screwtape immediately suggested that "it was just about time he had some lunch." Lewis wrote: "The Enemy presumably made the counter-suggestion (you know how one can never *quite* overhear what he says to them?) that this was more important than lunch" (*SL*, 13). Although in this case the patient eventually turned away from God, it wasn't because God had not presented him with opportunity. Finally, we see Lewis hinting at the presence of the Holy Spirit in the warnings against repeating a pleasure that were given to Ransom by an "inner adviser" after he had experienced the shower from the bubble tree and, later, after drinking from the gourd (which will be addressed in chapter six). In *Mere Christianity*, Lewis acknowledges the apparent tension between the charge that we "work out our own salvation with fear and trembling" and the promise that "it is God who is at work in you" (cf. Phil 4:12-13), essentially arguing that as a Christian he experienced both as equally true. But "even if we could understand who did what, I do not think human language could properly express it" (*MC*, 130).

Although many examples might be offered, here are four areas where putting his insights into practice can enhance our character, all drawn from what is perhaps the work that best captures the nature of spirituality and virtue, *The Screwtape Letters*.

1. Confronting debilitative emotions. When letter six opens, the patient, now a Christian, is struggling with feelings of worry and anxiety over the prospect that he will be called to military service in the war. Screwtape's advice to Wormwood on how to exploit those negative mental preoccupations and emotions gives us practical steps for facing the same challenge in our own lives. What the Christian in this situation needs to do, of course, is "accept with patience the tribulation which has actually been dealt out to him—the present anxiety and suspense," in other words, to exercise the virtue of courage in its classic sense, facing the reality of what one is called to do and, in spite of risk or fear, choosing to do it. In this moment, the anxiety that he is feeling about his future— that anxiety itself is his present cross, which he needs to acknowledge and ask God for the strength to bear. The first step in this process is to pray, "Thy will be done."[22]

Although Lewis did not use the technical language of enjoyment and contemplation here, the insight he gained from Alexander's *Space, Time, and Deity* appears just beneath the surface. In Alexander's terms, to this point the patient has been contemplating what serving in the war might mean for him and "enjoying" the accompanying feelings of distress. But if he becomes conscious of those feelings and brings them before God in prayer, that act of itself would turn his attention from the war to his negative feelings. And almost miraculously, by contemplating his anxiety (e.g., by acknowledging in prayer, "I feel such overwhelming anxiety"), he would actually begin to find relief from those feelings! So Screwtape's advice, not surprisingly, is for Wormwood to encourage him to do the opposite. Wormwood's task is to get the patient to think not "of the present fear as his appointed cross" but rather to imagine all the things

---

[22]*SL*, 34.

that *might* happen and to try and accept all of them as "his crosses: let him forget that, since they are incompatible, they cannot all happen to him, and let him try to practice fortitude and patience to them all in advance."[23] In other words, get him to obsess about future hypothetical horrors instead of simply acknowledging his fear and asking God for help. If Wormwood succeeds, the patient will likely be overcome with anxiety at the prospect of these anticipated disasters.

To anyone familiar with the contemporary concept of emotional intelligence, this should sound familiar. The first line of defense against negative emotions is simply to identify and name them. The moment I am able to say, "I am really feeling angry" (or jealous, or defensive, etc.), I have stopped contemplating whatever stimulated my anger and am now contemplating the emotions themselves. This insight leads Screwtape to articulate what he calls "an important spiritual law":

> In all activities of mind which favor our cause, encourage the patient to
> be un-self-conscious and to concentrate on the object. . . . Let an insult or
> a woman's body so fix his attention outward that he does not reflect "I am
> now entering into the state called Anger—or the state called Lust."[24]

In other words, when we are under the influence of debilitative emotions or states of mind, our temptation will be to focus on the thing that is evoking that state of mind—the body of the person after whom we are tempted to lust, the actions of the person against whom we feel anger or some other emotion—rather than attending to the emotion itself.

As a way of helping students understand the immense value of this insight, I often talk about the overwhelming anxiety I have sometimes felt when traveling—something I love to do but that is also a source of great stress and apprehension for me. I vividly remember once being on the London Underground with my family, trying desperately to find our way to the right subway line so that we could get to the train station and then to the airport to catch our flight home. I could feel anxiety over the

---

[23]*SL*, 35.
[24]*SL*, 35.

possibility of missing the train begin to envelop me—the fluttering in my stomach, the shakiness in my hands, the inability to think clearly, the overwhelming sense of panic. As I told my students in retrospect, it felt in the moment that if I missed that train, I would die right there on the platform. But something almost miraculous happened the moment when I said, "I'm really feeling anxious about this," and then began to pray. For, as Lewis realized, you can't contemplate the emotion or state of mind and the object producing that state of mind at the same time. In the very instant that you turn your attention from the original stimulus to the emotions themselves, the emotions lose their power. They cease to be an ocean engulfing you and now become something separate from you that you can examine. From that moment of self-awareness, it is but a small journey to the next step—choosing to bring these emotions before God in prayer.

2. Nurturing appropriate "self-forgetfulness." As we have emphasized, a key dimension of expanding our consciousness is developing greater self-awareness. But it is also important to note that Lewis did not view constant obsession with ourselves and our own emotional states as the key to spiritual growth. In fact, he knew that at times what was needed was the opposite, a kind of self-forgetfulness. This comes through beautifully in Screwtape's advice on humility, given later in the book after the patient has experienced a "relapse" into Christian faith marked by the absence of the fervor and "lavish promises of perpetual virtue" that had characterized his initial conversion. Screwtape observed that the patient had become humble and then immediately asked, "Have you drawn his attention to the fact?" What follows is both humorous and deeply insightful. Wormwood's task is to catch the patient at a moment when he is being truly humble and then to "smuggle into his mind the gratifying reflection, 'By jove! I'm being humble.'"[25] Immediately pride—in this case, pride at his own humility—will come over him. If he is at all self-aware, he might realize what has happened and fight against it, but, here

---

[25]*SL*, 71.

again, Wormwood can make him proud of the fact that he recognizes and is fighting against pride. In this way, Screwtape suggests, the self-awareness so crucial to spiritual formation at some points becomes a perverse source of temptation at others.

This insight reflects a corollary to the "important spiritual law" explained above, by which attending to negative emotions helps to diminish their power. Lewis knew that the same dichotomy between contemplation and enjoyment could be exploited in the opposite direction, as a way of extinguishing emotions and states of consciousness that the patient *should* possess. Whereas in the case of negative emotions he wants the patient to ignore them and stay focused on what is producing them, now "in all activities favorable to the Enemy [e.g., God] bend his mind back on itself. . . . Let the reflection 'My feelings are now growing more devout, or more charitable' so fix his attention inward that he no longer looks beyond himself to see our Enemy or his own neighbors."[26] As an illustration of this principle, Screwtape tells Wormwood how to weaken the patient's prayers. What the patient ought to be doing when he prays is focusing on God and not on himself. Of course, the by-product of contemplating God may well be the enjoyment of feelings of comfort and security. Wormwood aims to divert the patient's attention from God to his own states of mind *about* God, with the result that he loses that precious sense of God's presence.

Similarly, in his advice on humility, Screwtape recognizes that God would like for humans to be able to lose themselves joyfully in whatever work is before them. He wants them to be able to acknowledge that whatever talents they possess are gifts from God for which they could no more be proud than they could be of the color of their hair, and to be so centered in their identity as God's beloved that they no longer feel a need to prove themselves but instead can feel "charity and gratitude for all selves, including their own."[27] When we experience these moments, we continue to be attentive, but not primarily to ourselves. Rather, we are

[26]*SL*, 35.
[27]*SL*, 73-74.

intentionally present to the world around us and, especially, to the work we are doing. This kind of self-forgetfulness, Screwtape warns, would allow the patient to experience a "state of mind in which he could design the best cathedral in the world, and know it to be the best, and rejoice in the fact, without being any more or less or otherwise glad at having done it than he would be if it had been done by another."[28] In this case, the patient contemplates the work he is called to do and contemplates God, who has given him the ability to do it and enjoys the timeless bliss that comes when we are immersed in meaningful work.

This possibility represents the other side of that equation in the spiritual law Screwtape identified: in the case of positive emotions and dispositions, we risk undermining them when we turn our attention to them and away from the object that is producing them. When, for example, we find ourselves turning our contemplation from the God we are worshiping to the fact that we sound good or are performing well, our challenge is to be aware of it and to intentionally turn our gaze back to the One who merits our praise. In fact, this is the very example I use when I explain this concept to my students. Imagine, I ask, that I'm in church singing one of my favorite hymns, perhaps one with particularly rich harmonies. I am directing my attention to God and am lost in feelings of elation and well-being. I am contemplating God and enjoying those good feelings as a by-product of my contemplation. But as often happens, I get distracted. I say, "Wow, I'm in top form today!" Or worse, I begin to focus on the quality of my own voice ("I sound good!"). The instant I have turned my attention away from God, I lose that precious sense of communion with God. The striking thing about the scenario I just described is that it happens so quickly and imperceptibly.

Yet, even here, self-awareness and choice can be our aide when they are mingled with a healthy ability to laugh at ourselves. In his advice on humility, Screwtape encouraged Wormwood to get the patient caught

---

[28]*SL*, 73.

up in a perverse cycle in which he was fighting against pride and simultaneously feeling pride at his efforts. But he also warned that the entire effort can fall like a house of cards. As Screwtape put it, "Don't try this too long, for fear you awake his sense of humor and proportion, in which case he will merely laugh at you and go to bed."[29] What should I do when I become conscious that I have turned my attention from God to the quality of my own worship? I probably need to laugh at myself just a bit and then intentionally return to directing those words and notes to God.

3. Overcoming negative attitudes. Lewis also recognized the central place that consciousness and choice played in confronting and overcoming the negative attitudes with which we sometimes approach the world and other people. As an example of this, Screwtape offered Wormwood guidance on how to exploit the patient's peevishness—the petty irritability we feel in response to the small annoyances and interruptions that come to us many times each day. His discussion provides a helpful counterpoint to the old woman Lewis meets in *The Great Divorce*, mentioned above, who has given herself over to that irritability for so long that she now risks becoming not a grumbler but merely a grumble. His example also highlights the mundane nature of the choices on which our characters and eternal destinies are built.

Screwtape began by stating the general principle that our anger does not so much arise from misfortune itself but rather from "misfortune conceived as injury," that is, when we experience misfortunes that go against our expectations or our sense of entitlement. It is in response to these, Screwtape counseled, that the patient can be induced to feel more and more injured and ill-tempered. He then observed how quickly the patient's mood would turn sour whenever he found "a tract of time which he reckoned on having at his own disposal unexpectedly taken from him." The uninvited visitor who arrives when he was looking forward to a quiet evening, perhaps, or a friend with whom he had

[29]SL, 71-72.

expected an intimate conversation showing up with his talkative wife. They irritate him because "he regards his time as his own and feels that it is being stolen."[30]

Lewis here illuminated the source of our negative reactions to others and to the world—that they are driven not so much by the events we experience or the people we encounter as by the unexpressed and un-examined beliefs or expectations we hold about them, the "lenses" with which we are looking out at the world.[31] And so, for Wormwood, the key to nurturing the patient's growing peevishness is to encourage this sense of entitlement:

> Let him have the feeling that he starts each day as the lawful possessor of twenty-four hours. Let him feel as a grievous tax that portion of this property which he has to make over to his employers, and as a generous donation that further portion which he allows to religious duties. But what he must never be permitted to doubt is that the total from which these deductions have to be made was, in some mysterious sense, his own personal birthright.[32]

As Screwtape admits, of course, this belief is ludicrous. This man has absolutely no power to manufacture or control one minute in time. In theory at least, he has committed his life completely to God. Were God to show up and demand his service for even a day he would gladly submit—indeed, he would be relieved if that service meant something as simple as listening for an hour to the prattle of a conversation in which he had no interest. In the face of those realities, how could he ever, with a straight face, claim one second of time as his personal possession? Screwtape recognized the absurdity of this expectation, and so his challenge to Wormwood was to keep this preposterous assumption in the patient's mind, but not in his conscious awareness: "Don't let his thoughts come anywhere near it. Wrap a darkness about it, and in the center of

---

[30]*SL*, 106.

[31]For an insightful and practical treatment of how our hidden beliefs shape our perspectives on the world, see Chris Thurman, *The Lies We Believe* (Nashville: Nelson, 1989).

[32]*SL*, 107.

that darkness, let his sense of ownership-in-Time lie silent, uninspected, and operative."[33]

What we find embedded in this conversation is, again, practical wisdom about overcoming negative emotions and attitudes. Although Lewis does not explicitly address it here, we may assume that the patient has become sufficiently aware of his own emotions that he can begin to examine what lies beneath them. So, the first step in the process of dealing with our own negative attitudes is being carefully attentive to the emotions that come over us when our expectations are frustrated. Most of the time, of course, we just experience them unreflectively. They are the result of all of these irritating people and situations that plague our existence! But if we can attend to them and identify them, then we are ready to examine the beliefs that are provoking them—which is the second step in the process and the one to which Lewis devotes most of his attention in this letter. He assumes that if the patient ever examines this expectation, "my time is my own," he will see the absurdity of that illusion and will embrace what he knows to be the reality—that all time and all things are God's. Lewis even suggests where this process might lead. After having examined his emotions and the false beliefs that underlie them, and then having embraced the truth, he might even take the kind of action that would grow out of his embrace of that truth—giving his full and charitable attention to what he otherwise would have written off as "the conversation of a foolish woman."[34]

As I think about this, I am immediately struck by how often I have failed to embrace this practice in my own life, but I am also heartened by memories of times that I have. I remember one day walking across campus and saying "hello" to a student who passed me on the sidewalk and who seemed to ignore my friendly greeting completely. I immediately felt irritation and unkindness toward that person. Most of the time, that would have been that. I would have gone on with my day in a slightly worse mood than when I began. But this once, prompted I believe by the

[33]SL, 108.
[34]SL, 107-8.

Holy Spirit, I caught myself. I felt embarrassed at my feelings of un-kindness, at my assumption that her neglect had been intentional and at the unexamined expectations with which I had uttered that greeting. It was a moment of clarity for me—and also of repentance. As Lewis would observe, it was also a micro-level moment of choice with the potential to turn my character in the direction of God.

4. *Embracing compassion.* Lewis believed not only that awareness and agency were important for avoiding negative emotions and attitudes but that they also played a crucial role in nurturing positive qualities, compassion among them. It is a quality of character that builds on ele-ments of consciousness and choice that we have already emphasized, especially being aware of our negative emotions and being willing to challenge the beliefs that underlie them. But it adds to these the quality of empathy, which has to do with a consciousness of the circumstances and feelings of others, as well as the determination to seek their well-being. Lewis highlighted the virtue of compassion in Screwtape's advice about the patient's difficult relationship with his mother.

Screwtape's advice, as we noted in the previous chapter, centers on building up between the patient and his mother a "settled habit of mutual annoyance,"[35] using the following strategy. The patient must be encouraged to focus on the things she does that cause him irritation and inconve-nience, and to think the worst of those actions—to assume that she does them deliberately, for the express purpose of offending him. The patient must not be allowed to consider the implausibility of this assumption, and in no case should he entertain an awareness that he, too, does things that irritate other people. Finally, he should be induced to respond to her with the same vindictiveness that he imagines she directs toward him, by saying things that, on the surface, seem innocent but are deliberately said in a manner to give such offense that, in Lewis's words, "they are not far short of a blow in the face."[36] What makes the whole scheme work is the patient's reluctance to see the truth about both himself and his mother.

---

[35]*SL*, 20.
[36]*SL*, 22.

Lewis's masterful account of Screwtape's guidance for cultivating this "domestic hatred" also points to habits that nurture compassion. One of those habits involves being willing to ask oneself painful questions: How do I irritate others? What if others construed my actions in the same way that I construe theirs? These questions help us to be aware of our own need for forgiveness, which Paul emphasized in his command, "Bear with one another and . . . forgive each other; just *as the Lord has forgiven you*" (Col 3:13 NIV, emphasis added). Further, Lewis's account challenges us to examine our own tendency to place the actions of those we do not like in the worst possible light, as intentional and as qualities of flawed character (that is, the acts of a bad person rather than a good person having a bad day). Finally, Screwtape's advice points to the alternative, which is choosing to place that person's behavior within a benevolent narrative, assuming the best of them that we possibly can and then actively seeking that person's good. Lewis speaks of how the patient might determine to be attentive not to the imaginary mother he has constructed in his mind but to the real mother—the dear old woman across the table who experiences every day the persistent physical suffering of rheumatism. By deliberately entering her world and considering her true situation, his prayers for her would become not simply a catalog of her "sins" (e.g., those behaviors he personally finds irritating) but a compassionate plea for her well-being. And in practicing these habits of consciousness and choice, he would find himself becoming a compassionate—and indeed a happier—person.

No Ordinary People

In a famous passage from "The Weight of Glory," Lewis vividly captured the possible destinations to which we, over the course of our lives, are heading:

> It is a serious thing to live in a society of possible gods and goddesses, to remember that the dullest and most uninteresting person you talk to may one day be a creature which, if you saw it now, you would be strongly tempted to worship, or else a horror and a corruption such as you now

meet, if at all, only in a nightmare. All day long we are, in some degree, helping each other to one or other of these destinations. It is in the light of these overwhelming possibilities, it is with the awe and the circumspection proper to them, that we should conduct all our dealings with one another, all friendships, all loves, all play, all politics. There are no *ordinary* people.[37]

The gravity of these possibilities and especially the splendor of what we might become, of what God intends us to become, is the *weight* or the burden of glory. But as we have also observed, this ultimately glorious or horrific outcome does not happen all at once. Rather, it is the result of the small choices, the split-second decisions, that often we are not even aware we are making. It is in this sense that "all day long we are . . . helping each other to one or other of these destinations"[38]—or going there ourselves.

At the heart of that process lies the multitude of tiny choices that we each make every day, the choice to give ourselves over to anger or to step away and cool down, the choice to brag or gossip or even bolster our self-image by putting others down in our own thoughts, the decision to allow our eyes to rest on an image or another person in a way that is lustful or to turn our gaze away, the decision to welcome or turn away from someone who needs us, even the choice of the disposition we will carry through the day. If we look closely enough, we will see that in every case we are making choices. Our character and the direction of our lives will reflect the accumulation of these decisions. In 1 Corinthians 10:13, a passage that offers us assurance in the face of temptations "common to everyone," Paul promised that a "way out" would always be provided in our time of testing. Although he did not explain precisely how that way of escape would come to us, surely it did not mean that God would override our wills; rather, it would mean that God was constantly working to bring these choices into our conscious awareness and prompting us toward decisions that would turn our hearts and lives toward God.

---

[37] *WG*, 14-15, emphasis in original.
[38] *WG*, 15.

For Lewis, this was the key to transformation, progressing in these two qualities of spirituality: awareness and choice. As we grow ever more aware of ourselves, our world, others, and especially God and, in that growing awareness, as we freely choose the will of God under the gracious tutelage of the Holy Spirit, we become more spiritual. Thus, as it turns out, we become more fully persons. To the degree that these qualities of true spirituality are growing within us, we also find ourselves more and more attuned to the life of God, at whose right hand are joys forever more. And as chapter six will show, one of the most important sites for the practice of these joys is our own bodies, wonderfully endowed by our glad Creator with retinas and palates.

CHAPTER SIX

RETINAS AND PALATES

SPIRITUALITY AND THE EARTHY LIFE

The story is told that Bob Jones, president of the notoriously conservative college that still bears his name, strict teetotaler, and self-proclaimed "outspoken fundamentalist,"[1] once had lunch with C. S. Lewis. Jones had been deeply impacted by Lewis's writings, especially *The Screwtape Letters*, and was traveling in England. Through the help of an Anglican bishop known to both of them, he arranged to have lunch with Lewis at one of Oxford's pubs. Jones was shocked by what he saw. As they ate, Lewis drank a pint of ale and smoked his pipe, which prompted Jones to say years later that it was "very difficult for me to reconcile the pipe and the tankard of ale with a Christian testimony."[2] And yet, they also seemed to enjoy rich conversation about spiritual matters. At one point, as the

---

[1] I am drawing on the account of this story told by Burton K. Janes in the essay "Sightings," in *We Remember C. S. Lewis: Essays and Memoirs*, ed. David Graham (Nashville: Broadman & Holman, 2001), 146-48. As the author notes, the encounter is attested in a number of sources; see p. 162 n. 4, for other references to this meeting between Jones and Lewis. The introduction to the collection *C. S. Lewis and the Church: Essays in Honour of Walter Hooper*, also records a conversation recalling that meeting and Lewis's expression of surprise that anyone could become head of a college without knowing Greek. See Andrew Cuneo, "Introduction: Oxford, 1963, and a Young Boswell," in *C. S. Lewis and the Church: Essays in Honour of Walter Hooper*, ed. Judith E. Wolfe and Brendan N. Wolfe (London: T&T Clark, 2011), 7n12.

[2] Janes, "Sightings," 147.

story goes, Lewis "pushed his chair back and re-lit his pipe," and asked
Jones, "Which of my books do you like the best?" Jones answered,
somewhat apologetically, that his favorites were the ones in Lewis's
science fiction trilogy. Lewis clapped his hands and exclaimed, "Good
show! Those are my own favorites." Sometime later Walter Hooper asked
Jones what he thought about Lewis and recalled that "a severe look
crossed Jones's face" as he said, "That man smokes a pipe . . . and that
man drinks liquor." He paused and then continued, "But I *do* believe he
is a Christian."[3]

By all accounts, Lewis loved life, and especially the earthy dimensions of our lives as created beings. He loved being outdoors. He had
a particular fondness for dogs and cats, and, as he told his god-
daughter Sarah in a letter, he had made friends with an old rabbit that
he named Baron Biscuit, who lived in a wood near Magdalen College
and who would eat out of his hand. He loved laughter, especially
laughter among good friends. One of his students recalled a gathering
where Lewis told a story about a bishop who was giving out prizes at
a girls' school after a student performance of *A Midsummer Night's
Dream*. Lewis said, "The poor man stood up afterwards and said
[here, Lewis imitated the Bishop's piping voice], 'I was very interested
in your delightful performance, and among other things I was very
interested in seeing for the first time in my life a female Bottom.'"[4]
The group erupted in guffaws. He also loved food and drink, as
Lindvall noted:

> Lewis suggested that if you ever happened to pass a café door when you
> were sweat-sodden, hungry, and footsore, "and heard the plates clink and
> the music play, with laughter," would you not, then, "run to [a] table and
> become its happy guest?" This habit was certainly not foreign to Lewis
> and his brother, Warnie, who, after a long walk one day, "ate our egg
> sandwiches and pork pies and drank our bottled beer, . . . behaving just

---

[3]Janes, "Sightings," 146, emphasis in original.
[4]Bruce L. Edwards, *Not-a-Tame Lion: Unveil Narnia Through the Eyes of Lucy, Peter, and Other
Characters Created by C.S. Lewis* (Wheaton, IL: Tyndale House, 2005), 126.

as we would have done fifteen years earlier. Having eaten everything in sight, we are now finished."[5]

In one quip that combines both his wit and his love of food, Lewis described how, when he was recovering from the mumps as an adult, the desire for food would set him to salivating, which would only increase the discomfort brought on by his illness: "Verily 'He that but looketh on a plate of ham and eggs to lust after it, hath already committed breakfast with it in his heart.'"[6]

Although this love of the earthy may have been Lewis's natural inclination, it also became a central dimension in his picture of the spiritual life. As he remarked,

> The angels . . . have not senses; their experience is purely intellectual. . . . That is why we know something about God which they don't. There are particular aspects of His love and joy which can be communicated to a created being only by sensuous experience. Something of God which the seraphim can never quite understand flows into us from the blue of sky, the taste of honey, the delicious embrace of water whether cold or hot, and even from sleep itself.[7]

The challenge of spirituality, he believed, was to open ourselves up to the presence of God communicated to us in the often simple, mundane beauties of sight, smell, and especially taste.

In the previous two chapters, we examined what Lewis offered as an alternative to the negative spirituality that cuts us off from our embodied nature. In his view, true spirituality was marked by an expanding capacity for both self-awareness and the consciousness of others, of the world, and of God, joined with an ever-increasing exercise of agency, in which we choose the will of God in a way that is truly free. In this chapter, we explore how this spirituality embraces and sanctifies the physical, especially the earthy business of eating.

---

[5]Terry Lindvall, *Surprised by Laughter* (Nashville: Nelson, 1996), 153-54.
[6]C. S. Lewis, *Letters to an American Lady*, ed. Clyde S. Kilby (Grand Rapids: Eerdmans, 1967), 21.
[7]Quoted in C. S. Lewis, *A Mind Awake: An Anthology of C. S. Lewis*, ed. Clyde S. Kilby (New York: Harcourt, Brace & World, 1969), 103.

There, as in so many other physical aspects of our lives, Lewis believed that we find impetus for worship and adoration, even in the humblest pleasures that we enjoy. Through the attentive, disciplined embrace of these gifts, we draw close to God and we live out Paul's claim that our own bodies can become "temple[s] of the Holy Spirit" (1 Cor 6:19).

"TAKEN UP"

Whereas negative spirituality involved moving away from the physical, Lewis believed that true spirituality, exercised through awareness and agency, embraced the physical. As he saw it, nature could be "taken up" into the higher realm of the spiritual through the sanctifying influence of consciousness and choice.[8] His view was rooted in his understanding of the Christian doctrine of the incarnation, which held that God had embraced the physical by coming among us as a person in a body.[9] For Lewis, this was the lynchpin of the Christian story, the "Grand Miracle":

> The central miracle asserted by Christians is the Incarnation. They say that God became Man. Every other miracle prepares for this, or exhibits this, or results from this. . . . The fitness, and therefore credibility, of the particular miracles depends on their relation to the Grand Miracle; all discussion of them in isolation from it is futile.[10]

As this passage shows, Lewis believed that for Christianity the incarnation was "the chapter on which the whole plot of the novel really turned, . . . the main theme of the symphony."[11] But the incarnation, he

---

[8]On the idea of the lesser being "taken up" into the greater, see *FL*, 184; *RP*, 115; *M*, 176-78; and *T*, 180.

[9]Lewis's view resonates with the Orthodox tradition's doctrine of theosis, the belief that in salvation and in the resurrection of the body, humans experience something like "divinization." As Habets pointed out, Lewis's works are saturated with "theotic language and concepts," which he uses to express "the ineffable mystery and magnitude of life in union with Christ." Myk Habets, "Mere Christianity for Mere Gods: Lewis on Theosis," in *A Myth Retold: Re-encountering C. S. Lewis as Theologian*, ed. Martin P. Sutherland (Eugene, OR: Wipf & Stock, 2014), 21.

[10]*M*, 131.

[11]*M*, 132.

believed, did more than help us understand the Christian story; it also helps us understand the nature of our own existence:

> If the Christian doctrine is true, . . . [then] our own composite existence is not the sheer anomaly it might seem to be, but a faint image of the Divine Incarnation itself—the same theme in a very minor key. . . . Everything hangs together and the total reality, both Natural and Supernatural, in which we are living is more multifariously and subtly harmonious than we had suspected. We catch sight of a new key principle—the power of the Higher, just in so far as it is truly Higher, to come down, the power of the greater to include the less.[12]

Note especially that last phrase—"the power of the greater to include the less."

Lewis especially saw this dynamic reflected in the ascension of Christ. He emphasized that biblical accounts of that event described Christ as being "caught up" or "lifted up" into the sky, indicating that in the resurrection his very body, which had been mortal, had somehow been itself taken up into Christ's glorified existence.[13] In the ascension, then, Lewis found the ultimate instance of a process through which God was everywhere "taking up" the natural into the spiritual. For example, in *The Four Loves* he argued that divine love, *agape*, should "take up" into itself the other, natural loves. He critiqued as a "very doubtful maxim" Emerson's claim that "when half-gods go, the gods arrive," and he countered with his own: "'When God arrives (and only then) the half-gods can remain.' Left to themselves they either vanish or become demons. Only in His name can they with beauty and security 'wield their little tridents.'"[14] This understanding also informed his view of biblical inspiration, a view that was at odds with a fundamentalist or literalist view of Scripture. As he said in his *Reflections on the Psalms*, he saw no problem with the Bible incorporating elements of pagan mythology, where "something originally merely natural . . . will have been raised by

---

[12]*M*, 134.
[13]*M*, 177.
[14]*FL*, 166.

God above itself, qualified by Him and compelled by Him to serve purposes which of itself would not have served."[15] As I will argue in chapter eight, he also believed that this dynamic would see its consummation in our own resurrection. He held that our present physical experiences are transpositions of the greater realities that we will know in that moment when the breach between the physical and spiritual is at last healed.

Lewis believed that this understanding of nature and spirit had enormous implications for how we view and live in our bodies now. Even in our present, shadowland existence, as we await the consummation, sensuous experience plays an integral role in the development of our spiritual lives. Christians, of all people, must not retreat into negative spirituality, conceiving "spiritual joy and worth as things that need to be rescued or tenderly protected from time and place and matter and the senses."[16] Our God, after all,

> is the God of corn and oil and wine. He is the glad Creator. He has become Himself incarnate. The sacraments have been instituted. Certain spiritual gifts are offered us only on condition that we perform certain bodily acts. After that we cannot really be in doubt of His intention.[17]

Reflecting this understanding, temptation is never merely the lure of physical pleasure per se. As Screwtape warned Wormwood, "When we are dealing with any pleasure in its healthy and normal and satisfying form, we are, in a sense, on the Enemy's ground." On the other hand, he counseled, "sinful pleasures" actually involve taking gratifications that God has created, but "at times, or in ways, or in degrees, which He has forbidden."[18] Lewis's view, however, rises above even that of many Christians who might allow themselves to enjoy physical pleasure as a neutral phenomenon, something they experience alongside of but separate from whatever constitutes "spiritual life."

---

[15]*RP*, 110.
[16]*M*, 194.
[17]*M*, 194.
[18]*SL*, 49.

Since redemption and the enjoyment of God's presence in heaven would be in some sense an embodied experience, then physical pleasure provides the Christian with both an avenue for adoration in the present and a tangible source of hope, a "signpost" pointing to what awaits us.

Bearings on the Bright Blur

In *Letters to Malcolm*, Lewis addressed a problem that most Christians have dealt with in their prayers, which has to do with their efforts to try and picture or "conceive of" the God to whom they are praying. We feel that we ought to have some kind of mental representation of God when we pray. Lewis captured his own struggle with this problem when he referred to God as the "Bright Blur."[19] That phrase expressed his sense of God's transcendent glory but also the reality that God is infinitely beyond any kind of mental representation that we might conjure up in an effort to fulfill the instruction of Saint François de Sales, "*Mettez-vous en la présence de Dieu*"—put yourself in the presence of God—an instruction about which Lewis quipped, "I wonder how many different mental operations have been carried out in intended obedience to that?"[20] He went on to use the metaphor of a play set on a stage, in which we are actors playing a part before each other. But "in prayer," he said, the "real I struggles to speak, for once, from his real being, and to address, for once, not the other actors, but—what shall I call Him? The Author, for He invented us all? The Producer, for He controls all? Or the audience, for He watches, and will judge, the performance?"[21] Lewis recognized that perhaps his only hope was to try to reawaken within himself an awareness of the gravity of the situation in which a human creature addresses its Creator, and to find there "a possible theophany. Here is the holy ground; the Bush is burning now." But beyond that, the reality is that every idea that we form of God, God "must in mercy shatter." For all the representations and

---

[19]*M*, 91; cf. 78, 83.
[20]*LM*, 78.
[21]*LM*, 81.

explanations we try to form of God in our minds fall so far short that in the end we say of them with Thomas Aquinas, "It reminds me of straw." The "most blessed result of prayer," Lewis concluded, "would be to rise thinking 'But I never knew before. I never dreamed. . . .'"[22]

At the same time, Lewis found in his response to physical pleasures, often simple and mundane delights of the kind that typically pass unnoticed, a way of getting, as he put it, his "bearings on the Bright Blur."[23] Part of this involved learning the true meaning of praise. For many Christians, praise is simply something God demands of us, perhaps on pain of damnation. But Lewis offered the stunning insight that praise is actually connected integrally to our experiences of enjoyment.

> The world rings with praise—lovers praising their mistresses (Romeo praising Juliet and vice versa), readers their favorite poet, walkers praising the countryside, players praising their favorite game—praise of weather, wines, dishes, actors, motors, horses, colleges, countries, historical personages, children, flowers, mountains, rare stamps, rare beetles, even sometimes politicians or scholars. . . . Except where intolerably adverse circumstances interfere, praise almost seems to be inner health made audible.[24]

What is more, we not only praise all of these, we invite others to praise with us: Isn't she lovely? Wasn't it glorious? Don't you think that magnificent? He eventually came to see that praise does not merely express enjoyment; it actually completes enjoyment. Praise is enjoyment's "*appointed consummation.*"[25] In other words, we haven't fully enjoyed anything until we have praised it.

The truth of this insight hit me as I thought back on my memories of when our family would get a new car (a rare occurrence) and all pile in and drive it to church for the first time. We would invite friends (usually guys) from church to come out and see our new car. We'd lift the hood

---

[22]*LM*, 82.
[23]*LM*, 91.
[24]*RP*, 94-95, emphasis added.
[25]*RP*, 95.

and all huddle around the engine, and someone else might slide in behind the steering wheel and remark on the luxury of the new-car smell. The entire experience would be enveloped with praise—praising the car, how it drove, the advantages of this brand over the competition, the good deal we got, how cold the air conditioner blew. We praised our new car, and we invited our friends to praise it with us. Only when we had all gathered in praise was our enjoyment of our new car complete. For Lewis, this explained why God invites us to praise, not because God is somehow deficient and in need of an ego boost but because it is only in the praise of God that we enjoy God. The invitation to praise is, at its heart, an invitation to delight in God.

Central to that experience of praise, however, is learning to worship God in response to the physical pleasures that God grants us, which Lewis explained in great detail in letter seventeen of *Letters to Malcolm*. He began by recalling to his imaginary conversation partner, Malcolm, what Malcolm had taught him about prayer as adoration, which he had done on a walk one day through the Forest of Dean. As we noted in chapter three, where Lewis had been attempting to generate feelings of adoration in response to abstract theological concepts, Malcom pointed him to the sensation of splashing cool water on his burning face. It worked, Lewis said.

> Apparently you have never guessed how much. That cushiony moss, that coldness and sound and dancing light were no doubt very minor blessings compared with "the means of grace and the hope of glory." But then they were manifest. So far as they were concerned, sight had replaced faith. They were not the hope of glory; they were an exposition of the glory itself.[26]

From that moment on, he said, "I have tried . . . to make every pleasure into a channel of adoration."[27]

Lewis went on to make a distinction between thanksgiving and adoration. When we give thanks—as of course we should—our focus is still in some sense on the gift. But when we adore, we turn our attention

---

[26]*LM*, 88-89.
[27]*LM*, 89.

from the gift to the giver. Where gratitude exclaims, "How good of God
to give me this," adoration says, "What must be the quality of that Being
whose far-off and momentary coruscations are like this!" In other words,
we intentionally make the connection between that pleasure and the
character of God: "One's mind runs back up the sunbeam to the sun."[28]
And with practice, we might actually grow to the point when receiving
the pleasure and recognizing its divine source "are a single experience.
This heavenly fruit is instantly redolent of the orchard where it grew.
This sweet air whispers of the country from whence it blows. It is a
message."[29] To explain this, Lewis pointed to the universal experience
of hearing a bird or reading words on a page. We do not actually "hear
a bird." Rather, we hear a sound, and our mind searches through its
stored memories in order to identify that sound. We've just had so much
practice that our minds make the connection instantaneously: we "hear"
the bird. Similarly, once we have learned to read, it is difficult to go back
to just seeing marks on a page. We see words. In the same way, Lewis
said, we can actually learn to "read" a pleasure by being fully present to
it, by taking it in completely, and then by making the connection to
God.[30] Done repeatedly, this connection might actually become second
nature to us. "There need be no question of thanks or praise as a separate event, something done afterwards. To experience the tiny
theophany is itself to adore." Lewis made clear that although this seems
like hedonism, it is also difficult work—we are not attentive, or instead
of making the connection to God we simply say "encore." Yet the
practice of this difficult work held wonderful possibilities for the quality
of our lives.[31]

One benefit of practicing the "arduous discipline" of adoration is that
it answers the problem of how we understand or sense the presence of
God in our prayers. If we could actually develop the habit of "reading

---

[28]*LM*, 90.
[29]*LM*, 89-90.
[30]*LM*, 89.
[31]*LM*, 90.

pleasures" in the way he suggested, we would find that "every day furnishes us with, so to speak, bearings on the Bright Blur."[32] What evades us when we try to form a mental conception or theological definition of God—the sense of God's presence and the assurance of God's protection—becomes real to us when we practice adoration by fully enjoying physical pleasures and by connecting those pleasures to God in the worship that says, "God, how wonderful you are." This practice captures the understanding of spirituality that has been the focus of this book. Although clearly our minds are involved in the process, it is not the mind divorced from the body. God is not simply a mental abstraction. But neither does the practice represent simply an abandoned plunge into bodily sensation, where one "loses oneself" in the physical and sensual. Rather, it is the body taking in and the mind making sense of physical experience, where physical sensation is "taken up" into a disciplined habit of prayer that says at every turn: "This also is Thou."[33] Through that disciplined habit of adoration, which combines sensual experience with the cognitive work of adoration, God begins to be present to us, not just mentally but viscerally. We come to know God's presence not simply as a point of Christian doctrine but in our guts. One obvious place where Lewis believed heaven could meet earth and where earth could be taken up into heaven is in our experience of eating.

Eating as a Spiritual Experience

Lewis considered the capacity to enjoy food a special gift bestowed on humans by God. Whereas angels are "pure intelligences" who know taste as an abstract concept—"they *understand* . . . tastes better than our greatest scientists"—to humans God has given the gift of palates.[34] Lewis often depicted humans exulting in the enjoyment of food. At the end of *The Last Battle*, when the children found themselves in the true Narnia, of which all their previous experiences had been but a shadow, the first

---

[32]*LM*, 91.
[33]*LM*, 91.
[34]*LM*, 17, emphasis in original.

thing they encountered was a grove of fruit trees. They wondered if they were allowed to pluck the fruit, but Peter reassured them, "I've a feeling we've got to the country where everything is allowed." And so they began to eat. As Lewis described it, compared to that fruit even "the freshest grapefruit you've ever eaten was dull, and the juiciest orange was dry, and the most melting pear was hard and woody, and the sweetest wild strawberry was sour."[35]

But for Lewis, eating was more than simply a source of sensual pleasure. It also represented par excellence an avenue through which we might expand consciousness and exercise agency—in short, a site for spiritual practice in the way that Lewis understood spirituality, where physical action was "taken up" into the spiritual. Specifically, Lewis envisioned that the act of eating food could contribute to spiritual growth by prompting three intentional human responses to physical sensation that are each connected to consciousness and choice, the responses of attention, gratitude and adoration, and self-discipline.

1. Attention. When we watch Jesus move through his days, one thing about him that stands out is how present he is to everything and everyone around him. In the Sermon on the Mount, he called attention to flowers ("consider the lilies of the field," Mt 6:28). At another point, as Jesus made his way within the press of a crowd, he was able to sense when a woman, hoping to be healed from a persistent hemorrhage, touched the fringe of his robe (Mt 9:20). To Simon the Pharisee, his heart full of condemnation toward both Jesus and the sinful woman who had just anointed Jesus' feet, Jesus posed this question, "Do you see this woman?" (Lk 7:44). An odd question—who could have missed her? But perhaps Jesus was pressing Simon to *see* her, to see the person she was, the story she was living, and not just to dismiss her as a category or label, "a sinner" (Lk 7:39). And to the surprise of his own disciples, he engaged with a Samaritan woman they would have written off. Jesus tells them, "Wake up and look around. The fields are already ripe for harvest" (Jn 4:35 NLT).

---

[35]*LB,* 172.

And yet, how often do we go through our days not noticing the beauty around us, not tasting the food we eat (and sometimes not even remembering having eaten), not being present to the people in our lives.

Lewis fervently believed, as we have observed, that this attentiveness was crucial to living the spiritual life—and that food offered one rich opportunity to practice expanding our awareness. He often portrayed the sensation of taste and the act of eating as important physical activities through which we can become intentionally present to ourselves and our world as the first step toward developing the habits of both adoration and self-control. In *Perelandra*, after Ransom was first dropped onto the watery surface of Venus and found himself swimming in a vast ocean with mountainous waves, he took in a mouthful of water and discovered that it was fresh and rather good to drink: "Though he had not been aware of thirst till now, his drink gave him quite astonishing pleasure. It was almost like meeting Pleasure itself for the first time."[36] The simple drink awakened him to a faculty of taste that before seemed asleep. Similarly, in *The Screwtape Letters*, Wormwood's primary task was to keep his patient from awakening to his true condition, and when he did experience what is tantamount to a "second conversion," the event that brought it about was a pleasurable afternoon in which food played a central part. The patient read a book he really liked, "because he enjoyed it and not in order to make clever remarks about it to his new friends," and then he took a walk by himself—creating the perfect condition for reflection and attentiveness—down "to the old mill . . . through country that he really likes," where he had tea.[37] Enjoying a good meal in a setting of beauty created the kind of positive pleasure that, unbeknownst to Wormwood, had the power to "peel off from his sensibility the kind of crust you have been forming on it, and make him feel that he was coming home, recovering himself."[38] In other words, positive pleasures, including food, taken with an openness to reflection, have the power to wake us up.

---

[36]*P*, 35.
[37]*SL*, 67.
[38]*SL*, 68.

When, on the other hand, food is a source of temptation and sin, it becomes so in Lewis's view precisely because of the failure to be attentive. An example was the patient's mother, whose belly, Screwtape said, "now dominates her whole life." But in her case, it is not gluttony of excess but rather a "gluttony of delicacy":

> The woman is in what may be called the "All-I-want" state of mind. *All* she wants is a cup of tea properly made, or an egg properly boiled, or a slice of bread properly toasted. But she never finds any servant or any friend who can do these simple things "properly"—because her "properly" conceals an insatiable demand for the exact, and an almost impossible palatal pleasure she imagines she remembers from the past; a past described by her as "the days when you could get good servants" but known to us as the days when her senses were more easily pleased.[39]

His mother, in other words, had so fixated on an imagined delicacy that she could not be present to the pleasures of taste that were before her, and as a result she became discontented, ungrateful, and ill-humored. The character Edmund experienced the same thing in *The Lion, the Witch, and the Wardrobe*; his obsession with Turkish Delight spoiled his capacity for enjoying a plain, hearty supper provided by Mr. and Mrs. Beaver. In both cases, their habits of consumption embodied the opposite process through which the Green Lady in *Perelandra* came to understand faith as willingly embracing the fruit she was offered rather than holding tightly to the expectation of the fruit she hoped for. Gluttony had dulled their consciousness and weakened their ability to choose. For Lewis, then, the sensation of taste presented the Christian with an opportunity to enhance the spiritual quality of consciousness, and as he made clear in *Letters to Malcolm*, attentiveness to pleasurable sensation, including the sensations of taste and aroma, is the prerequisite to prayer as worship or adoration.

2. Gratitude and Adoration. When intentionality is combined with attentiveness to pleasurable sensations, including the sensations of

---

[39]*SL*, 87-88, emphasis in original.

aroma and taste that accompany eating, we find before us the opportunity for gratitude and adoration. Although he saw these as different acts, with adoration being the higher of the two, Lewis believed that both flow from a gracious openness to gifts of beauty, received attentively. For example, at one point in *Perelandra*, Ransom came across some bushes on which grew "oval green berries, about three times the size of almonds." When he ate one, he found the flesh to be "dryish and bread-like, something of the same kind as a banana." Though good to eat, the fruit "did not give the orgiastic and almost alarming pleasure" of some of the planet's other fruit "but rather the specific pleasure of plain food—the delight of munching and being nourished." Quoting John Milton's drama, *Comus*, Lewis described how Ransom received this plain food with gratitude as a "sober certainty of waking bliss" and felt prompted "to say grace over it; and so he presently did."[40] Thus, "gratitude exclaims, very properly, 'How good of God to give me this.'"[41]

In *Perelandra*, Lewis also depicted the kind of experience in which the rich pleasure of taste provides an earthly glimpse of heavenly bliss and a window into the glory of God, which he believed opened us to the possibility of prayer as worship. When Ransom was first exploring one of Venus's floating islands, he came upon a grove of trees with yellow gourds hanging from their branches, "clustered as toy-balloons are clustered on the back of the balloon-man and about the same size."[42] He picked one, turned it over, and discovered an aperture in the fruit that allowed him to taste the juice inside. He put the gourd up to his lips, intending only to take a small sip, and was flooded with a pleasure beyond anything he had ever known:

> It was like the discovery of a totally new *genus* of pleasures, something unheard of among men, out of all reckoning, beyond all covenant. For one draught of this on earth wars would be fought and nations betrayed. It could not be classified. He could never tell us, when he came back to the

---

[40]*P*, 49.
[41]*LM*, 90.
[42]*P*, 42.

world of men, whether it was sharp or sweet, savory or voluptuous, creamy or piercing. "Not like that" was all he could ever say to such inquiries.[43]

As we noted in our discussion of prayer as adoration, the physical sensation of taste offered more than just a transcendent experience but could also be a prelude to worship. By being fully present to taste, and by doing the mental work of connecting that blissful sensation to the character of God, we learn the habit of making "every pleasure into a channel of adoration" in a way that connects our sensation of pleasure with its divine source.[44] Practiced diligently, we can come to experience pleasure, including the presence of eating, as an immediate, visceral sensation of God's presence, and we know instantaneously, "This also is Thou."[45] The work required to develop this sense of God's presence, finally, hints at the third way that Lewis believed mindful eating could help the Christian develop spiritually, through the practice of self-discipline.

3. *Self-Control.* One theme that ran through much of Lewis's writings had to do with the temptation to try to duplicate an experience of pleasure immediately after it has been felt, to utter, as he put it, "the fatal word, *Encore.*"[46] To do so was an expression of desire for control and thus, as Ransom realized, a lack of faith, a "defense against chance, a security for being able to have things over again."[47] But it was also a descent into animality and greed. The impulse to say "encore" represents the opposite process of spiritual growth. Whereas the spiritual brings the physical into itself, with expanding levels of consciousness and agency (receiving the pleasure with the knowledge, "This also is Thou"), the demand to repeat the pleasure makes the physical sensation *itself* of highest importance while ignoring "the smell of Deity that hangs about it."[48] In so doing, the impulse to say "encore" drags the spiritual down into the physical and animal, where the possibility of conscious, intentional adoration is

---

[43]*P*, 42, emphasis in original.
[44]*LM*, 89.
[45]*LM*, 90.
[46]*LM*, 90.
[47]*P*, 48.
[48]*LM*, 90.

overwhelmed by physical sensation. Here we see the fragile delicacy of the spiritual, how easily it can be overwhelmed by the rush to experience mere physical sensation.

In *The Abolition of Man* Lewis stated his famous axiom, "The head rules the belly through the chest," meaning that it is through "just sentiments" and "trained emotions," nurtured by instruction and experience, that our rational selves bring our animal selves into subjection.[49] But at other points in his writings, he depicted the opposite process, where the belly, rather than being a conduit through which physical pleasure is taken up into the spiritual life, comes to rule a person's life so that he or she loses the qualities that make one human, those of awareness and choice. He thus hinted that food might lead in a long-term way to the same kind of decay of personality that someone who is drunk undergoes temporarily, the loss of sense and self-control. The patient's mother described in *The Screwtape Letters* was one example. Another was the character Edmund in *The Lion, the Witch, and the Wardrobe* when he first encountered the White Witch. She gave him hot chocolate and Turkish Delight, and he began to stuff himself with the candy. One can almost see him becoming more and more "beastly" with every bite, as he lets his manners fall by the wayside, talks with his mouth full, and whines for more. The White Witch had told him that he was the "cleverest and handsomest young man I've ever met," but Lewis offered this far more blunt assessment: "His face had become very red and his mouth and fingers were sticky. He did not look either clever or handsome, whatever the Queen might say."[50]

We find the opposite reaction, the self-controlled rejection of "encore," at several points in *Perelandra*. One occurs after Ransom had the ecstatic experience of drinking the juice from the gourd. He dropped the empty shell and was about to pick another when Lewis described this

---

[49]*AM*, 10, 15-16. On the role of poetry and literature in nurturing just sentiments, see Charlie W. Starr, "So How *Should* We Teach English?" in *Contemporary Perspectives on C. S. Lewis' "The Abolition of Man*," ed. Timothy M. Mosteller and Gayne John Anacker (London: Bloomsbury Academic, 2017), 63-81.

[50]*LWW*, 34.

thought—suggesting the prompting of the Holy Spirit and signaling both Ransom's self-awareness and the exercise of his will:

> It came into his head that he was now neither hungry nor thirsty. And yet to repeat a pleasure so intense and almost so spiritual seemed an obvious thing to do. His reason, or what we commonly take to be reason in our own world, was all in favor of tasting this miracle again; the childlike innocence of fruit, the labors he had undergone, the uncertainty of the future, all seemed to commend the action. Yet something seemed opposed to this "reason." It is difficult to suppose that this opposition came from desire, for what desire would turn from so much deliciousness? But for whatever cause, it appeared to him better not to taste again. Perhaps the experience had been so complete that repetition would be a vulgarity—like asking to hear the same symphony twice in a day.[51]

Later, Ransom would have the same experience with the "plain meal" described above, consisting of the almond-like berries.[52] He gave thanks and began to eat, but he discovered that he occasionally came across a berry with a bright red center "so savory, so memorable among a thousand tastes" that he was tempted to pick them out from among the others and eat them exclusively, but he was "once more forbidden by that same inner adviser which had already spoken to him twice since he came to Perelandra." He was again aware of himself experiencing the temptation to say "encore," and he chose to heed the "inner adviser" cautioning him against it.[53]

For Lewis, then, discipline was the essential element through which eating became a spiritual practice. There is discipline in the process of mindfully tasting and enjoying food. There is discipline in the work of always expressing gratitude and, even more, of constantly making the connection between the pleasures of taste and aroma and the nature of the God who has created such wondrous gifts. And, finally, there is

---

[51]P, 42-43.

[52]P, 49.

[53]P, 50. Although Lewis did not often write in great detail about the Holy Spirit, the presence of this "inner adviser" guiding Ransom toward the better choice signals his awareness of the vital role that the Spirit plays in the formation of Christian character.

discipline in the setting of limits, avoiding the demand for the encore and, in its place, welcoming and being content with what has been given, and trusting that God will provide more in God's own way. In *The Problem of Pain*, Lewis described how the sacrifice of Christ may be "repeated, or re-echoed, among His followers" even in what appears to be a very minor "self-submission of intention whose outward signs have nothing to distinguish them from the ordinary fruits of temperance and 'sweet reasonableness.'"[54] In other words, the kinds of actions that one might take for any number of reasons can be offered as a conscious, willful submission to God and in this way may rise to the level of a participation in the cross. Lewis believed that self-discipline in food might function in the same way. People can exercise self-control in their eating for many reasons that have nothing to do with spirituality. But when it is practiced attentively, for the purpose of adoring God and living by faith, the practice of self-control itself is taken up into the spiritual, and the act of eating now becomes a practice that brings us closer to God.

THE LORD IS NEAR

In Philippians 4:4-7, Paul wrote:

> Rejoice in the Lord always; again I will say, Rejoice. Let your gentleness be known to everyone. The Lord is near. Do not worry about anything, but in everything by prayer and supplication with thanksgiving let your requests be made known to God. And the peace of God, which surpasses all understanding, will guard your hearts and your minds in Christ Jesus.

Paul described a way of life marked by the capacity to be joyful in every situation, by a gentleness or resilience so rooted in our character that it becomes obvious to everyone around us. This life contains a freedom from all anxiety and a peace so great that it is beyond our ability to understand or explain. But at the center of his account of the good life—and the reality that gives rise to all of those other qualities—was this one small statement: "The Lord is near." To the degree that we know and feel

---

[54]*PP*, 92.

the nearness of the Lord, we will find joy, gentleness, freedom from anxiety, peace that transcends understanding. The nearness of the Lord drives away worry and anxiety, restless competitiveness, selfish ambition, and all other qualities that steal our joy. Truly, "where the Spirit of the Lord is," as Paul said, "there is freedom" (2 Cor 3:17). But how does that sense of God's presence become real to us? Negative spirituality—the idea that we live in our minds, attempting to generate fervor in response to abstract ideas—holds little promise for most of us. Rather, we find an answer in what Lewis viewed as genuine spirituality and especially in the discipline of adoring God as we experience physical pleasures of sight, sound, smell, touch, and taste.

Lewis recognized that we exist within a tension, brought on by the fall, between nature and spirit. But for him that tension was not simply between physical and "non-physical" but rather between consciousness and agency on the one hand and their degradation and loss on the other. We live on the razor's edge between the possibility of being raised to an attentive and thoughtful engagement with the physical that opens us to the worship and enjoyment of God, or of descending into a state where our spirits have been taken over by the desires and impulses of the flesh. Within that understanding, spirituality did not mean renouncing the body but, rather, living in a way that prefigured the moment when the body would be "inside of" the spirit and not the other away around, when we would enjoy the bliss that even now is hinted at in physical pleasure but without the pain and the limitations that come with living in our bodies. In the meantime, there is a place for discipline, not a discipline aimed at eliminating the physical but one that intentionally connects physical pleasure to adoration and faith. As Lewis put it in *Letters to Malcolm*, "If I could always be what I aim at being, no pleasure would be too ordinary or too usual for such reception; from the first taste of the air when I look out of the window—one's whole cheek becomes a sort of palate—down to one's soft slippers at bedtime."[55]

---

[55]*LM*, 90.

As Lewis learned from his lifelong friend, Arthur Greeves, even the simplest pleasure, received attentively and in adoration, now held out the opportunity to taste God's goodness. For most of his life, he said, "My feelings for nature had been too narrowly romantic. I attended almost entirely to what I thought awe-inspiring, or wild, or eerie, and above all to distance." In other words, what Lewis had looked for in his search for inspiration in those early years was the exotic. What he learned from Arthur was the glory of the ordinary, an attentiveness to the beauty that exists in "homeliness," in the "rooted quality [present in] . . . all our simple experiences, to weather, food, the family, the neighborhood."[56] If it had not been for Arthur, he would never have learned to recognize the glory of such simple things as vegetables, "ordinary drills of cabbages." Arthur would often draw Lewis's gaze back from the distant mountains to peer through a hedge at "nothing more than a farmyard in its mid-morning solitude, and perhaps a gray cat squeezing its way under a barn door, or a bent old woman with a wrinkled, motherly face coming back with an empty bucket from the pigsty."[57] What Lewis came to see, and what he invited us to see, was that all around us, in our mundane, earthy surroundings, even in our daily bread, lies ample cause for praise and thanksgiving if we will but open our eyes. By developing the habit of awareness, made second nature through constant practice, and by choosing always to give thanks for what we taste and see, we come to know the joyful presence of God.

---

[56]*SJ*, 152.
[57]*SJ*, 157.

CHAPTER SEVEN

THOSE WE HAVE HITHERTO AVOIDED

SPIRITUALITY AND THE OTHER

In the third book of Lewis's science fiction trilogy, *That Hideous Strength*, we meet a comical hodgepodge of personalities who form the small religious community of St. Anne's—among them, a stodgy old professor and his matronly wife, the Dimbles; an obstinate, argumentative hyperrational Scottish atheist named Andrew MacPhee (who many believe was patterned after Lewis's tutor, William T. Kirkpatrick); Ivy Maggs, a stock working-class figure and the former maid of Jane Studdock, who is one of the book's main characters; Grace Ironwood, a stern psychologist whose personality fits her name to a T; and even a large, ungainly bear named Mr. Bultitude. As the book unfolds, this unlikely patchwork of characters is arrayed against a formidable and highly organized foe in the trilogy's climactic battle between good and evil. They have all gathered around a single, charismatic leader, Elwin Ransom—the central character in all three books in the series.

And what a character he is! We first meet him through the eyes of Jane, who has been reluctantly yet inexorably drawn into the community of St. Anne's. In her visits to the community so far, he has been vaguely referred to as "the director." But now she has finally been summoned to meet him face to face. Jane is not prepared for the person she meets. With one look, "instantly her world was unmade." All the light in the room "seemed to run toward the gold hair and the gold beard" of the man before her. His skin made him appear boyish, and yet his strength, visible in his arms and shoulders, seemed sufficient to "support the whole house."[1] When he spoke to her, his voice was "like sunlight and gold."[2] He was charismatic, fearless, and winsome, instantly inspiring confidence. As the book continues, it becomes clear that his company of friends, even crusty old MacPhee, is fiercely devoted to him. They trust him completely.

How different he is from the Ransom we encountered in the first book of the trilogy, *Out of the Silent Planet*. When that book opened, he was a lone, stoop-shouldered Cambridge professor, somewhat fussy and provincial, with no real social or familial attachments, out on a walking tour trying to find lodging. He passed the house of an old woman anxiously watching for the return of her son, "my Harry," who worked for the two mysterious men at the next place along the road and who was late in coming home.[3] More to quiet her than anything, Ransom promised to look in on him, but now, standing outside the gate where he presumed the boy worked, he regretted this "troublesome duty on behalf of the old woman. . . . A nice fool he would look, blundering in upon some retired eccentric . . . with this silly story of a hysterical mother in tears because her idiot boy had been kept half an hour late at his work!"[4] Nevertheless, he went ahead and squeezed through the hedge, where he came upon Devine and Weston, the story's two villains, trying to force Harry into a spaceship. What Ransom would have liked in that moment was to thunder, in a commanding voice and with a physical presence marked by confidence and power, "What are you doing with that boy?" But what actually came out, "in a rather unimpressive voice," was more a sheepish whimper: "Here! I say! . . ."[5]

---

[1] *THS*, 159.
[2] *THS*, 160.
[3] *OSP*, 8.
[4] *OSP*, 10.
[5] *OSP*, 12.

To what do we owe Ransom's dramatic transformation from book one to book three? Certainly, he was exposed to all manner of extraordinary physical phenomena—exotic food and drink unknown on earth, unfiltered solar radiation, daily exertions that only a professional athlete might undergo. He had directly encountered the angelic beings, the Oyarsa, charged with guiding and protecting the planets. He had courageously faced the prospect of his own death and prevailed in an epic struggle against evil, something that would give any person an air of coolness under pressure. Surely all of these played a role. But if we take seriously what Lewis said elsewhere about the importance to our own spiritual growth of seeking community with people who are different from us, at least part of the transformation came as a result of Ransom's journey to Malacandra in *Out of the Silent Planet*, where he formed intense, personal relationships, not merely across barriers of gender and ethnicity and culture but with "persons" from a totally different planet.

Ransom's transformation mirrors the one that Lewis himself went through in his own convictions about diversity. In *Surprised by Joy* he described himself as "the product of long corridors, empty sunlit rooms, upstairs indoor silences, [and] attics explored in solitude."[6] He hated being dragged to social gatherings by his father and couldn't wait to get back home where it was just him and his brother, Warnie. His ideal day, he said, was spent mostly in solitude or in the company of a couple of friends who shared the same interests and background as himself. But after his conversion, Lewis went from being a solitary believer, determined to avoid people outside of his own circle, to someone who saw being in community with people unlike himself not simply as a Christian duty but as an essential ingredient in his own spiritual formation. To be sure, Lewis lived his life within an extremely parochial world—white, male, highly educated, and privileged—and that context shows its influence in his writings, for example, in the disparaging stereotypes of strong women that appear in what he wrote before he met and married

---

[6]*SJ*, 9.

a strong woman, Joy Davidman. (It was likely her influence that led to the development of one Lewis's most sympathetic and fully developed characters, the noble and strong Queen Orual in *Till We Have Faces.*[7]) And yet he also came to recognize his need not simply to tolerate but to welcome people who were different from him, who could draw him out of his safe and comfortable context. Such encounters, he would learn, would be crucial to his own life as a Christian.

To this point in our study, much of what we have explored seems to be very individually focused, as if spiritual growth were merely a matter of the solitary exercise of consciousness and choice. And certainly those practices do often grow out of micro-level choices that we make within ourselves. But Lewis was also clear that spiritual growth has a vital communal element to it.[8] We cannot do it on our own. Rather, an essential part of our development as Christians involves a mindful engagement with other people, especially with people who are different from us. Those encounters provide avenues for exercising consciousness and choice and, when we open ourselves to them, have an uncanny power to expand our awareness of ourselves, of God, and of our world. In this chapter, we explore the gifts that come to us when we engage people we might otherwise have sought to avoid.

DOING IT ON OUR OWN

When he was once asked whether attending worship at a local church was necessary to being a Christian, Lewis told of how at first, after his conversion, he had assumed he would just "do it on my own," nurturing

---

[7]On the influence of Davidman on *Till We Have Faces* and especially on the character of Orual, see Scott Calhoun, "C. S. Lewis and Joy Davidman: Severe Mercies, Late Romances," in *C. S. Lewis: An Examined Life*, vol. 1 of *C. S. Lewis: Life, Works, and Legacy,* ed. Bruce L. Edwards, 274-93 (Westport, CT: Praeger, 2007), 290.

[8]Drawing on an abundance of data from neuropsychological research, Brown and Strawn argue convincingly that the process of adult spiritual formation mirrors the process by which our personalities are formed in the early years of our lives, through such social mechanisms as reciprocal imitation, shared attention, empathy, and attachment. In other words, spiritual formation is fundamentally a socially embedded process. See Warren S. Brown and Brad D. Strawn, *The Physical Nature of Christian Life: Neuroscience, Psychology, and the Church* (New York: Cambridge University Press, 2012).

his faith by retiring to his rooms at the college to read theology all by himself. He found the prospect of church profoundly distasteful: "I disliked very much their hymns, which I considered to be fifth-rate poems set to sixth-rate music." But even worse, he would be forced to "come up against different people of quite different outlooks and different education."[9]

Lewis also recognized that this aversion to people who are different from us can shape the organizations and social formations we are part of. He frequently wrote about the allure of what he called the "inner ring," the informal, implicit group of insiders who seem to those on the outside to have the real power or knowledge, the real sense of fashion or sophistication, or whatever else it is that binds them together as insiders against those excluded from the group. In the third book of his science fiction trilogy mentioned above, *That Hideous Strength*, the character Mark Studdock (Jane's husband) is so drawn to the possibility of being an insider at the university where he teaches that he is willing to sacrifice his career, his marriage, and even his morals in order to be included. Two of the main characters in the Chronicles of Narnia, Edmund (*The Lion, the Witch, and the Wardrobe*) and Eustace (*The Voyage of the Dawn Treader*) fall into rebellion against Aslan in part because of their resentment over being excluded from an inner circle. Lewis faced that same dynamic himself at boarding school, where all activity was driven by one master passion, to be included in the elite group, the Bloods, who embodied "all worldly pomp, power, and glory."[10]

Toward the end of his lecture "The Inner Ring," Lewis captured the essential element in this group dynamic when he warned his hearers that they would always find the inner ring difficult to enter "for a reason you very well know. You yourself, once you are in, want to make it hard for the next entrant, just as those who are already in made it hard for you." Of course, he observed, even healthy groups exercise some form

---

[9]C. S. Lewis, "Answers to Questions on Christianity," in *God in the Dock: Essays on Theology and Ethics*, ed. Walter Hooper (Grand Rapids: Eerdmans, 1970), 61-62.
[10]*SJ*, 83.

of exclusion—the small musical ensemble you join limits its size if for no other reason than that the room where it meets is only so big. But it's different for the inner ring. For the inner ring, exclusion is the whole point. "There'd be no fun if there were no outsiders. The invisible line would have no meaning unless most people were on the wrong side of it. Exclusion is no accident: it is the essence."[11] In short, the group owes its very existence to the exclusion of those who are kept outside of its boundaries.

This process Lewis described so incisively is what psychologists and sociologists have called "Othering." It's the tendency to find your sense of personal identity and well-being by emphasizing the distance between you and those who are different from you—and especially by emphasizing some kind of superiority you possess over them. Have you ever found yourself driving along the highway and looking across the median strip at the fender-bender that has created a miles-long traffic jam? You gaze ahead in your lane and, as far as you can see, it's wide open. If you're like most people, you will feel a sense of contentment settle over you as you gently push down on the accelerator and feel your car surge ahead. You might even entertain some judgment toward the people who caused the accident—serves them right for not paying attention. Do you see what has just happened? By accentuating the distance between you and those people in the opposite lane, you've just made yourself feel better. As that example shows, it's not just social comparison—it's actually "downward comparison." We make ourselves feel better by looking for those who are worse off than we are, in precisely the way the Narnian horse Bree had done when he imagined himself to be a "great horse" by comparing himself with the "poor dumb horses" among whom he had lived for so long.[12] At times, we even actively disparage those who are

---

[11] C. S. Lewis, "The Inner Ring," in *They Asked for a Paper: Papers and Addresses* (London: Geoffrey Bles, 1962), 148.

[12] *HB*, 161-62. One study examined what affected people's levels of unhappiness with standing in long lines and discovered that the key variable wasn't how many people were in front of the subjects they surveyed, between them and the front of the line. It was actually how many people were *behind* them. To the degree that they could compare their situation with others who were worse off, they felt greater well-being. Rongrong Zhou and Dilip Soman, "Looking Back:

different, putting them in the worst possible light in order to bolster our own self-identity.

The same process happens in groups when we form "in-groups" by excluding the "out-groups." Through processes of communal social comparison, we tend to accentuate our group solidarity—our sense of "us-ness"—by choosing the most undesirable qualities of the excluded group and exaggerating them, making that caricature the lens through which we see everyone in that group. This is what Screwtape tells Wormwood to seize on by calling the patient's attention to the grocer's "oily expression,"[13] or what Lewis himself first reacted against when his eyes fell on his fellow worshipper's "elastic side boots."[14] These are caricatures of a lower socio-economic class from the patient and from Lewis, conveying a stereotype of people who lack education and sophistication and whose religion must therefore be ridiculous. Sometimes we even find those differences threatening to us, and in these cases our discourse will emphasize how dangerous those people are to us, as a way of encouraging us to band together. Listen carefully to the language in your church or circle of friends, all the way up to national politics, and this is what you'll find: one way that we often emphasize our own well-being and minimize internal differences within our group is by banding together against common enemies and by emphasizing how different we are from those on the outside or, worse, how much more righteous we are than they.

Lewis knew that same propensity in his own life, so it is not surprising that his first impulse after becoming a Christian was to carry that isolation into his own spiritual practice. But very soon he came to realize that if he was going to take his Christian faith seriously, then he would have to be involved in the community of believers. As he put it, it was "the only way of flying your flag." He understood that participating in Communion, or the Lord's Supper, was a clear obligation for the Christian

---

Exploring the Psychology of Queuing and the Effect of the Number of People Behind," *Journal of Consumer Research* 29 (March 2003): 517-30.
[13]*SL*, 15.
[14]"Answers," 62.

set forth in the New Testament and "you can't do it without going to Church." What's more, he began to find some of that initial conceit "peeling off," as he came to realize that those sixth-rate hymns were being "sung with devotion and benefit by an old saint in elastic-side boots in the opposite pew"—boots, he realized, he wasn't "fit to clean."[15] That was the very awareness Screwtape warned Wormwood to keep from his patient's consciousness, the possibility that the pew next to him contained "a great warrior" on God's side.[16]

As Lewis bluntly concluded, "The New Testament knows nothing of solitary religion. We are forbidden to neglect the assembling of ourselves together. Christianity is already institutional in the earliest of its documents. The Church is the bride of Christ. We are members of one another."[17] But beyond that sense of "Christian duty," he would eventually come to realize that the membership that brought him into relationship with those who were different from him would play an essential role in his own spiritual formation. This theme appears in numerous of his writings (for example, in the wonderfully diverse communities that form across the Narnia books). But the work where he illustrated the process of a healthy engagement with the Other in greatest detail was his science fiction fantasy, *Out of the Silent Planet*.

EXTRATERRESTRIAL OTHERNESS

Lewis's account of Ransom's interplanetary journey to Malacandra is delightful and engaging—many find it the most enjoyable read of all three. What might not be so obvious is the uncanny way it models the research of cultural anthropology, embedding in a sci-fi fantasy what ethnographers would call a "thick description" of an unknown culture's behaviors, practices, and artifacts, and a rich account of how these all fit

---

[15]"Answers," 61-62. For a delightful account of Lewis's life as a church member, written by his former minister, see Ronald Head, "C. S. Lewis as a Parishioner," in *C. S. Lewis and His Circle: Essays and Memoirs from the Oxford C. S. Lewis Society*, ed. Roger White, Judith E. Wolfe, and Brendan N. Wolfe (Oxford: Oxford University Press, 2015), 179-86.

[16]*SL*, 16.

[17]*MP*, 30.

the context of that culture. Lewis described the tools, the common food and drink, the social structures, even the arts practiced among the different peoples on the planet. But most striking is the way the book captured the evolution of Ransom's own regard for beings who were so different from him in appearance and culture. One of the axioms of cross-cultural study is that interaction with people of a different culture or ethnicity can help a person become more open to difference, more cosmopolitan in the literal sense of being what the ancient philosopher Diogenes Laertius called "a citizen of the world." But cross-cultural contact doesn't guarantee it—and can actually make things worse. *Out of the Silent Planet* is remarkable for the way it charts with stunning accuracy the actual experience of encountering the Other in a way that reduces social and psychological distance and embraces community.

During his sojourn, Ransom came to know members of three different rational species. The *hrossa* (the plural of *hross*), among whom he spent the bulk of his time on the planet, were six or seven feet tall, with a "gleaming . . . coat of thick black hair, lucid as a sealskin, very short legs and webbed feet, a broad beaver-like or fish-like tail, [and] strong forelimbs with webbed claws or fingers." The *hross* was "something like a penguin, something like an otter, something like a seal," but with the slenderness and flexibility that suggested a giant stoat or weasel.[18] A second species, the *sorns*, had the more human-like appearance—and yet grotesquely altered in a way that made them appear "closest to the traditional 'science fiction' outer space creatures pictured on pulp magazines."[19] Twice the height or more of a human, they had long legs, an elongated face—"too long, too solemn and too colorless, . . . much more unpleasantly like a human face than any inhuman creature's face ought to be," with tiny eyes that made the creature seem like a goblin. A *sorn's* legs and arms were covered with what looked like cream-colored feathers, it had fan-shaped, seven-fingered hands with skin that barely

---

[18]*OSP*, 54.
[19]Martha C. Sammons, *"A Far-Off Country": A Guide to C. S. Lewis's Fantasy Fiction* (Lanham, MD: University Press of America, 2000), 115.

covered the bones like a leg of a bird, and it maneuvered with "strange, spidery movements."[20] Toward the end of the book, Ransom interacted briefly with the third species, a comical creature known as the *pfifltrigg*, more "insect-like or reptilian" than any other he met, built distinctly like a frog, with long forelegs leading to an elbow on which it walked, attached to "thin, strong forearms ending in enormous, sensitive many-fingered hands." The *pfifltriggi* had heads like a tapir and moved with rapid and jerky movements that suggested an insect. "It was rather like a grasshopper, rather like one of Arthur Rackham's dwarves, rather like a frog."[21]

Over the course of the book, Ransom came to respect the intelligence and unique gifts of these creatures, even to the point where he felt deep affection for each, despite—or perhaps because of—all their differences. But that is not how he began. Rather, he brought to his journey the popular-culture perceptions of the Other, in this case, aliens in outer space. He also brought a set of assumptions from his own culture that he naively believed were reality, for example, that competition for scarce resources was inevitable in all social interaction, that different cultures could not coexist without one seeking power and dominance over the others, and that hostility and war were unavoidable elements of all social experience. And, of course, he brought the sense of superiority that is all too common in cross-cultural interactions.

Before they even arrived on Mars, Ransom overheard Devine and Weston having a conversation that clearly signaled their identity as representatives of colonial exploitation, as they discussed "meeting the brutes" that lived on the planet.[22] Devine told Weston, "When the time comes for cleaning the place up we'll save one or two for you, and you can keep them as pets or vivisect them or sleep with them or all three—whichever way it takes you."[23] Ransom's mind was "richly furnished

---

[20]*OSP*, 92-93.
[21]*OSP*, 112-13.
[22]*OSP*, 33.
[23]*OSP*, 34.

with bogies" by science fiction writers like H. G. Wells, and he was instantly overcome with horror at the prospect of encountering these creatures himself:

> He saw in imagination various incompatible monstrosities, bulbous eyes, grinning jaws, horns, stings, mandibles. Loathing of insects, loathing of snakes, loathing of things that squashed and squelched, all played their horrible symphonies over his nerves. But the reality would be worse: it would be an extraterrestrial Otherness—something one had never thought of, never could have thought of.[24]

Later, after landing on the planet and starting to set up their camp, they looked up to see a group of creatures coming toward them, "so crazily thin and elongated in the leg, so top-heavily pouted in the chest, such stalky, flexible looking distortions of earthly bipeds . . . like something seen in one of those comic mirrors." It was a group of *sorns,* and Ransom assumed he was about to be handed over to them, with their "thin and unnaturally long" faces, with their "long, drooping noses and drooping mouths of half spectral, half-idiotic solemnity."[25] In terror, he tore himself away from Devine and ran for his life into the Malacandrian forest, putting several miles between him and his captors before collapsing into exhausted sleep. The next day, he set out in search of food and water, and at one point, lying down on his stomach to drink, he was startled by a disturbance in the water nearby. "Circles shuddered and bubbles danced ten yards away from his face. Suddenly the water heaved and a round, shining, black thing like a cannonball came into sight. Then he saw eyes and mouth—a puffing mouth bearded with bubbles."[26] It was a *hross.*

Ransom lay motionless, hoping not to be seen, when something happened that completely changed everything. The *hross* began to make noises that, to Ransom's trained ears as a linguist, were clearly language. Instantly, his intellectual curiosity overcame his fear and he leaned up on an elbow to stare at the beast who, seeing him, stopped and stared back.

---

[24]*OSP*, 35.
[25]*OSP*, 45.
[26]*OSP*, 54.

Thus, "in utter silence the representatives of two so far-divided species stared into the other's face."[27] They began a halting process of introducing themselves—each tensed, ready to run or perhaps fight in self-defense, in what was strangely like a dance of courtship. After a few moments of this, the creature turned away and Ransom, feeling despair, cried "Come back."[28] The creature said something, walked twenty yards away, stooped down and picked up what looked like a large oyster shell, which it dipped in the water and then added some drops from a pouch suspended around its waist (Ransom's first, disgusting thought was that the creature was urinating in the shell), took a drink, and then handed it to Ransom, an unmistakable invitation to drink himself. "His fingertips touched the webbed membrane of the creature's paws and an indescribable thrill of mingled attraction and repulsion ran through him; then he drank." He realized immediately that what the creature had added was alcoholic. "He had never enjoyed a drink so much."[29]

Thus began Ransom's true introduction to Malacandrian civilization— the first step in the evolution of his encounter with the Other. As Lewis described it, in his early interactions with the *hrossa* Ransom was fearful of and even repulsed by the planet's inhabitants, and he clearly operated from a position of ethnocentrism (the belief that one's own culture is superior to all others). Yet, over the course of the story, he came to a stance that anthropologists call "cultural accommodation"; he recognized differences between his culture and the cultures of the various races of the planet where he was a sojourner, where he moved easily among them, where he appreciated the unique qualities that each brought to the whole, and where he was even able to critique his own culture from the perspective of the host culture that had welcomed him.

One of the key elements in that transformation was simply Ransom's acceptance that, although starkly different from him, the creatures who lived on Malacandra were *persons*, a development Lewis signaled

---

[27]*OSP*, 55.
[28]*OSP*, 56.
[29]*OSP*, 57.

through a subtle shift in the terms used to describe the *hrossa*. In the account of his first encounter cited above, Ransom clearly perceived the *hross* as an animal lacking personhood, a perception reflected in the persistent use of two terms to describe the *hross*: *it* and *creature*. But later, when the narrative jumps ahead to a point when Ransom has become habituated to life on Mars (with his favorite walks, favorite foods, etc.), Lewis indicates that Ransom has come to experience the *hrossa* as persons. He could tell males from females and even distinguish differences in personality between individuals in the community: "Hyoi who had first found him—miles away to the north—was a very different person from the grey-muzzled, venerable Hnohra who was daily teaching him the language."[30] Each *hross* now had a name and a distinct identity. From this point on, the narrator uses personal pronouns, *he* and *she* rather than *it*, in order to describe these creatures. Here is a classic element in developing a healthy regard for the Other—accepting the Other's full personhood. It seems too obvious to say, but the fact is that we often see people who are different from us as less than fully persons—as animals or children, for example. Maybe you've had the experience of interacting with someone from a different culture who was just learning English—and whose English vocabulary is limited—and finding yourself interacting with that person as if he or she were a child when in fact that person might have been a scientist, philosopher, or doctor in his or her home country. Unless we are vigilant and intentional about our perceptions, we will do this almost unconsciously. And, of course, viewing the Other as less than human has given rise to our world's ugly history of racial oppression and colonial exploitation. Lewis thus captured a key element in fostering respect across ethnic, gender, and cultural boundaries—consciously acknowledging the full personhood of the Other.

As he became more and more familiar with the *hrossa*, Ransom even came to accept how strange *he* must seem to them, as a "hairless goblin."[31] Lewis here signaled a second fundamental dimension of a healthy

---

[30]*OSP*, 67.
[31]*OSP*, 65.

encounter with the Other. Our usual tendency, depending on where we are on the cultural hierarchy, is to see our cultural identity, or gender, or ethnicity, as the norm, as simply reality, whereas any other cultural identity, gender, or ethnicity is a deviation from that norm. (As an example of this, note how we have historically labeled sports traditionally reserved for men without a gender qualification whereas if women were playing, we would qualify it with a gender designation. Think basketball and women's basketball, or volleyball and women's volleyball. The norm is male so that when women play the same sport, it's somehow a deviation from that norm.) Lewis brilliantly captured that tendency—and shows Ransom growing out of it, to the point that he accepts that his appearance or identity isn't the norm against which all others are judged. He realizes that he seems as strange to them as they do to him!

But perhaps the most difficult part of Ransom's experience was simply letting go of his sense of cultural superiority, something that Lewis depicts in several humorous exchanges. Ransom had mastered their language sufficiently to begin satisfying his hosts' curiosity about himself, and when they asked him where he had come from, he told them that he had come from the sky, on the assumption that, given their lack of intelligence, such an answer would suffice. So he was

> a little annoyed to find Hnohra painfully explaining to him that he could not live in the sky because there was no air in it; he might have come through the sky, but he must have come from a *handra* [their word for "planet"]. He was quite unable to point Earth out to them in the night sky. They seemed surprised at his inability, and repeatedly pointed out to him a bright planet low on the western horizon.[32]

Ransom could tell that what they were pointing to was clearly a planet rather than a star, and he was astonished at how adamantly they stuck to their choice. "Could it be possible that they understood astronomy?" he wondered.[33] Upon identifying the planet from which he had come, they

---

[32]*OSP*, 67.
[33]*OSP*, 67.

concluded that he needed to be taken to Oyarsa, the angelic being who protected and ruled their planet. What follows is a comical account of their struggle to help him understand what we would call their "religion," and Ransom's irritation at the very idea that *they* would need to instruct *him* about spiritual matters:

> Ever since he had discovered the rationality of the *hrossa* he had been haunted by a conscientious scruple as to whether it might not be his duty to undertake their religious instruction; now, as a result of his tentative efforts, he found himself being treated as if *he* were the savage and being given a first sketch of civilized religion—a sort of *hrossian* equivalent of the shorter catechism.[34]

Again, Lewis masterfully captures the ethnocentric response to the Other—his assumption of superiority—as well as the painful process of discovering that he might not be superior after all. Ransom began to realize that the cultures of Malacandra were actually above his own in some important ways. In one conversation with his friend Hyoi about the *hrossas'* view of sex, he discovered that, although they found it immensely pleasurable and experienced it as an integral element of love, it did not rule their lives in the way it seemed to among humans. It was a moment of sharp awakening for Ransom: "Here, unless Hyoi was deceiving him, was a species naturally continent, naturally monogamous."[35] His thoughts turned instantly to his own "civilization": "It dawned on him that it was not they, but his own species, that were the puzzle."[36] Still later he concluded that his persistent assumption that three rational species could not live as equals without one seizing power over the others was actually a sign of fallenness in human culture rather than a fixed rule of all interaction between rational beings.

Ransom also came to see how the three species on the planet each made unique and indispensable contributions to the well-being of all the others—something that he learned in hearing them affirm their need for

---

[34]*OSP*, 68.
[35]*OSP*, 77.
[36]*OSP*, 78.

what the others brought to the life of the whole. The *sorns*, it turned out, were the scientists and philosophers of the planet, but they had no capacity for making things, and, as Ransom's friends among the *hrossa* pointed out, they were completely useless in a boat. The *pfifltriggi* were the planet's craftsmen and technicians—so when Ransom's journey to see the Oyarsa took him up into altitudes where the air was too thin for human lungs, he used an oxygen machine designed by a *sorn* but crafted by one of the *pfifltriggi*. And, of course, the *hrossa* were the planet's poets. Although each species had its own tongue, they all used the language of the *hrossa* because of its rich and beautiful vocabulary. When members of all three groups were together, he discovered, Malacandrian humor made its appearance, growing out of the drollness of their differences. As Lewis put it, "Apparently the comic spirit arose chiefly from the meeting of the different kinds of *hnau*."[37] One can imagine the good-natured ribbing that might break out when three so different rational beings came together who had first taken each other seriously. But it is also a sign of the breadth of their consciousness—a key dimension of spirituality—that they were able to observe themselves in relation to the Other and to appreciate difference.

Finally, Ransom came to see that his own perceptions of the inhabitants on the planet had changed. At one point in his journey to Oyarsa he rode on the shoulder of a *sorn*, one of the creatures he had so dreaded to meet at the beginning of the story. With new eyes he saw a group of three *sorns* coming to meet them down a steep slope. They seemed to be "skating rather than walking," with bodies perfectly fitted for their world, which allowed them to "lean forward at right angles to the slope," making their way swiftly down the hill "like full-rigged ships before a fair wind." This moment marked for Ransom the "final transformation" in his feeling toward their race, as he wondered at "the grace of their movement, their lofty stature, and the softened glancing of the sunlight on their feathery sides."[38] Lewis wrote,

---

[37]*OSP*, 117.
[38]*OSP*, 101.

"Ogres" he had called them when they first met his eyes as he struggled in the grip of Weston and Devine; "Titans" or "Angels" he now thought would have been a better word. Even the faces, it seemed to him, he had not then seen aright. He had thought them spectral when they were only august, and his human reaction to their lengthened severity of lines and profound stillness of expression now appeared to him not so much cowardly as vulgar. So might Parmenides or Confucius look to the eyes of a Cockney schoolboy![39]

Ransom even came to appreciate Malacandrian music, which had always been a mystery to him. In a telling moment, Lewis wrote, Ransom had come to know and to love these creatures so deeply that "he began, ever so little, to hear it with their ears." It was as if "the gate of heaven had opened before him."[40]

What we find in *Out of the Silent Planet* is a remarkably accurate portrayal of healthy intercultural interaction. It is almost as if Lewis had an intercultural communication textbook opened before him as he wrote, for Ransom comes to demonstrate all the key transitions that we look for in healthy cross-cultural exchange. He recognizes and embraces the full personhood of the inhabitants of Mars, resisting the impulse to see them as animals, children, or in some other non-personal way. He comes to realize that his own culture isn't the standard against which all cultures should be judged, and he can appreciate the ways that the cultural values and practices he discovers on Mars fit the physical and social contexts in which he finds them. He allows his assumptions about them to be challenged, especially his sense of superiority, as he moves deeper into community with them. He even enters the world of his host culture so deeply that he finds a standpoint from which to observe and critique his own culture. How completely he has adapted to Malacandrian culture becomes clear toward the end of the story. He was at Melidorn, about to meet the Oyarsa, when he saw a group of *hrossa* guarding two creatures that he could not remember having seen on the

[39]*OSP*, 101.
[40]*OSP*, 131.

planet before, and therefore did not recognize. Lewis described the moment:

> They were much shorter than any animal he had yet seen on Malacandra, and he gathered that they were bipeds, though the lower limbs were so thick and sausage-like that he hesitated to call them legs. The bodies were a little narrower at the top than at the bottom so as to be very slightly pear-shaped, and the heads were neither round like those of the *hrossa* nor long like those of *sorns*, but almost square. They stumped along on narrow, heavy-looking feet which they seemed to press into the ground with unnecessary violence. And now their faces were becoming visible as masses of lumped and puckered flesh of variegated color fringed in some bristly, dark substance.[41]

As you read his account, you wonder at the manner of strange creature Lewis is describing, when suddenly it hits you: Ransom is staring at his two fellow humans, Weston and Devine! It's just that he has become so accustomed to the creatures on Mars that members of his own species have now become strange to him. In ethnographic research, we call this "problematizing the mundane." The goal is to get to the point where we can step back from the everyday taken-for-grantedness of our day-to-day lives in order to really examine our own culture carefully. Clearly, Ransom has come to that point, and as a result he will never look on himself or his world in quite the same way again.

WELCOMING THE OTHER

For a number of years, I taught in a study-abroad program that took US students to East Africa, where we would explore intercultural communication and experience a culture radically different from our own native culture. We saw firsthand some of the challenges facing the developing world, but we also formed deep and lasting friendships and came to see ourselves and our own culture with new eyes. At the end of their time in college, many of our students looked back on their brief sojourn in Africa as the most formative experience of their lives.

---

[41]*OSP*, 125.

As we helped them process their experience, we were painfully aware of the risk that they could easily come back more ethnocentric and fearful of other cultures than before they left so we constantly emphasized several "stances" toward the people and practices that they would encounter in their host culture, among them these three:

1. Curiosity. We would warn them that they would often feel negative "gut reactions" to what they saw in this new culture. They might feel discomfort or even outright revulsion. We encouraged them instead to be curious without automatically judging, to say to themselves, "Hmmmm. That's interesting. I wonder what's behind that."

2. Empathy. As an outgrowth of curiosity, we would challenge them to ask themselves, "What does the world look like from this person's perspective?" Our usual tendency is to witness actions or appearances that put us off and then immediately to judge that person's character or even apply what we see in that individual to that person's entire culture (which is the definition of stereotyping). Instead, we urged them to ask, "What does this person see and feel as she or he looks out at the world?" We found that when students practiced "intentional empathy," the people they encountered in their cross-cultural experiences seemed so much less threatening. In fact, they discovered so much that we shared in common.

3. Humility. At the heart of ethnocentrism is the belief that one's native culture is the standard against which all other cultures should be measured and that other cultural values and practices are deviations from that standard. So, for example, US students might see several people in East Africa working together on a task easily done by one person and make a judgment about how inefficient and even backward they are. Instead, we would encourage students to see that efficiency is an important cultural value but not the only, or even the highest, value. Community and friendship are also important, and the actions they had labeled as inefficient and backward might actually indicate that the folks they were observing simply prized community more than efficiency. That might open a conversation about how we in the United States often sacrifice community in the name of efficiency—a conversation that would help us realize that although our native culture has so much that we value, we also could learn from other cultures! Ultimately, of course, we hoped that by taking stances of curiosity, empathy, and humility, our students would be prepared to form relationships with people from the cultures among whom they were guests. When that happened, their lives were changed.

Lewis's *Out of the Silent Planet* models these core dimensions of healthy cross-cultural exchange. In that very first encounter with Hyoi, the *hross* who becomes his good friend, it is his curiosity that first drives him to reach out to this being who is so different from him. As the story unfolds, even though it means challenging some of his prior assumptions, he asks questions and turns possibilities over in his mind. Ransom engages in the ultimate expression of empathy, learning his host culture's language and seeking to understand how the world looks through their eyes. As he moves deeper into community, he comes to realize things about his own culture, and even to critique unhealthy attitudes and behaviors from the world he left behind.

Behind these essential elements of intercultural competence lie the core dimensions of spirituality that we have emphasized throughout this book, consciousness and choice. Although not as obvious in *Out of the Silent Planet* as in other books by Lewis, the importance of choice or agency lies just beneath the surface. Ransom's first encounter with Hyoi signaled a crucial moment of choice, when he made the split-second decision to reach out to this alien creature who became his dear friend. That decision, in turn, opened the door to all the other choices that would shape his time on Malacandra—his willingness to put out his hand in greeting, to receive a "cup" offered him by his alien host, to get into Hyoi's boat, and so forth. In a sense, Ransom's entire journey—and the secret of all that came to him as a result—was simply a succession of choices to open himself up to each new encounter, each new experience.

Lewis also depicted Ransom's dramatic expansion of consciousness that resulted from his decision to embrace the Other. Of course, from his very first moment on the planet, his mind is racing to make sense of all he sees—what manner of creatures live here, the nature of their language, how they organize themselves socially, and so on. But he is also growing in self-awareness with each new encounter. As he learns their language and is welcomed into their community, he has enough awareness of his own irritation and defensiveness at being instructed about space travel, planets and stars, and "religion" that he continues in dialogue with the *hrossa* and later the *sorns,* who are his hosts. In so doing, he learns not only about their world but also about himself and his world. He comes to perceive his own culture's preoccupation with sex and its obsession with power and domination. As he comes to know a *sorn,* he is able to observe the evolution of his own perception of these creatures from being "ogres" to "Titans" or "Angels," and from his new perspective he critiques his former one as "vulgar," in the way that a Cockney schoolboy might have viewed Parmenides or Confucius.[42]

As we have also emphasized in this book, Ransom's spiritual growth is integrally connected to physical experiences, except that in this case they are embodied within community. A turning point in his drastically altered view of the *sorns* comes when he assents to climb onto one's shoulder in order to be carried to the Oyarsa—an experience that he at first finds ghastly but that eventually he comes to greatly enjoy. Perhaps the most poignant of these moments of communal embodiment, however, is when he first receives from Hyoi the shell-like cup with the drink in it. Lewis often emphasized that community is born in the sharing of food and drink (think of how Mr. Tumnus repents of his plan to betray Lucy to the White Witch as a result of sharing tea with Lucy in his home). In the case of Ransom, it is almost as if he and the stranger were sharing Eucharist. Hyoi prepares the cup, takes a drink, and then offers it to Ransom, who also drinks. That moment changes their relationship forever. Of course, it didn't hurt that what Hyoi had added to the water was plainly alcoholic; "he had never enjoyed a drink so much."[43] Lewis thus depicts Ransom's spiritual journey as holistic and incarnational,

[42]*OSP,* 101.
[43]*OSP,* 57.

integrally tied to relationships in community with spiritual beings who are radically different from him. What Lewis captured imaginatively in this popular sci-fi fantasy he would also emphasize about our need for the Christian community, the church.

THE FANTASTIC VARIETY OF THE SAINTS

In Colossians 3:15, Paul invites us to "let the peace of Christ rule in [our] hearts," a statement that may sound like something we do privately, on our own. But then, in the next phrase, he urges us to "teach and admonish one another" and to sing together (Col 3:16)—reflecting his conviction that participation in community is essential to what happens inside us individually. Lewis came to embrace a similar conviction that being part of a diverse community was an essential prerequisite for our own spiritual formation. As he emphasized in his essay "Membership," the people around us who are different from us are not just a burden to be tolerated; they are ministers of God for our own growth as Christians. To explain this, Lewis first used the analogy of the family, emphasizing the vital importance of difference within the Christian community. As he pointed out, the grandfather, the parents, the adult children, the younger children—even the dog and the cat—are all members precisely because they are not "units of a homogeneous class. They are not interchangeable."[44] So, he continued,

> The mother is not simply a different person from the daughter, she is a different *kind* of person. The grown-up brother is not simply one unit in the class children, he is a separate estate of the realm. The father and grandfather are almost as different as the cat and the dog. If you subtract any one member you have not simply reduced the family in number, you have inflicted an injury on its structure.[45]

Thus, he concluded, the unity they experience is a "unity of unlikes, almost of incommensurables."[46] As a further analogy, Lewis mentioned

---

[44]*MP*, 34.
[45]*MP*, 34, emphasis added.
[46]*MP*, 34.

one of his favorite children's works, *The Wind in the Willows*, where the unity shared by such incommensurable characters as Rat, Mole, and Badger gives us "a dim perception of the richness inherent in this kind of unity."[47]

To what end does God invite us into community with those who are different from us? One obvious purpose is for the sharing of diverse strengths and gifts, a "continual interchange of complementary ministrations." Where one person is weak, another is strong. Where one is immature, another is wise. But for Lewis it went even deeper. He came to realize that there was something about living in community, with all its messiness, bumping up against each other, that was necessary for our own development. As he put it, "We are all constantly teaching and learning, forgiving and being forgiven, representing Christ to man when we intercede, and man to Christ when others intercede for us." To be sure, he admitted, true community demanded the "sacrifice of selfish privacy," but that sacrifice would be "daily repaid a hundredfold in the true growth of personality which the life of the Body encourages."[48]

After many years of serving in a diverse Christian community, I came to see the church like the rock tumblers many of us had when we were children. We were like those unpolished stones, rough and featureless. God puts us in the rock tumbler with some sand and grit and a little water, shuts the door, turns it on, and just lets it run for weeks or months (or in my case, two decades). Like the pebbles in the rock tumbler, we roll and bang against each other and we feel the grit rubbing us raw. But eventually it is as if God turns the motor off, opens the door, and lets us see what we are becoming—precious stones, with elegant and diverse striations shining forth beneath a brightly polished surface.

Against the influence of his own temperament and background, Lewis believed that we needed to be in community with people who are different from us, and, given the narrowness of his own cultural context, he lived that conviction out in remarkable ways. There was his faithful

---

[47] *MP*, 34.
[48] *MP*, 36.

attendance at his local Anglican church. Lewis believed that going "all over the neighborhood" to find a church that "suited him" would reduce him into a mere "taster or connoisseur of churches" and would also prevent his rubbing shoulders with "people of different classes and psychology . . . in the kind of unity" God desires.[49] At great cost to his academic career, he embraced a calling to make the deep truths of Christian theology accessible to the "masses" through his radio addresses and writings, and when the public responded with an incessant torrent of letters, Lewis, with the help of his brother, Warnie, would spend several hours every day writing back. (His letters to the children who wrote to him are models of how to treat people with respect and care.[50]) And of course, there was his marriage to Davidman, a most unlikely life partner—and yet someone whose influence on Lewis was simply incalculable. These relationships help us see how deeply Lewis believed that crossing boundaries is the secret to our growth as persons. As "obedience is the road to freedom" and "humility the road to pleasure," unity within diversity is "the road to personality." It is only as we embrace the Other, as we learn to savor the "almost fantastic variety of the saints," that we become fully the persons we were meant to be.[51]

---

[49]SL, 81.
[50]See C. S. Lewis, C. S. Lewis Letters to Children, ed. Lyle W. Dorsett and Marjorie Lamp Mead, with a foreword by Douglas H. Gresham (New York: Macmillan, 1985).
[51]MP, 36.

CHAPTER EIGHT

THE BEGINNING OF ALL THINGS

SPIRITUALITY AND THE LIFE OF HOPE

In his sermon "Transposition," Lewis tells a parable about a woman and her son who have been cast into prison. The son has never been in the outside world and so has grown up "seeing nothing but the dungeon walls, the straw on the floor" and—recalling Lewis's earlier poem, "Dungeon Grates"—only a "little patch of the sky seen through the grating." His mother had managed to sneak a drawing pad and a box of pencils into the prison and, using them, has tried to keep before her son a vision of the outside world. "With her pencil," Lewis wrote, "she attempts to show him what fields, rivers, mountains, cities and waves on a beach are like." One day she realizes that he cannot imagine the reality of the outside world existing without the presence of lines from the pencil. "What?" he exclaimed. "No pencil-marks there?" Without pencil lines "instantly his whole notion of the outer world becomes blank."[1] He did not realize that the lines were merely a transposition of reality,

> the waving tree-tops, the light dancing on the weir, the colored three-dimensional realities which are not enclosed in lines but define their own shapes at every moment with a delicacy and multiplicity which no

---

[1]*T*, 178.

drawing could ever achieve. The child will get the idea that the real world is somehow less visible than his mother's pictures. In reality it lacks lines because it is incomparably more visible.[2]

The young man had somehow gotten the impression that the real world outside of his prison walls would be less real than what had been conveyed in his mother's drawings so that, in some sense, going there would mean the loss of what had been most meaningful in his life in the dungeon.

In the young man's reaction to his mother's drawings, Lewis sought to capture the impression he believed many Christians had of heaven. We have fallen prey, he said, to the "philosophically respectable notion" that heaven would be devoid of "most of the things our nature desires." The son thought the absence of pencil marks would make the world outside of his prison less substantial, less compelling. In the same way, because we know that the Bible's images of gold streets and pearly gates are mere symbols, we automatically imagine heaven in terms of "perpetual negations: no food, no drink, no sex, no movement, no mirth, no events, no time, no art."[3] At one point in *Perelandra*, Lewis humorously put this view on the lips of one of his characters, the Scottish skeptic MacPhee, when he told of how Ransom and his friends had been debating the resurrection of the body. MacPhee scoffed at the absurdity of retaining in heaven such bodily functions as sex and eating: "So you think you're going to have guts and palate forever in a world where there'll be no eating, and genital organs in a world without copulation? Man, ye'll have a grand time of it!"[4]

Given this view of heaven as the negation of all that we find meaningful in this life, it is not surprising that even we who claim the hope of the resurrection often see our lives here as moving inexorably toward a dreaded end: minute by minute, day by day, we come closer and closer to drawing our final breath and leaving behind the people

---

[2]*T*, 178.
[3]*T*, 176.
[4]*P*, 32.

and the world we love. Lewis believed that the opposite was true, that we were moving not toward the end but toward the beginning. History itself marches toward a commencement of the true life before which all else will be prologue, and against which our richest joys here will appear as mere shadows. We move toward that moment when, in Paul's words, "this perishable body must put on imperishability, and this mortal body must put on immortality," when at last that saying will come true, "Death has been swallowed up in victory" (1 Cor 15:53-54). It will not be the end but only the beginning.

In chapter six, we explored the tantalizing possibility that in our moments of pleasure we are receiving in our minds and bodies the actual life of God, coming to us from its source "at a thousand removes."[5] Where our attempts to conjure a mental conception or theological definition of God fail, we said, we might actually come to know the presence and protection of God deeply, viscerally, by being fully present to physical pleasures and by engaging in the hard work of persistently connecting those pleasures to their source in God in the worship that says, "God, how wonderful you are." Practiced consistently, we might actually become habituated to "reading" even the simplest, most mundane pleasure as the touch of the "finger of that right hand at which there are pleasures forevermore."[6]

In this chapter, we explore Lewis's invitation to connect these same experiences to the life that awaits us in heaven, and we explore the implications of this invitation for the way we live our lives now, in the present. Certainly, Lewis admitted that even the faint glimmers of God's glory are almost "too much for our present management."[7] We struggle to receive them with the kind of awareness and choice that avoids the temptation of "encore." We fight against the impulse to lose ourselves in the sensation itself instead of lifting our eyes from the gift to the giver in the conviction that what we ultimately long for is God. But granting all

---

[5] WG, 14.
[6] LM, 90.
[7] WG, 14.

this, Lewis still raised this provocative question: If, so far removed from their actual source in God, these gifts are still *this* rich and exquisite and overwhelming, what would it be like to come face to face with their source? Lewis posed the question this way: "What would it be to taste at the fountain-head that stream of which even these lower reaches prove so intoxicating? Yet that, I believe, is what lies before us. The whole [person] is to drink joy from the fountain of joy."[8] As he put it a few lines later, citing Augustine, the experience of the presence of God will be nothing less than a *torrens voluptatis*—a torrent of pleasure.[9]

As the writer of the epistle to the Hebrews recognized, few things are more important for the Christian life—indeed, for human life—than hope. Repeatedly he urged his hearers to "seize the hope set before us" (Heb 6:18), to "hold fast to the confession of our hope without wavering" (Heb 10:23), for he knew that only in hope could we be steadfast in pursuing Christ until "the very end" (Heb 6:11). Jürgen Moltmann wrote in his classic work *Theology of Hope* that the "sin of unbelief is manifestly grounded in hopelessness," giving rise to "weakness, timidity, weariness, not wanting to be what God requires of us."[10] By contrast, our confident expectation for the fulfillment of God's vision draws us forward, holding out the possibility of meaning and redemption in the face of suffering and tragedy, causing us to be impatient with and to work against the pain and injustice we see around us, and giving us endurance in the face of the weariness that we all feel at points in our lives. "Living without hope," Moltmann said, "is like no longer living. Hell is hopelessness." But the hope God brings "becomes the happiness of the present" embracing "all

---

[8] *WG*, 14.

[9] The phrase *torrens voluptatis* appears, among other places, in Augustine's commentary on Psalm 35:14 (numbered in contemporary English translations as 36:8), where he renders the verse as, "Thou shalt make them drink of the torrent of thy pleasure," and then explains, "Torrent is the name for a rushing stream of water. The stream will be God's mercies, flowing to refresh and inebriate those who now put their trust beneath the shadow of His wings. What is this *pleasure*? A torrent to inebriate the thirsting." Augustine, "Discourse on Psalm 35," in *St. Augustine on the Psalms*, trans. Scholastica Hebgin and Felicitas Corrigan, 2 vols. (New York: Paulist Press, 1961), 2:243.

[10] Jürgen Moltmann, *Theology of Hope: On the Ground and the Implications of a Christian Eschatology*, trans. James W. Leitch (New York: Harper and Row, 1975), 22.

things in love, abandoning nothing to annihilation but bringing to light how open all things are to the possibilities in which they can live and shall live."[11]

In response to the hopelessness that he believed resulted from negative spirituality, Lewis called us to the virtue of hope and, in what he wrote, pointed us to the kind of concrete practice that would help make that hope real in our experience. That practice involves learning to welcome the joys God grants us here on earth as signs of the new heaven and new earth that God is preparing for us.

HOPE AS VIRTUE

Lewis made clear that Christian hope, the "continual looking forward to the eternal world,"[12] was not simply a feeling that came over us. It is a *virtue* of the Christian life. In other words, it is a settled, persistent trait of personality or character that we are called by God to cultivate intentionally and diligently. We *work* at it. As he reminded us, hope is one of three core "theological" virtues (along with faith and love) that Scripture points to as the unique markers of the Christian life (1 Cor 13:13). If we are to be true to our calling as Christians, we have no choice but to cultivate our hope of heaven.

As he pointed out in *Mere Christianity*, however, "most of us find it very difficult to want 'Heaven' at all,"[13] in large part because we have been so profoundly influenced by the negative spirituality that leads us to imagine the heavenly life as some kind of disembodied, ghostlike existence, devoid of all that makes life beautiful and joyful here. Because heaven is "spiritual," we imagine it being less than what we enjoy on earth, as an emptying of all sensuous life. The prospect of that sort of "heaven" holds little appeal.

Not surprisingly, for an answer Lewis called us back to those experiences of longing that we discussed at the outset of this book. The "real

---

[11]Moltmann, *Theology of Hope*, 32.
[12]*MC*, 118.
[13]*MC*, 119.

want for Heaven is present in us," but we simply "do not recognize it."[14] If we would look into our own hearts, we would find that we all possess a profound ache for something that cannot be had in this world, evoked by the kind of desire that we feel "when we first fall in love, or first think of some foreign country, or first take up some subject that excites us." We find, of course, that "no marriage, no travel, no learning, can really satisfy. . . . There was something we grasped at, in that first moment of longing, which just fades away in the reality."[15] He went on to talk about the ways people try to deal with that longing, some by flitting from possession to possession, relationship to relationship, or achievement to achievement, in the hope of finally catching "the mysterious something we are all after." Others simply opt to lower their standards and give up the search entirely, which he calls "the Way of the Disillusioned 'Sensible Man.'" Of the two options, he said, the latter would be the more logical if we did not live forever. "But supposing infinite happiness *is* there, waiting for us? Supposing one really *can* reach the rainbow's end?" This led Lewis to a third way, the Christian way, which held that earthly pleasures were never meant to satisfy this longing, "but only to arouse it, to suggest the real thing."[16] The task for the Christian, then, is first of all never to mistake these pleasures for their ultimate fulfillment: they are "good images of what we really desire; but if they are mistaken for the thing itself, they turn into dumb idols, breaking the hearts of their worshippers." But this does not mean we ignore or suppress them. To the contrary, we welcome them and attend to them with deep gratitude, for while not heaven itself, they nonetheless offer us the "scent of a flower we have not found, the echo of a tune we have not heard, news from a

---

[14]*MC*, 119.

[15]*MC*, 119. In his essay, "On Stories," Lewis identified the same reality as a chief obstacle to writing good fiction, the inability of a story to fulfill the sense of longing that it has evoked in its opening pages: "We grasp at a state and find only a succession of events in which the state is never quite embodied. The grand idea of finding Atlantis which stirs us in the first chapter of the adventure story is apt to be frittered away in mere excitement when the journey has once begun. But so, in real life, the idea of adventure fades when the day-to-day details begin to happen. . . . The bird has escaped us." C. S. Lewis, "On Stories," in *Of Other Worlds: Essays and Stories*, ed. Walter Hooper (London: Geoffrey Bles, 1966), 20.

[16]*MC*, 120, emphasis added.

country we have never yet visited."[17] Here is how he described that task in *Mere Christianity*:

> I must keep alive in myself the desire for my true country, which I shall not find till after death; I must never let it get snowed under or turned aside; I must make it the main object of life to press on to that other country and to help others to do the same.[18]

We must cultivate hope. And for most of us, the secret to nurturing that virtue will lie in the spiritual embrace of what we now enjoy in our bodies, even as we also keep before us the reality that our deepest longing will never be fulfilled in this life. By living in the delicate tension between the rich sensations of physical pleasure and the knowledge that they do not finally satisfy our deepest hunger, we can learn to see even simple joys and pleasures as "transpositions" from the heavenly glory of our glad Creator into our earthly plane of existence.

TRANSPOSITION

As we have emphasized throughout this book, Lewis believed that physical experiences could be "taken up" into the higher realms of the spiritual through the sanctifying influences of consciousness and choice. That view, we pointed out, was rooted in Christianity's claim that God had embraced the physical by taking on flesh, which led Lewis to suggest that our own "composite existence" might actually be a "faint image of the Divine Incarnation itself—the same theme in a very minor key." In the incarnation "we catch sight of a new key principle—the power of the Higher, just in so far as it is truly Higher, to come down, the power of the greater to include the less."[19] As his parable of the mother and her son illustrated, he viewed the art of drawing as a perfect example of what he called the process of "transposition," where the "higher reproduces itself in the lower."[20] The artist employs what, from one perspective, are

---

[17] *WG*, 5.
[18] *MC*, 120.
[19] *M*, 134.
[20] *T*, 173.

mere lines and angles and cubes in order "to represent a three-dimensional world on a flat sheet of paper."[21] When an artist uses shading, the brightest part of the drawing is literally "only plain white paper," but in the artist's hand, it becomes "the sun, or a lake in the evening light, or human flesh."[22] "Taken up" within the drawing, lines and shapes and shading come to have a higher purpose, pointing beyond themselves to a rich, enthralling vision.

Lewis, however, found the strongest evidence for this principle in the New Testament's accounts of the resurrection and ascension of Christ. He observed that modern readers, steeped in negative spirituality, tend to conceive of the resurrection as merely "the reversal or undoing of the Incarnation" in a way that overlooks the "risen *manhood*" of Jesus.[23] We tend to assume that Jesus was raised to some kind of shadowy, ghost-like existence and that in his ascension he simply faded away or was somehow "dematerialized" into the heavens. In that view, the references to the risen *body* of Christ

> make us uneasy: they raise awkward questions. For as long as we hold the negatively spiritual view, we have not really been believing in that body at all. We have thought (whether we acknowledged it or not) that the body was not objective: that it was an appearance sent by God to assure the disciples of truths otherwise incommunicable. But what truths? If the truth is that after death there comes a negatively spiritual life, an eternity of mystical experience, what more misleading way of communicating it could possibly be found than the appearance of a human form which eats boiled fish?[24]

And in the ascension itself, Lewis insisted, the Gospels record that the apostles somehow perceived "the Ascending Christ . . . in a three-dimensional space." He was quick to say that this is not a matter of "a human body as we know it existing in interstellar space as we know it."[25]

---

[21]*T*, 171.
[22]*T*, 181.
[23]*M*, 176, emphasis in original.
[24]*M*, 175-76.
[25]*M*, 187.

In the ascension, rather, we witness the first glimpse of the "new Nature," a nature in which Jesus occupies space and yet is no longer bound by its limitations. Lewis believed that the accounts of Jesus' resurrection and ascension provided clues to the nature of the heavenly existence that awaits the faithful, where the physical will likewise be taken up into the spiritual. In that existence, the physical is not less but more real.

By extension, Lewis saw in Jesus' resurrection and ascension crucial clues to the nature of the heavenly existence that awaits us who are in Christ. In a dramatic reversal prefigured by Christ's resurrection, the physical will no longer rule the spiritual. Instead, the spiritual will now take up and rule the physical. As he put it in *Letters to Malcolm*, "At present we tend to think of the soul as somehow 'inside' the body. But the glorified body of the resurrection as I conceive it—the sensuous life raised from its death—will be inside the soul. As God is not in space but space is in God."[26] In this view, our present physical experiences are transpositions of the greater realities that we will know in that moment when the breach between the physical and spiritual will, at last, have been healed.

Growing out of this view, he sought to convey that the heavenly existence would not be less real than our earthly one but more real, more substantial and solid, in the way that the mother's pencil marks could only hint at how real, how beautiful, the outside world was. The analogy he used in his sermon "Transposition" to explain this process captures the idea beautifully: "If you are making a piano version of a piece originally scored for an orchestra, then the same piano notes which represent flutes in one passage must also represent violins in another."[27] In other words, musical transcription involves taking a score that might be intended for full orchestra and attempting to play it using a single instrument in a way that suggests but could never do full justice to the listening experience. As an analogy, imagine using a midi program (short for "musical instrument digital interface") to create a recording of a

---

[26]*LM*, 122.
[27]*T*, 171.

classic piece of music like the opening strains of Beethoven's Fifth Symphony. You can almost hear those opening notes (Da-da-da-DAAAAH . . . Da-da-da-DAAAAH) coming out in the shrill tones of a cheap electric piano. It has certainly lost much of its grandeur. Yet even here you catch a hint of the haunting note progression and rhythms that make this piece a classic. Now imagine going from hearing that midi version to sitting before a full orchestra in a majestic, acoustically perfect concert hall, hearing those opening notes. The midi version hinted at but could never capture the beauty and power of the real thing. In the same way, Lewis believed that our richest experiences of pleasure and beauty here on earth are but faint glimpses of the life that awaits us, where sensuality has been taken up into the spiritual. He put it this way:

> "We know not what we shall be"; but we may be sure we shall be more, not less, than we were on earth. Our natural experiences (sensory, emotional, imaginative) are only like the drawing, like penciled lines on flat paper. If they vanish in the risen life, they will only vanish as pencil lines vanish from the real landscape, not as a candle flame that is put out but as a candle flame which becomes invisible because someone has pulled up the blind, thrown open the shutters, and let in the blaze of the risen sun.[28]

We no longer hear the midi version of Beethoven because it has been engulfed in the swelling sounds of the orchestra. Or consider his illustration of a candle in a dark room, around which we huddle as a source of precious light. Such are even the richest of pleasures we experience in this life. But imagine throwing back the curtains and flooding the room with sunlight. The light of the candle hasn't been extinguished. Rather, it's been engulfed, overwhelmed by the far greater light of the sun. In this way, the joys of our lives here exist in strong continuity to those of the heavenly life to come, but only as the flickering light of a small candle exists in relation to the full blast of glorious sunlight. Heaven will not be less, but so much more, than what we know here.

---

[28]*T*, 178-79.

At a number of points in his imaginative writings, Lewis sought to depict this principle whereby the embodied heavenly existence was the reality, of which our richest experiences on earth were faint transpositions. In *The Great Divorce* the visitors from hell are ghosts, "smudgy and imperfectly opaque, . . . man-shaped stains on the brightness of that air,"[29] in comparison to the far more "solid" substantiality of heaven. At one point the narrator, himself a ghostly visitor from hell, reached down to try and pick a daisy growing at his feet: "The stalk wouldn't break. I tried to twist it, but it wouldn't twist. I tugged till the sweat stood out on my forehead and I had lost most of the skin off my hands. The little flower was hard, not like wood or even like iron, but like diamond." When he tried to walk, the grass, "hard as diamonds to my unsubstantial feet," made it feel like he was walking on sharp rocks.[30] In stark contrast to the ghostly visitors from hell, the "bright people," who would be their heavenly guides whose task was to guide them toward heaven, were overwhelming in their solidity and dazzling radiance. As they came toward the ghostly visitors, "the earth shook under their tread as their strong feet sank into the wet turf."[31] As Lewis depicted it, the narrator and the other visitors from hell are only on the outermost edge of the heavenly land, and not even in heaven proper. Yet how firm and rock-solid, and how beautiful and vivid it all was even at this distance. Behind his depiction, of course, is this question: What must it be like to go "further up and further in"?[32]

But perhaps Lewis's most captivating depictions of heaven come in the Narnia books, where we catch stirring glimpses of Aslan's country. One of these comes at the end of *The Voyage of the Dawn Treader*, where the youngest two Pevensie children, Lucy and Edmund, their cousin Eustace Scrubb, and the brave and chivalrous mouse, Reepicheep, join Caspian, now the king, on a voyage to the eastern end of the world in search of the seven lost lords of Narnia. As they drew closer to their destination,

---

[29]*GD*, 18.
[30]*GD*, 19.
[31]*GD*, 21.
[32]*LB*, 206.

they found the sunlight becoming brighter and more intense, as if the sun were two or three times its size, and they heard the sound of white birds singing in what sounded like human voices. When Reepicheep jumped into the sea (to avenge the honor of Caspian and his crew when he thought they had been threatened by a kingdom of mermen and mermaids) and was hauled out of the water, soaked and gasping for breath, he blurted out, "Sweet! Sweet! . . . I tell you, the water's sweet."[33] They put down a bucket and discovered that the water around them was beyond fresh; it was like "drinkable light."[34] "It's the loveliest thing I have ever tasted," Lucy exclaimed. Then, after they had all drunk, they were silent for a long time, feeling "almost too well and strong to bear it."[35] Like the "solid people" in *The Great Divorce* who are gradually able to tolerate the excruciating hardness and beauty of the outer fringes of heaven, Caspian and his friends found that, after drinking the water, they were able to bear the brightness of the sun, even though it seemed to be growing ever brighter. As Lewis described it,

> No one ate or slept and no one wanted to, but they drew buckets of dazzling water from the sea, stronger than wine, more liquid than ordinary water. . . . One or two of the sailors who had been oldish men when the voyage began now grew younger every day. Everyone on board was filled with joy.[36]

As their voyage continued, they came to an expanse of lilies as far as they could see, from which rose "a fresh, wild, lonely smell that seemed to get into your brain and make you feel that you could go up mountains at a run or wrestle with an elephant." Caspian exclaimed, "I feel that I can't stand much more of this, yet I don't want it to stop."[37]

Finally, when the ship could go no further because the sea had grown so shallow, the three children and Reepicheep said their farewells to

---

[33] *VDT*, 247.
[34] *VDT*, 248.
[35] *VDT*, 249.
[36] *VDT*, 255.
[37] *VDT*, 258.

Caspian and his crew and climbed into a small boat for the final part of their journey, Reepicheep to the land of Aslan and the children to their home in England. They came to a wave of water extending some thirty feet into the air, giving off colors like a rainbow, and then through the shimmering water they saw the land beyond. There were mountains, "warm and green and full of forests and waterfalls however high you looked." Suddenly, they felt a breeze blow over them from that land. It lasted only a second, but they would remember it forever. "It brought both a smell and a sound, a musical sound. Edmund and Eustace would never talk about it afterward. Lucy could only say, 'It would break your heart.'"[38] As they drew near to Aslan's country, their senses were flooded with sights and smells and tastes and sounds that were agonizing in their beauty and sweetness. With but a momentary touch of the breeze from that far country, they were overcome with longing. In this way, Lewis sought to evoke our own longing for the far country that awaits us, that far country for which we were made.

Lewis especially captured what he believed about the "supra-physical" character of heavenly existence at the end of *The Last Battle*, when the children are finally allowed to enter the true Narnia, of which the beloved country of their magical visits had been a mere "shadowland." They recognized familiar landmarks, and yet what they saw was also somehow different. Lucy exclaimed,

> "They have more colors on them and they look further away than I remembered and they're more . . . more . . . oh, I don't know . . ."
> "More like the real thing," said the Lord Digory softly.[39]

Like the risen Christ, the children had bodies that occupied space, and, like Jesus, they ate. Yet they were not bound by the limitations of physicality. So they ran like the wind, the air flying in their faces "as if they were driving fast in a car without a windscreen. The country flew past as if they were seeing it from the windows of an express train. Faster and

---

[38] *VDT*, 265.
[39] *LB*, 210.

faster they raced, but no one got hot or tired or out of breath."[40] When they came to a great, roaring waterfall cascading over "high, unclimbable cliffs," they simply swam up the falls, "as if one could swim up the wall of a house."[41] Lewis thus attempted to express imaginatively what he believed was an essential reality in God's creation, represented in the incarnation and, especially, in the resurrection of Christ—that the miracle of creation is the joining together of spiritual and physical, and that at the consummation the conflict unleashed between them by the fall would be overcome and they would be rejoined as God intended them to be.

WHAT MUST IT BE LIKE?

Lewis believed that our experiences of physical pleasure, of taste and sight, hearing and touch and smell, gave us avenues for cultivating a visceral sense of God's presence around us and in us. But he also believed that they were our best hints of the nature of eternal life. Since redemption and the enjoyment of God's presence in heaven would be in some sense an embodied experience, physical pleasure, he believed, provides the Christian not only an avenue for adoration in the present but also a tangible source of hope, a signpost pointing to what awaits us in the future. In order to make that connection, Lewis most often used a classic mode of "if-then" logic, arguing from the lesser to the greater. As Aristotle explained in his treatise on rhetoric, one powerful form of argument is to start with something that people agree on as being good and to use that as the basis for considering the comparative benefit or beauty or wealth of the *surpassing* good:

> Now to call a thing "greater" or "more" always implies a comparison of it with one that is "smaller" or "less," while "great" and "small," "much" and "little," are terms used in comparison with normal magnitude. The "great" is that which surpasses the normal, the "small" is that which is surpassed by the normal; and so with "many" and "few."[42]

---

[40]*LB*, 214.
[41]*LB*, 217.
[42]Aristotle, *Art of Rhetoric*, 1.7.

In other words we come to appreciate the surpassing good by imagining it against the good to which it is so far superior. If a tiny taste of perfectly cooked filet mignon is exquisite, what would it be like to sit down to the whole steak? If a photograph of snow-covered mountains stirs our hearts, how much more beautiful would it be to stand before them in person? This is exactly the kind of operation of thought and imagination that Lewis invited us to perform in "The Weight of Glory." Our experiences of physical pleasure here are merely the "faint, far-off results" of God's creative energy; we experience them in the same way that we experience the rays of the sun on a cloudy day, diluted by the layers and layers of atmosphere through which they must pass before they reach us. And yet, "even thus filtered they are too much for our present management." We struggle to welcome them with anything like moderation and discipline, so wonderful and delicious are they now. But then Lewis asked, "What would it be to taste at the fountain-head that stream of which even these lower reaches proves so intoxicating?"[43] Similarly, his analogy of musical transcription suggested the same work of imagination: If even the midi version of Beethoven's Fifth is this good, how much greater would it be to have a front-row seat at a live performance in one of the world's great concert halls? As he asked in *Letters to Malcolm*, "What must be the quality of that Being whose far-off and momentary coruscations are like this!"[44] We see here but momentary coruscations, faint and ephemeral glitters or sparkles that come to us "from a thousand removes."[45] What would it be like to be in the presence of God if the faint and far-off glimpses are this good?

Using the "lesser to the greater" argument as a model, then, Lewis gave us one additional dimension of spiritual practice with which to engage physical pleasures. As we attend to them and connect them to God in

---

[43] *WG*, 14. Again, we hear the influence of Augustine, who exclaimed the wonders of nature that come to humans living "under condemnation" and then asked, "What then will those rewards be, if the consolations are so many and so wonderful?" Augustine, *City of God*, trans. Henry Bettenson (Harmondsworth, UK: Penguin Books, 1972), 22.24.

[44] *LM*, 90.

[45] *WG*, 14.

adoration, he also invited us to imagine the eternal existence to which they point. In one sense, he admitted, we do live in a "'valley of tears,' cursed with labor, hemmed round with necessities, tripped up with frustrations, doomed to perpetual plannings, puzzlings, and anxieties."[46] And yet, even here, in the midst of all that weighs us down, we are given gifts of intense beauty and pleasure. If we choose to, we can pay attention to them, welcome them, and enjoy them fully as glimpses of what awaits us.

This discipline, of course, can have tremendous practical value for our lives since, if we are attentive, we are daily presented with pleasurable experiences. But one area where we might find it particularly helpful is in our experience of memory, specifically in those happy memories of people or experiences or periods of our lives that have passed, to which we can never return. It might be a time in youth or a particular journey we once took or a time in the lives of our children. We all have them, and we often experience their passing with great sadness. It is as if a door has been firmly shut and bolted behind us on a room to which we can never return. That reality can paralyze us with deep sadness and even despair as we obsess over the past or as we try somehow to recapture and relive memories of moments gone forever. In *Letters to Malcolm* Lewis captured the futility of that attempt by comparing it to trying to recapture the scent of last year's flowers by digging up the bulbs from the dirt in the middle of winter: "Grub them up and hope, by fondling and sniffing, to get last year's blooms, and you will get nothing."[47]

But what would it mean to embrace even these memories from the vantage point of hope? What if we were able to look at them with a perspective that acknowledges that these experiences were never intended to fulfill our deepest longings but instead were signposts to something greater? What if we learned to savor those memories, to give thanks for the experiences that they recall, but then to imagine the life to which they, like all pleasures, are pointing? What if we said, "If the moment

---

[46]*LM*, 92.
[47]*LM*, 27.

I remember is this sweet, how much better will be that land to which this memory is ultimately directing me?" I have a sweet recollection from when my boys were small of the time we went sledding on a hill behind one of those big-box stores in the town where we lived. Over and over we would climb up the hill, pile onto the saucer, and laughing with glee fly down again. Looking back, I miss that moment dearly, and it is painful to realize that whatever other good comes to me in my life, I will never go back to that time. It's gone forever. I am learning to embrace it, to give thanks for that glad moment and for my rich memory of it, even though the remembering is tinged with sadness. But I also realize that the experience and the memory are pointing me to heaven, and to the eternal life that I will know there. And so I look back, but in order to look ahead, with hope. As Lewis wrote, "Properly bedded down in a past which we do not miserably try to conjure back, they will send up exquisite growths."[48] We look back on them, but always as a sign of the life that we believe lies ahead. To be sure, nothing completely removes the sting of the staggering reality that the past is gone, that those moments will never return. But, taken up within the life of hope, even our memories of a joyful past, like our tastes of pleasure in the present, become sources of hope for life eternal.

A Gallop with the King

When we turn to the very last page of the Chronicles of Narnia, we find the children we met at the beginning of *The Lion, the Witch, and the Wardrobe* now in the true land of Narnia, which is heaven. Although they felt an overwhelming joy, they did not yet fully realize where they were. Aslan saw that they were troubled and said to them, "You do not yet look so happy as I mean you to be." "We're so afraid of being sent away, Aslan," they replied. "And you have sent us back into our own world so often." "No fear of that," he answered. "Have you not guessed?" At his question, "their hearts leaped and a wild hope rose within them."[49]

---

[48]*LM*, 27.
[49]*LB*, 228.

Aslan began to explain that the shaking and crashing from their last memory of earth was a railway accident. "You are—as you used to call it in the Shadowlands—dead." But then he said these words that poignantly capture Christianity's hope of eternal life: "The term is over: the holidays have begun. The dream is ended: this is the morning."[50] Lewis ended the treasured series of children's books with these words:

> And for us this is the end of all the stories, and we can most truly say that they all lived happily ever after. But for them it was only the beginning of the real story. All their life in this world and all their adventures in Narnia had only been the cover and title page: now at last they were beginning Chapter One of the Great Story, which no one on earth has read: which goes on for ever: in which every chapter is better than the one before.[51]

We close the book with sadness at the ending of the story, but for the characters themselves it is not the end but only the beginning. The story is just starting.

That hope of eternal life is perhaps the happiest outcome of Lewis's understanding of spirituality as the full, glad embrace of the gifts of physical pleasure and enjoyment that God places in our lives. When welcomed through the disciplined exercise of attention, gratitude, and adoration, they give us a tangible encounter with the presence and creative energy of God. No longer are we merely thinking *about* God's glory as an abstract theological concept; rather, we hear its music, we smell its aroma, we feel its touch. When we practice this spiritual life with diligence, we find ourselves growing in our capacity for wonder and worship and for living joyfully as we become more and more aware of the gifts God constantly showers on us in even the most mundane moments of our lives. But beyond all of this, our present moments of pleasure and enjoyment thus received hold out for us the potential for nurturing Christian hope.

To be sure, for physical pleasures to be taken up into the spiritual life—the life of awareness and agency—they must be subjected to

---

[50]*LB*, 228.
[51]*LB*, 228.

discipline. And yes, part of that discipline has to do with exercising self-control, with rejecting the impulse for the "encore," for to do so would be to allow consciousness and choice to be engulfed within physical sensation, causing us, literally, to lose ourselves in an orgy of satiation. But the discipline we exercise toward physical pleasure is never restraint alone. Rather, it is restraint combined with the active connection we make in our minds between the gift and the giver. In the same way that we take only a morsel of cake and eat it slowly and attentively, savoring each delicious taste, the practice of moderation in pleasure can actually heighten our enjoyment, even as it allows us to connect that physical sensation to the greater joy of God's presence. We thus encounter the glory with our whole being, body, mind, and soul. We "taste and see that the LORD is good" (Ps 34:8). But what is more, as Lewis emphasized, we can do the imaginative work of connecting even the tiniest epiphany of pleasure to what awaits us in heaven by asking this question: If it is this good here, how much greater will it be there? Biblical scholars and theologians have long emphasized that eternal life is not something that begins after death, in heaven; rather, it begins here and now. Lewis in the same way repeatedly emphasized the continuity between this life and the life to come, but he also gave us a practical way to take that truth into ourselves by challenging us to see pleasures here as pointers to the life beyond this life.

Lewis captured that vision of a heavenly future, and his conviction about how that vision might bring joy and hope to us in the present, in his book *Miracles*:

> To shrink back from all that can be called Nature into negative spirituality is as if we ran away from horses instead of learning to ride. There is in our present pilgrim condition plenty of room (more room than most of us like) for abstinence and renunciation and mortifying our natural desires. But behind all asceticism the thought should be, "Who will trust us with the true wealth if we cannot be trusted even with the wealth that perishes?" Who will trust me with a spiritual body if I cannot control even an earthly body? These small and perishable bodies we now have were given to us as

ponies are given to schoolboys. We must learn to manage: not that we may some day be free of horses altogether but that some day we may ride bareback, confident and rejoicing, those greater mounts, those winged, shining and world-shaking horses which perhaps even now expect us with impatience, pawing and snorting in the King's stables. Not that the gallop would be of any value unless it were a gallop with the King; but how else—since He has retained His own charger—should we accompany Him?[52]

We learn to live within our bodies now, practicing attentiveness, adoration, and self-control in a way that opens us to a tangible, bodily sense of joyful God's presence in this life. But by connecting those joys to the life that is to come, we also "seize the hope set before us" (Heb 6:18). We are renewed in our conviction that death is not the end, that God will redeem all suffering, and that even creation itself will be liberated from its bondage of decay (Rom 8:21). And we find a reason to live with joyful expectation as we face our own future and even the prospect of our physical death. For we have glimpsed the unspeakable bliss that awaits us when we "gallop with the King."

---

[52]*M*, 194-95.

CONCLUSION

THE JOY OF THE LORD
IS MY STRENGTH

Imagine this scenario: a small community of Christians is facing discrimination because of their faith, perhaps in the form of intimidation, slander, or verbal insults. Or worse, they are being threatened with physical harm, or even with persecution at the hands of the state. But then the oddest thing happens. Some of their opponents begin to observe them up close and are so perplexed by the sheer optimism and joyfulness they see that they end up asking, "What is it with you Christians? What's your secret?"

That's precisely the situation Peter envisions in 1 Peter 3:15. Earlier in the epistle he had praised God for the gift of new life, a life infused with a vibrant and energizing confidence—a "living hope" (1 Pet 1:3). He had described their experience of this new life as one of "inexpressible and glorious joy" undiminished by "grief in all kinds of trials" (1 Pet 1:8, 6 NIV). But then, as he warned them of the persecution that they would likely encounter, given their political and social context, he counseled them to keep Christ in their hearts and to be ready always to explain their hope. "For there will be some who, when they see your unquenchable hope, will want to know your secret. Be prepared to answer," Peter says, "but do so with gentleness and respect."

What a contrast between this hypothetical scenario, where even bitter opponents are enthralled by the joy they see in Christians' lives, and the way that many in our society actually see Christians today. As research into the public's perceptions of Christianity has shown, we Christians are known more for being judgmental and uncaring than for our gentleness and respect.[1] Instead of demonstrating the kind of optimism that sustains us through disappointments and difficulties, what they have seen in us has led them to believe that faith doesn't really help one live a better, more fulfilling life. Instead of encountering us as people filled with living hope and inexpressible joy, many in our world—even many who grew up in church—see us as boring, irrelevant, lacking vitality.

A big part of what lies behind that perception, I have argued, has been an approach to Christianity centered in an unhealthy view of "spirituality." We have too often exchanged the vibrant, hopeful life in Christ for what C. S. Lewis called "negative spirituality," viewing the spiritual life as a negation, as the renunciation of all that is pleasurable here on earth. Negative spirituality tells us to empty ourselves as if emptiness were the highest good, rather than being the prerequisite to finding ourselves filled with the joy of God's love. Like the second-century Gnostics, we have tended to set the spiritual against the physical, with the result that we assume spiritual growth to entail an ever-increasing distance from physicality. We have been given a miraculous capacity to enjoy delights of taste, touch, sound, sight, and smell, and yet tragically we have gotten the impression that the quest for holiness involves turning away from these gifts and retreating into the world of abstract, theological ideas. In this view, heaven is the place where our richest experiences of pleasure are lost to us. We are like the proverbial little boy that loved chocolate more than anything else in the world who, when told that sex didn't involve eating chocolate, declared that he

---

[1]David Kinnaman and Gabe Lyons, *Unchristian: What a New Generation Really Thinks About Christianity . . . and Why It Matters* (Grand Rapids: Baker Books, 2007).

wanted nothing to do with it.[2] In the same way, we come to see heaven as the place where we are deprived of all that is most precious to us here on earth. No wonder even we Christians cling to life here so desperately. And of course, in this view, God is the great killjoy or, as Lewis saw God in the earlier years, the divine interferer.

Lewis was convinced that this whole understanding of Christianity was profoundly mistaken, and in this book I have sought to unfold what he advanced as the alternative. He invited us to start by paying close attention to our richest experiences of delight and then to consider the possibility that our capacity to experience this pleasure is a gift from God. He challenged us to ask ourselves what the character and nature of God must be to have created us with such appetites and then to have strewn along our way such gifts of beauty and gladness. He invited us to imagine what it might be like to be in the presence of this God, at whose "right hand are pleasures forevermore" (Ps 16:11). It would be nothing less than a *torrens voluptatis*, a torrent of pleasure.[3]

But Lewis also gave us a practical way for living into this picture of spirituality, a way of living that embraced the physical and earthy. For Lewis, true spirituality had nothing to do with turning away from our bodies and from contact with the physical world. Rather, it centered on the expansion of consciousness and agency, by which we become ever more aware of ourselves, others, and God, allowing us to act more and more out of free choice. This picture of the spiritual embraces rather than shuns our nature as embodied creatures, and it welcomes—it relishes— the gifts of sensory delight. When we receive them through the disciplines of awareness, gratitude and adoration, and self-control, these gifts of sensuous pleasure are taken up into the spiritual life, as the resurrected body of Christ was taken up into heaven at his ascension. Lewis's view brought together mind and body: with our bodies we take in physical

---

[2]Lewis gave this analogy in *Miracles* (190-91), where he quipped that the little boy comes to "regard the absence of chocolates as the chief characteristic of sexuality. In vain you tell him that the reason why lovers in their carnal raptures don't bother about chocolates is that they have something better to think of."

[3]*WG*, 14.

pleasure and beauty, and with our minds we connect those sensations to the God who gave them to us. To the degree that we become more and more habituated to receiving every gift from God as a theophany, we move deeper and deeper into the life of God. Our lives become marked by a living hope that endures even when we face "grief in all kinds of trials" (1 Pet 1:8, 6 NIV). And at the center of it all, of course, is the joy of the Lord.

For me, as for so many who have discovered this secret of joyful life, Lewis's picture of spirituality has been truly life changing. The Bible now makes sense. The core dimensions of Christian theology all fit together. And we find a way to live that is joyful in the present and filled with hope for the life to come. In the introduction to this book, I talked of how my students find in Lewis a theological coherence; the biblical narrative and their own personal experiences of joy and longing all come together. Now, at the conclusion of our journey through Lewis's view of spirituality, we return to that theme by exploring how Lewis's conception of the spiritual life enables us to see anew the message of Christianity, what the New Testament writers called, simply, "the faith." At the center is what one ancient leader of Israel, Nehemiah, promised would sustain God's people through whatever trials they faced: "The joy of the LORD is your strength" (Neh 8:10).

THE GOLDEN THREAD

What Lewis called "Joy," that fleeting sensation of bliss and delight mingled with sadness and intense longing, so beautiful that it hurts, became the theological center of his life. It was the thread that ran through all his writings about the spiritual life, both fiction and non-fiction. In the same way, our own glimpses of joy are our clue to the meaning of the universe. They expose our ultimate longing, our ache for God, and they point us to the nature of the God for whom we ache. Every experience of pleasure, even stolen pleasure, is a glimpse of the divine presence. As Lewis discovered in his own spiritual journey, they are not themselves the fulfillment, and any attempt to satisfy our hunger by grasping at whatever has evoked the longing will ultimately break our hearts, leaving us empty and unfulfilled. Instead, they point beyond themselves to their maker, who uses them to woo us and draw us deeper and deeper into the life of God. And miraculously, as we learn to live more and more into the nearness of God, we find ourselves filled with that "inexpressible and glorious joy" (1 Pet 1:8 NIV) that is our strength.

The joy of the Lord was the missing piece that gave coherence to the rest of Lewis's theological universe, and for me it has become the lens through which I see the entire biblical narrative and the "Christian system." In a word, it has been the biggest aha of my life as a Christian, the same kind of aha Lewis captured when he told the story of his very first visit to Oxford.[4] It seems that when he stepped out of the train station he inadvertently turned in the wrong direction and started walking so that he completely missed the towers and spires of the famous university town. He kept walking, wondering when he would finally see Oxford's storied skyline, when it occurred to him to turn around. And there it was. Discovering the joy of the Lord has been, for me, that same kind of experience. Now I see.

One way this has impacted me is in how I read the Bible. The joy of the Lord has become my lens for reading Scripture, with the result that I discover texts I never noticed before and see familiar ones in a new way. Space doesn't permit anything like a full account of those passages, but here are a few examples.

Consider the creation story of Genesis 2, where God fashions a man and a woman, Adam and Eve, and puts them in the Garden of Eden, literally, the garden of delight, the garden of ecstasy. In the last verse of Genesis 2, the biblical narrative says that they were "naked, and were not ashamed" (Gen 2:25). Think about what that meant—totally unafraid, completely unselfconscious and uninhibited in each other's presence. And consider what was lost when Adam and Eve rejected God, the tragic event recorded in the very next chapter: they experience death, the

---

[4]*SJ*, 184.

fracturing of all the relationships that had marked their lives. Now they hide from themselves by covering their bodies, they hide from God, they blame each other, and they are set in conflict with the created order. What, then, was Eden all about? It was God's vision of humans living in a perfect relationship with God, with the created order, with each other, and within themselves. All is peace and harmony. It is the place where humans know the presence of God, unmarred by sin or corruption. Literally, the whole earth is full of the glory of God. And the Bible calls that experience Eden, the place of ecstasy.

Then there is the story of the Exodus, where God promises to lead the people out of the drudgery, oppression, and hopelessness of slavery in Egypt to the Promised Land, the land flowing with milk and honey. And think about that moment in the life of their leader, Moses, when he actually saw the presence of God (Ex 33). It was shortly after the golden-calf disaster, and Moses is at a low point. At first, he wants a simple guarantee from God: "Promise you'll go with me. Don't leave me alone with these people." God responds, "My Presence will go with you" (Ex 33:14). But then Moses asks what is really on his heart: "Show me your glory" (Ex 33:18). In other words, "I want to see your presence!" In response, God explains that the divine presence, straight on, is more than Moses can handle so instead, as the story is told, God places Moses in a crevice in the rock and covers him with a hand, hiding Moses from the full brunt of that glory. Only after God has passed by is the hand of God removed and Moses allowed to look upon the glory (Ex 33:20-23). I believe that this was the climactic moment of Moses' life as a human, excruciating in its beauty. I believe that he never forgot it, that it became the event against which Moses measured every other experience of his life. And in those times when Moses became tired or discouraged, this was the memory he ached for and that sustained him, that day he saw the backside glory of Yahweh.

Think about Job. His life has fallen apart and, in his anger, he cries out to God, "God what are you doing? God, are you enjoying this? Is this your idea of fun?" But mostly he cries, "God, I want answers. I demand that you explain yourself." In a way, the entire book is about the demand for answers, for an explanation of why, after Job had done everything right, his life had still fallen apart.[5] But the fascinating thing is that when you come to the end of the book, Job gets something he's not ready for. He gets God. God comes to Job and displays the divine presence as awesome and powerful—God speaks to Job from out of the whirlwind (Job 38:1). I imagine Job tottering on a bare, rocky hill, so small and vulnerable against the background of the storm, trying to stay upright while the wind churns his hair and his robes and the dark clouds swirl around him. God, awesome and powerful, begins to interrogate Job:

> "Who is this that obscures my plans
>   with words without knowledge?
> Brace yourself like a man;
>   I will question you,
>   and you shall answer me." (Job 38:2-3 NIV)

If you're Job, this is the moment when you think, "Oh my. I've done it now."

Then God begins to ask Job some questions. At first, it seems as if you can hear sarcasm in God's voice, and certainly there is some chiding. "Job, are you big enough to handle the answer you've demanded from me?" But then the oddest thing happens. As you read along, you detect a twinkle in God's eye:

> "Where were you when I laid the earth's foundation?
>   Tell me, if you understand.
> Who marked off its dimensions? Surely you know!
>   Who stretched a measuring line across it?
> On what were its footings set,
>   or who laid its cornerstone—

---

[5]For examples of this questioning, see Job 3:11-26, where Job asks why he was allowed to live, if this suffering was to be his destiny (e.g., "Why is light given to one who cannot see the way, whom God has fenced in?" v. 23); 7:20, where Job asks God, "Why have you made me your target?"; 9:21-24, where Job accuses God mocking "the calamity of the innocent" and then asks, "If it is not he, who then is it?"; and especially, 10:3, where Job asks of God, "Does it seem good to you to oppress, to despise the work of your hands and favor the schemes of the wicked?"

while the morning stars sang together
    and all the angels shouted for joy?" (Job 38:4-7 NIV)

Here we see God the glad Creator and God's act of creation as a spectacle that prompts the giddy applause of heaven. When I read this, I think about being at a fireworks display—as rocket after rocket shoots up in the air and lights up the sky with a burst of color and all in the audience involuntarily cry out "Oooooh" and "Aaaaah" and break into applause. That's Job's creation account!

As part of Job's interrogation, God takes him on a tour of creation, where God joyfully shows off the glory of all that has been made. Of course, behind the tour is God's question to Job, "Can you do this?" But we also get a sense that God is having a grand time showing Job the wonders of creation. My favorite moment in the tour is when they come upon an ostrich. God directs Job to look at the ostrich. Her wings

flap joyfully. . . .
She lays her eggs on the ground
    and lets them warm in the sand,
unmindful that a foot may crush them. (Job 39:13-15 NIV)

For, God says, I

did not endow her with wisdom. . . .
Yet when she spreads her feathers to run,
    she laughs at horse and rider. (Job 39:17-18 NIV)

Imagine this stop on the tour: God is standing with an arm around Job's shoulder, pointing off into the distance. "Look, Job. Look at that ostrich. She's not the smartest animal in creation." Then, just at that moment something startles her and she takes off, running like the wind. And God says, "But look at her go!"

At the end of the book Job simply says,

Surely I spoke of things I did not understand. . . .
I despise myself
    and repent in dust and ashes. (Job 42:3, 6 NIV)

Job has come to God demanding an explanation, demanding answers. And if you read to the very final verse, what you realize is that God never answers Job's question. Job never gets his explanation. Instead, what he gets is the presence of God, the glad Creator. And that turns out to be all he needs.

I think of all the references to joy in the Psalms. Earlier we highlighted Psalm 81, where we hear the divine frustration at Israel's stubborn refusal to trust God and enter God's joy. God calls out to the people,

> Open your mouth wide and I will fill it. . . .
> I would feed you with the finest of the wheat,
> and with honey from the rock I would satisfy you. (Ps 81:10, 16)

In the Exodus story, the people had known water from the rock, but what God really longed to give them was so much more—it was honey. And at several points, we've recalled the final verse of Psalm 16, where David exclaims to God,

> You show me the path of life.
> In your presence there is fullness of joy;
> in your right hand are pleasures forevermore. (Ps 16:11)

Of course, there are repeated invitations to praise God with joy and enter God's presence with thanksgiving (Pss 5:11, 21:6, 28:7, 33:1, 47:1, 65:8, 81:1, 95:1, and 100:1-2). But I think my favorite is Psalm 4:7, where David says to God, "You have put gladness in my heart / more than when their grain and wine abound." What a thing to say. In an agricultural economy, what you live for is the completion of the harvest. Up to that point, you're on the edge of your seat, praying for a good crop, hoping that bad weather or an infestation or some other disaster doesn't come along because if the harvest fails, you don't eat. So you hold your breath until that moment when the crops are safe in the barn, and then you throw a party! You celebrate. I remember as a kid watching beer commercials on TV. People would tap their glasses together, and the narrator would say something like, "Go for the gusto." It always seemed to me that those people in the commercial had achieved the pinnacle of human happiness. That's what the celebration of grain and new wine was like. Imagine people clinking glasses together and saying, "It doesn't get any better than this." But David exclaims, almost incredulously, "It actually does. There is actually something even better than what I thought was the high point of my life—and that is your presence, God."

When we come to the New Testament, we have this amazing, mysterious event that we call the incarnation, God becoming flesh, God who was the agent of creation coming among us as a person. In John's Gospel, here are the events that herald the coming of God among us. Water is turned to wine, and not just cheap wine, but the good stuff (Jn 2). There is a promise of living water, water so fulfilling that we will never thirst again (Jn 4). We find healing from our paralysis (Jn 5). We are offered the bread of life, an offer that recognizes our longing for sustenance that truly fills our deep hunger (Jn 6). We find the gift of sight (Jn 9) and the overturning of death itself (Jn 11). And in the midst of all of this, Jesus declares this to be his mission: "I came that they may have life, and have it abundantly" (Jn 10:10).

One final example. We concluded chapter six with Paul's invitation in Philippians 4:4-7 to "rejoice in the Lord always." He speaks of the joy that never goes away. He urges us to display gentleness, a calm sense of equanimity and composure, before all who see us. He invites us to a life that is free from anxiety—"do not worry about anything"—but instead, whatever comes along, to pass off all our concerns to God. And he concludes with the promise that God's peace, which is beyond understanding, will guard our hearts and minds in Christ. Isn't that the life all of us want? Constant joy. Resilience and poise. Freedom from anxiety. Peace. What makes all of this possible? The secret is that one short phrase in the middle of this beautiful passage: "The Lord is near." It is the presence of the Lord, the nearness of God, that brings us joy.

Like a golden thread, the joy of God is the theme that runs through all of Scripture. We are made to live in the presence of God, at whose right hand are joys forevermore. Here's how the very first question in the Westminster Shorter Catechism put it:

> What is the chief end of man?
>
> Man's chief end is to glorify God, and to enjoy him forever.

The joy of the Lord is our strength.

But not only does joy run like a golden thread through the Bible; it also makes sense of all those elements of Christian theology that otherwise might seem arbitrary or unintelligible to us. When we put the joy of the Lord at the center, suddenly everything else falls into place.

What is worship? Here's the conception I grew up with. I remember one summer day as a junior high kid being out in the backyard watching ants scurry around their anthill. It occurred to me that in some tiny way, in terms of size and power, I was to these ants as God was to me, and I imagined ordering the ants to line up and worship me—to tell me how great and wonderful I was—or I'd stomp on their anthill. I had somehow gotten the impression that God was insecure and needed us to boost God's ego with praise and adulation, or else God would throw fire at us and destroy us. What a view of worship! In dramatic contrast is Lewis's picture of the spiritual life, in which worship is the natural response to the joyful, awesome presence of God. At those moments in the Bible when the curtain is drawn back and humans get a glimpse of God—think Moses glimpsing God's glory from behind (Ex 33), Isaiah's vision of "the Lord high and lofty" (Is 6:1), and John the Seer's vision of the throne of God in Revelation—they certainly see God's awesome power, they feel the heat of God's purity, but they also hear exquisite music and see dazzling color, and they are overcome with ecstasy. Of course, in this life, where we feel the weight of duties pressing upon us and we daily face pain and loss, that reality is not usually present to us except in far-off and momentary glimpses, so Lewis challenges us to practice the discipline of attentiveness and adoration in order to tune our hearts to God's presence. But behind this is the conviction that worship, at its heart, is yet another gift that enables us to enjoy the presence of God fully.

And what of sin? As Lewis put it, we often think of sin as breaking the rules. Instead, he insisted that sin was actually the choice to settle for a cheap and tawdry imitation of the real thing that God longs to give us. Again, this is what we find in Psalm 81, where God pleads with the people to turn away from false, imitation gods, so that they might receive the "finest of the wheat" and "honey from the rock" God longed to give them (Ps 81:16). As we noted in chapter three, this is also what we find, for example, in the Sermon on the Mount, where Jesus tells us not to perform our acts of righteousness in order to be noticed and praised by others because then we "have no reward from [our] Father in heaven" (Mt 6:1). What is he saying? Simply this: when we perform our acts of religion in order to be seen by others, we have accepted a cheap imitation of what we really long for, which is the presence of God. As Lewis put it, we have settled for "mud pies in a slum" because we can't imagine "what is meant by a holiday at the sea."[6]

This understanding of sin also helps us make sense of temptation— that it is simply the allure of that imitation. Every day, I am bombarded with messages from without and impulses from within telling me that I would be happy and fulfilled, once and for all, if I just had *THIS . . .* whatever that thing is that presents itself to me as the answer to all my longings. Maybe it's a certain level of funds in my bank account, or a particular item of clothing, or the new boat, or a certain achievement, or a sexual encounter. In the moment of longing, the desire can seem so overwhelming and the promise so certain. Yet afterward, when I've gotten whatever it was that promised wholeness, I am still empty. Where does faith fit into this picture? Faith is simply a response to that temptation that says, "I refuse to believe that this thing will do for me what it promises; I will trust that what this offers me I can only find in God."

Lewis also wanted us to see the cumulative effect of accepting the cheap imitation. He warned us of what happens in our souls when we settle, how we turn ourselves more and more into the kind of person who is unable to enjoy the life of God. Think about it this way. Imagine that there is some "good" that I think I have to have in order to be whole and content, perhaps the next promotion or achievement. But to reach that

---

[6]*WG*, 2.

goal I determine that I need to lie or to undermine a colleague. What happens to my character, my spirit, what kind of person am I becoming in my pursuit of that goal? Someone a bit more suspicious, a bit more protective of my territory, a bit more dishonest. And how does that choice affect my capacity for trusting God and opening myself to the joy of God? I have, in some small way at least, closed myself off from the life of God. This is what we saw in character after character in Lewis's writings, from Orual to the grumbling woman in *The Great Divorce* to Edmund in *The Lion, the Witch, and the Wardrobe.* We see Edmund making a choice, perhaps just a small one to bend the truth or to act out of self-centeredness or to entertain just a sliver of malice, but that choice turns his soul, the deepest part of himself, into something slightly different than it was before; and of course, each small turning prepares him for the next choice, which takes him further away, and so forth. We sometimes feel resentment because someone appears to have "gotten away with" a sin. But when we understand the true nature of sin, we realize that no one ever escapes sin's consequences, for sin is simply the process of turning our hearts away from our true joy and deadening our capacity to receive the life of God—whether anyone ever finds out or not.

And conversely, what is holiness? It is simply the process of becoming more and more the kind of person who is able to receive the joy of the Lord. As many Christian writers have pointed out, the spiritual disciplines, those practices we engage in as Christians—prayer, meditation, Bible study, and so on—these are simply tools for setting our sails and putting our boats in a position to catch the wind! What Lewis wrote about adoration is a perfect example. We work hard to be conscious of the pleasures and delights that fill our days, especially the small ones that we might otherwise overlook. We are attentive to them, and as we savor them we choose to make the connection to God, to say, "God, how wonderful you are to have given me this. . . . This also is Thou."[7] That's work, but it's work that helps us tune more and more into God's joyful presence.

---

[7]*LM*, 90.

We sometimes think of the Christian life as if we were preparing for a big test, an entrance exam into heaven, and we just hope that we pass the exam and can get in. But that's not how it works at all. Rather, the pursuit of holiness is simply the process that I go through in order to prepare myself to receive the bliss of heaven. This is what we see in *The Great Divorce*, where the visitors from hell are overwhelmed by heaven's excruciating beauty, by its sheer "solidness"—and they're barely on the outskirts! They must become more solid themselves in order to be able to take in the otherwise unendurable ecstasy of that place.

Here's a way to think about it. One of the biggest joys of my life has been the arrival of four beautiful baby granddaughters, Ruby, Sadie, Joanna, and Juniper. I feel an overwhelming love for them. So naturally I would want to share the most delightful pleasures of my life with them— and among those pleasures is my absolute favorite dish, cream of crab soup, a soup made with heavy cream and full of the choicest backfin lump crabmeat, with just a hint of sherry mixed in. When done right, it's rich and exquisite, so thick your spoon will almost stand up in the bowl. How could I not want my precious granddaughters to experience *this*? But what would happen if, in my exuberance, I started feeding my baby granddaughters cream of crab soup? Assuming they even liked it, it's doubtful that they would be able to get more than two bites down before throwing it all up again. Why? Because they're just not ready to take it in. Their constitutions aren't strong enough yet to stomach, let alone enjoy, such rich fare. They need something far more bland right now. But one day their capacity for that delicacy will have developed so that they can enjoy it with me. I look forward to that day! That is how holiness works— it's not about trying to score a 75 on the entrance exam to heaven; it's about becoming the kind of person who can receive ever more fully the beauty and ecstasy of the joyful presence of God.

And, finally, where is God taking the whole story? What will heaven be like? When I was a child, I imagined heaven as a church service with no closing prayer. It's like you turn the page of your order of worship and there's more; it just goes on and on. As I tell people now, it seemed better than hell, but not much better. But Lewis gave us a different picture, one that highlights the continuity between our richest experiences here on earth and the life that awaits us there. He wanted us to see that heaven will be the unadulterated, unmarred experience of the joyful, ecstatic presence of God; it will be what, in our moments of greatest bliss, we only glimpse from a far distance. In our present existence it's as if we are outside a door, and on the other side a jubilant party is happening. We catch a hint of light through the crack in the door, and a faint sound of music filters through the wall. We catch the distant aroma of rich food. Even through the closed door, the hints of the party within are deliciously wonderful. And yet, as Lewis put it, "all the pages of the New Testament are rustling with the rumor that it will not always be so. Some day, God willing, we shall get *in*."[8] When the joy of the Lord takes its rightful place in the Christian story, everything makes sense—sin, temptation, faith, holiness, heaven. And the gospel truly becomes good news.

EMBRACING LIFE

A number of years ago, I spent a year teaching in a study-abroad program in Europe. That experience gave me a front-row seat in the lives of my students, many of whom had grown up in Christian homes. Although, on the whole, the experience was wonderful, there were times when I was dismayed at some of the patterns of behavior I saw them fall into, especially those who seemed determined to pursue a lifestyle of heavy partying. What I discovered as I got to know them better was that for many this was not just a year to go abroad. It was a year to "take a vacation from God." They didn't plan to leave God altogether. In fact, they fully intended to return to God at some point in the future. But for now, at least for this one year, this was their moment to have some fun, to really live, before they settled down to the drudgery of the "faithful Christian life." I remember being so puzzled by their behavior until one day it hit me. Just as I had not been taught to connect the joy I felt sitting around

---

[8]*WG*, 13, emphasis in original.

the Mossmans' dinner table with my sense of God's purpose for my life, so they had grown up with a theology in which God and joy are completely disconnected. God is *here*, and joy is *there*. They know they need God, and for those who still hold to some conception of hell, they don't want to go there. But they'd sure like to experience a little joy before they pack that away and get right with God. I realized that they were missing the centerpiece of Christianity, what is, tragically, Christianity's best-kept secret. At the center of it all is the presence of God at whose right hand are joys forevermore. How desperately we need to rediscover that center of our faith. For if it ever gets through, if the joy of the Lord ever truly gets hold of us, nothing will ever be the same. May that be true for us, may we open our lives to the presence of the glad Creator, and may this be our message to the world.

FOR FURTHER READING

WORKS BY LEWIS

King, Don W. *The Collected Poems of C. S. Lewis: A Critical Edition*. Kent, OH: Kent State University Press, 2015.

Lewis, C. S. *The Abolition of Man, or Reflections on Education with Special Reference to the Teaching of English in the Upper Forms of Schools*. New York: MacMillan, 1947.

———. "Answers to Questions on Christianity." In *God in the Dock: Essays on Theology and Ethics*, edited by Walter Hooper, 48-62. Grand Rapids: Eerdmans, 1970.

———. *C. S. Lewis Letters to Children*. Edited by Lyle W. Dorsett and Marjorie Lamp Mead, with a foreword by Douglas H. Gresham. New York: Macmillan, 1985.

———. *The Discarded Image: An Introduction to Medieval and Renaissance Literature*. Cambridge: Cambridge University Press, 2012.

———. "Dungeon Grates." In King, *Collected Poems*, 88-89.

———. "The Empty Universe." In *Present Concerns: Essays by C. S. Lewis*, edited by Walter Hooper, 81-86. San Diego: Harcourt Brace Jovanovich, 1986.

———. *English Literature in the Sixteenth Century, Excluding Drama*. Oxford: Clarendon Press, 1954.

———. *The Four Loves*. New York: Harcourt Brace Jovanovich, 1960.

———. *The Great Divorce*. New York: Macmillan, 1946.

———. *The Horse and His Boy.* Illustrations by Pauline Baynes. Chronicles of Narnia 5. New York: HarperCollins, 1994.

———. "In Praise of Solid People." In King, *Collected Poems,* 98-99.

———. "In Prison." In King, *Collected Poems,* 84.

———. "The Inner Ring." In *They Asked for a Paper: Papers and Addresses,* 139-49. London: Geoffrey Bles, 1962.

———. *The Last Battle.* Illustrations by Pauline Baynes. Chronicles of Narnia 7. New York: HarperCollins, 1994.

———. *Letters to an American Lady.* Edited by Clyde S. Kilby. Grand Rapids: Eerdmans, 1967.

———. *Letters to Malcolm: Chiefly on Prayer.* New York: Harcourt, Brace & World, 1964.

———. *The Lion, the Witch, and the Wardrobe.* Illustrations by Pauline Baynes. Chronicles of Narnia 1. New York: Collier Books, 1970.

———. *The Magician's Nephew.* Illustrations by Pauline Baynes. Chronicles of Narnia 6. New York: HarperCollins, 1994.

———. "Meditation in a Toolshed." In *God in the Dock: Essays on Theology and Ethics,* edited by Walter Hooper, 212-15. Grand Rapids: Eerdmans, 1970.

———. "Membership." In *The Weight of Glory and Other Addresses,* 30-42. 1949. Repr., Grand Rapids: Eerdmans, 1965.

———. *Mere Christianity.* New York: Macmillan, 1960.

———. *A Mind Awake: An Anthology of C. S. Lewis.* Edited by Clyde S. Kilby. New York: Harcourt, Brace & World, 1969.

———. *Miracles: A Preliminary Study.* London: Geoffrey Bles, 1947.

———. "On Stories." In *Of Other Worlds: Essays and Stories,* edited by Walter Hooper, 3-21. London: Geoffrey Bles, 1966.

———. *Out of the Silent Planet.* New York: Macmillan, 1965.

———. *Perelandra: A Novel.* New York: Macmillan, 1944.

———. *The Pilgrim's Regress: An Allegorical Apology for Christianity, Reason, and Romanticism.* 1943. Repr., Grand Rapids: Eerdmans, 1959.

———. *Prince Caspian: The Return to Narnia.* Illustrations by Pauline Baynes. Chronicles of Narnia 2. New York: HarperCollins, 1951.

———. *The Problem of Pain.* London: Geoffrey Bles, 1940.

———. *Reflections on the Psalms.* London: Geoffrey Bles, 1958.

———. *The Screwtape Letters.* London: Geoffrey Bles, 1942.

———. "Set on the Soul's Acropolis the Reason Stands." In King, *Collected Poems,* 238.

———. *The Silver Chair*. Illustrations by Pauline Baynes. Chronicles of Narnia 4. New York: HarperCollins, 1953.

———. *Spirits in Bondage: A Cycle of Lyrics*. Edited by Walter Hooper. New York: Harcourt Brace Jovanovich, 1984.

———. *Surprised by Joy: The Shape of My Early Life*. New York: Harcourt Brace, 1955.

———. *That Hideous Strength, a Modern Fairy-Tale for Grown-Ups*. New York: Macmillan, 1947.

———. *Till We Have Faces: A Myth Retold*. New York: Harcourt, Brace, 1956.

———. "Transposition." In *The Weight of Glory and Other Addresses*, 16-29. 1949. Repr., Grand Rapids: Eerdmans, 1965.

———. "Transposition." In *They Asked for a Paper: Papers and Addresses*, 166-82. London: Geoffrey Bles, 1962.

———. *The Voyage of the Dawn Treader*. Illustrations by Pauline Baynes. Chronicles of Narnia 3. New York: HarperCollins, 1952.

———. "The Weight of Glory." In *The Weight of Glory and Other Addresses*, 1-15. 1949. Repr., Grand Rapids: Eerdmans, 1965.

SECONDARY WORKS

Adwinkle, Stella. "Memories of the Socratic Club." In White, J. Wolfe, and B. N. Wolfe, *C. S. Lewis and His Circle*, 192-94.

Alexander, Samuel. *Space, Time, and Deity: The Gifford Lectures at Glasgow, 1916-1918*. Gloucester, MA: Peter Smith, 1979.

Aristotle, *The Rhetoric and the Poetics of Aristotle*. Translated by W. Rhys Roberts and Ingram Bywater. New York: The Modern Library, 1984.

Augustine of Hippo, Saint. *St. Augustine on the Psalms*. Translated by Scholastica Hebgin and Felicitas Corrigan. 2 vols. New York: Paulist Press, 1961.

———. *City of God*. Translated by Henry Bettenson. Harmondsworth, UK: Penguin Books, 1972.

———. *Confessions*. Translated by Henry Chadwick. Oxford: Oxford University Press, 1991.

Bailey, Sarah Pulliam. "C. S. Lewis Still Inspires 50 Years After His Death." Religion. Huffington Post. November 22, 2013. www.huffingtonpost.com /2013/11/22/cs-lewis-50-year-death_n_4325358.html.

Blake, John. "Surprised by C. S. Lewis: Why His Popularity Endures." *CNN Belief Blog*. December 17, 2010. http://religion.blogs.cnn.com/2010/12/17 /surprised-by-c-s-lewis-why-his-popularity-endures/.

"Books of the Century: Leaders and Thinkers Weigh in on Classics That Have Shaped Contemporary Religious Thought." *Christianity Today*. April 24, 2000. www.christianitytoday.com/ct/2000/april24/5.92.html.

Brazier, P. H. *C. S. Lewis—Revelation, Conversion, and Apologetics*. Eugene, OR: Pickwick, 2012.

Brown, Devin. *A Life Observed: A Spiritual Biography of C. S. Lewis*. Grand Rapids: Brazos Press, 2013.

Brown, Warren S., and Brad D. Strawn. *The Physical Nature of Christian Life: Neuroscience, Psychology, and the Church*. New York: Cambridge University Press, 2012.

Calhoun, Scott. "C. S. Lewis and Joy Davidman: Severe Mercies, Late Romances." In *C. S. Lewis: An Examined Life*, vol. 1 of *C. S. Lewis: Life, Works, and Legacy*, edited by Bruce L. Edwards, 274-93. Westport, CT: Praeger, 2007.

Carpenter, Humphrey. *The Inklings: C. S. Lewis, J. R. R. Tolkien, Charles Williams, and Their Friends*. London: HarperCollins, 1997.

Crawford, Matthew B. *The World Beyond Your Head: On Becoming an Individual in an Age of Distraction*. New York: Farrar, Straus and Giroux, 2015.

Cuneo, Andrew. "Introduction: Oxford, 1963, and a Young Boswell." In Wolfe and Wolfe, *C. S. Lewis and the Church*, 1-20.

Dorsett, Lyle W. *Seeking the Secret Place: The Spiritual Formation of C. S. Lewis*. Grand Rapids: Brazos Press, 2004.

Dreyfus, Hubert, and Charles Taylor. *Retrieving Realism*. Cambridge, MA: Harvard University Press, 2015.

Edwards, Bruce L., ed. *An Examined Life*. Vol. 1 of *C. S. Lewis: Life, Works, and Legacy*. Westport, CT: Praeger, 2007.

————. *Not-a-Tame Lion: Unveil Narnia Through the Eyes of Lucy, Peter, and Other Characters Created by C. S. Lewis*. Wheaton, IL: Tyndale House, 2005.

Frankl, Victor E. *Man's Search for Meaning*. New York: Pocket Books, 1984.

Graham, David, ed. *We Remember C. S. Lewis: Essays and Memoirs*. Nashville: Broadman & Holman, 2001.

Green, Roger Lancelyn, and Walter Hooper. *C. S. Lewis: A Biography*. New York: Harcourt, Brace, Jovanovich, 1974.

Guite, Malcolm. "Telling the Truth Through Imaginative Fiction: C. S. Lewis on the Reconciliation of Athene and Demeter." In *C. S. Lewis at Poets' Corner*, edited by Michael Ward and Peter S. Williams, 15-24. Cambridge: Lutterworth, 2016.

Habets, Myk. "Mere Christianity for Mere Gods: Lewis on Theosis." In *A Myth Retold: Re-encountering C. S. Lewis as Theologian*, edited by Martin Sutherland, 110-29. Eugene, OR: Wipf & Stock, 2014.

Head, Ronald. "C. S. Lewis as a Parishioner." In White, J. Wolfe, and B. N. Wolfe, *C. S. Lewis and His Circle*, 179-86.

Hooper, Walter. "Oxford's Bonnie Fighter." In *Remembering C. S. Lewis: Recollections of Those Who Knew Him*, edited by James T. Como, 241-308. San Francisco: Ignatius Press, 2005.

Janes, Burton K. "Sightings," in Graham, *We Remember C. S. Lewis*, 144-48.

Kinnaman, David, and Gabe Lyons. *Unchristian: What a New Generation Really Thinks About Christianity . . . and Why It Matters*. Grand Rapids: Baker Books, 2007.

Lindsley, Art. "C. S. Lewis: His Life and Works." *C. S. Lewis Institute*. Accessed September 14, 2018. www.cslewisinstitute.org/node/28.

Lindvall, Terry. *Surprised by Laughter*. Nashville: Nelson, 1996.

McGrath, Alister. *C. S. Lewis—A Life: Eccentric Genius, Reluctant Prophet*. Carol Stream, IL: Tyndale House, 2013.

Moltmann, Jürgen. *Theology of Hope: On the Ground and the Implications of a Christian Eschatology*. Translated by James W. Leitch. New York: Harper and Row, 1975.

Proust, Marcel. *Swann's Way*. Translated by C. K. Scott Moncrieff and Terence Kilmartin. New York: Vintage Books, 1989.

Sammons, Martha C. *"A Far-Off Country": A Guide to C. S. Lewis's Fantasy Fiction*. Lanham, MD: University Press of America, 2000.

Sayer, George. *Jack: A Life of C. S. Lewis*. Rev. ed. Wheaton, IL: Crossway, 2005.

Smilde, Arend. "Horrid Red Herrings: A New Look at the 'Lewisian Argument from Desire'—and Beyond." *Journal of Inklings Studies* 4, no. 1 (2014): 33-92.

Smith, James K. A. *Desiring the Kingdom: Worship, Worldview, and Cultural Formation*. Grand Rapids: Baker Academic, 2009.

———. *You Are What You Love: The Spiritual Power of Habit*. Grand Rapids: Brazos Press, 2016.

Starr, Charlie W. "So How *Should* We Teach English?" In *Contemporary Perspectives on C. S. Lewis' "The Abolition of Man,"* edited by Timothy M. Mosteller and Gayne John Anacker, 63-81. London: Bloomsbury Academic, 2017.

Thomas, Owen C. "Interiority and Christian Spirituality." *Journal of Religion* 80, no. 1 (2000): 41-60.

Thurman, Chris. *The Lies We Believe*. Nashville: Nelson, 1999.

Tillich, Paul. *The Essential Tillich: An Anthology of the Writings of Paul Tillich.* Edited by F. Forrester Church. Chicago: University of Chicago Press, 1999.

"Top 100 Religious Books." Religion, Huffington Post. Updated September 14, 2012. www.huffingtonpost.com/2012/09/14/top-100-influential-relig_n _1836687.html.

Ward, Michael. *Planet Narnia: The Seven Heavens in the Imagination of C. S. Lewis.* Oxford: Oxford University Press, 2008.

White, Roger, Judith E. Wolfe, and Brendan N. Wolfe, eds. *C. S. Lewis and His Circle: Essays and Memoirs from the Oxford C. S. Lewis Society.* Oxford: Oxford University Press, 2015.

Wolfe, Judith E., and Brendan N. Wolfe, eds. *C. S. Lewis and the Church: Essays in Honour of Walter Hooper.* London: T&T Clark, 2011.

Zhou, Rongrong, and Dilip Soman. "Looking Back: Exploring the Psychology of Queuing and the Effect of the Number of People Behind." *Journal of Consumer Research* 29 (March 2003): 517-30.

GENERAL INDEX

SCRIPTURE INDEX

Finding the Textbook You Need

The IVP Academic Textbook Selector
is an online tool for instantly finding the IVP books
suitable for over 250 courses across 24 disciplines.

ivpacademic.com